W9-BDM-006

The Versatile
Labrador Retriever

By Nancy Martin

Doral Publishing, Inc.
Wilsonville Oregon
1994

Published by Doral Publishing, 8560 S.W. Salish Lane, Suite 300, Wilsonville, OR 97070-9612.
Printed in the United States of America.

Copy edited by Marianne Foote, and Luana Luther.
Book design by Fred Christensen.

Cover photo by Brian Yeowart, Langshott Labradors, England.
"On the wild Scottish coast at Portsoy, Banffshire."
Left to right—Wynfaul Debit, Wynfaul Sasha, Eng. Sh. Ch. Cricklecreek Camomile of Wynfaul, Edenlea Sunrise at Wynfaul, Langshott Bramble, Wynfaul Overdraft, Wynfaul Hurricane, Chestnut Chaser around Wynfaul, Eng. Ch. Wynfaul Tobasco and Langshott Charm of Tina.

Back cover photo by Christine Watt.
Nancy Martin and Ayr's Sea Chanty of Kenbu C.D., JH, TDI (yellow), Ch. Ayr's Real McCoy C.D.X., JH (black), Ayr's Mr. Lucky, WC, TDI (chocolate).

Typesetting and formatting by MSF Computer Graphics, 531 Old Horseshoe Pike, Downingtown, PA 19335.

Library of Congress Card Number: 94-68115
ISBN: 0-9944875-31-9

Small Library Services:
Martin, Nancy A.
        The versatile Labrador retriever / by Nancy A.
    Martin. -- Wilsonville, Or. : Doral Pub.,
    1994
        p. : ill. ; cm.

        Includes bibliographical references and
    index.

        1. Labrador retriever   I. Title

    SF429.L3M   636.752 dc20

CONTENTS

SECTION IV   Breeders and Kennels

SECTION V   Labradors in Other Countries

SECTION VI   The Basis of Heredity

SECTION VII   Becoming a Breeder

Dedication

To all the good, kindly Labrador Retrievers in the world—past, present and future—and to those people responsible for them now and forever. May they strive diligently to preserve this wonderful breed's qualities.

Ch. Great Scot of Ayr (1964 - 1977)
(Ch. Lockerbie Sandylands Tarquin x Ch. Sandylands Spungold)
owned by Nancy Martin, bred by Mrs. Dorothy S. Franke.

The word *versatile* means adaptable to many uses or functions; many-sided in abilities. It is an adjective that can be applied without hesitation to the Labrador Retriever, and an appropriate title for this book. I am pleased to honor this wonderful breed of dog.

—*Nancy Martin*

PREFACE

It is a great delight for me to introduce this comprehensive book on my favorite breed. No one in America today is more qualified to write on the versatile aspects of this popular world-wide companion. Nancy Martin has never deviated in her personal loyalty to Labrador Retrievers. A beloved specialist judge, she is one most sought after for her opinion. This breed expert has traveled from Scandinavia to Down Under, rewarding her favorites at home and abroad.

Nancy acquired her first dog in 1960 and with succeeding generations of her dual-purpose Ayrs has achieved success. Obedience degrees, hunting test awards, gun dog titles, and show ring championships are only part of the proof of Nancy's success as a breeder. Some Ayrs have also led the blind, sniffed out drugs, met school busses and performed Best House Dog chores with relish. Her special empathy toward the "brown" ones (chocolates) has helped prove that no good Lab can be a bad color.

In *The Versatile Labrador*, which brings today's Labs to the forefront of all types of canines, we can follow the fruits of the prophetic "Legends." I refer, of course, to an earlier book by Nancy Martin, *Legends in Labradors*, that concentrated on the personalities and memories of pioneer breeders both here and in England. This privately printed and reprinted "sleeper" is proof of this talented writer's gift as a research recorder by both word and illustration.

This story is one that Nancy is uniquely qualified to tell, for she has participated as a founder and instructor for the Waterland Retriever Club, an active group of retriever owners that meets regularly in the greater Philadelphia area. These amateurs have produced many dual purpose winners, another proof that Nancy's enthusiastic leadership and integrity have a positive impact on owners, handlers, and dogs.

Joan R. Read
Chidley
Oyster Bay, New York

Shadowglen Joshua of Sundaze owned by Karen D. Christina and Deborah A. Whitehead; bred by Margaret and James Wilson, Shadowglen.

SECTION I
History

- **Chapter 1**

    Origin

- **Chapter 2**

    Early England

- **Chapter 3**

    Breed Development in England

- **Chapter 4**

    Breed Development in the United States

Logo from The Black Dog®, Martha's Vineyard, Massachusetts. Reproduction permission granted by The Black Dog restaurant.

Chapter 1

Origin

The history of the Labrador Retriever is filled with a variety of opinions on the origin of the breed. I have included several for conjecture.

Colonel Peter Hawker

Once there was a young sea captain who lived near the busy port of Poole in Dorset, southwestern England. He was the owner of a sailing ship that carried English goods to the hardy settlers of Newfoundland and returned with a hold full of salted cod and sometimes a black dog or two. This adventurous trader, Colonel Peter Hawker (1786-1853), an avid sportsman, has been called the great authority on working dogs. It was he who first used the term, "Labrador Breed," when referring to a dog, in his book, *Instructions to Young Sportsmen in all that relates to Guns and Shooting*, initially published in 1814 with ten more editions to follow over the years.

Colonel Hawker avowed that all he wrote was from "personal experience and not from hearsay" and that "everything here asserted has been the result of many years' trial and experience." The following quotes are taken from his chapter on "Newfoundland Dogs," second edition, 1816, and the last two paragraphs are from the third edition, 1824:

> Here we are a little in the dark. Every canine brute that is nearly as big as a jackass, and as hairy as a bear, is denominated a fine Newfoundland Dog. Very different, however, is both the proper Labrador and St. John's breed of these animals; at least many characteristic points are required to distinguish them.
>
> The one is very large: strong in the limbs; rough-haired; small in the head; and carries his tail very high. He is kept in that country for drawing sledges full of wood, from inland to the seashore, where he is useful by his immense strength and sagacity among wrecks and other disasters in boisterous weather.
>
> The other, **by far the best for every kind of shooting,** is oftener black than of another colour, and scarcely bigger than a pointer. He is made rather long in the head and nose; pretty deep in the chest; very fine in the legs; has short or smooth hair; does not carry his tail so much curved as the other; and is extremely quick in running, swimming and fighting . . ."
>
> "The St. John's breed of these dogs is chiefly used in their native country by fishermen. Their sense of smelling is scarcely to be credited. Their discrimination in following a wounded pheasant through a whole covert full of game, or a pinioned wild fowl through a furze brake or warren of rabbits appears almost impossible . . .

The real Newfoundland dog may be broken in to any kind of shooting; and without additional instruction is generally under such command that he may be safely kept in if required to be taken out with pointers. For finding wounded game of every description there is not his equal in the canine race, and he is a *sine qua non* in the general pursuit of wildfowl.

Poole was, till of late years, the best place to buy Newfoundland dogs; either just imported or broken in; but now they are becoming more scarce, owing (the sailors observed) to the strictness of those (blank) tax gatherers . . .

The following is added in the third edition:

For a punt or canoe always make choice of the **smallest** Newfoundland dog that you can procure; as the smaller he is the less water he brings into your boat after being sent out; the less cumbersome he is when afloat; and the quicker he can pursue crippled birds upon the mud . . .

If, on the other hand, you want only a Newfoundland dog as a retriever for covert shooting; then the case becomes different; as here you require a strong animal that will easily trot through the young wood and high grass with a large hare or pheasant in his mouth.

In the middle 1800s, the name *Labrador* in England came to include the smaller black dog—the St. John's breed of Colonel Hawker. W.E. Cormack describes the Labradors of St. Johns as small water dogs that are usually black, but once in a while a yellow or brown dog was seen.

Major Maurice Portal

Another theory was given by Major Maurice Portal in his book, *Guns at Home and Abroad*. He mentions that Blaine in his *Encyclopaedia of Rural Sports*, written in 1852, refers both to the Newfoundland retriever and the St. John's breed. The latter dog, Blaine says, is preferred by sportsmen on every account, being smaller, more easily managed, and sagacious in the extreme, his scenting powers being also very great.

Probably this latter is the ancestor of the Labrador as we know him today. How the breed was evolved it is hard to say, but the probabilities that the Fishermen of Newfoundland wanted a good strong water dog, since they are reported to have found them useful in cases of wrecks and wreckage on that coast, and crossed the heavy coated, strong black Newfoundland Retriever with a black Pointer, and evolved in time a hard, short coated dog with great staying powers. That this is probably the origin is borne out by the fact that if Labradors are inbred, the result is often a light-made dog, long on the leg, light of bone, with a thin tail and Pointerlike ears.

"... the black hounds of St. Hubert were much prized and it is well within the bounds of possibility that some of these dogs found their way back to Labrador and that they were the ancestors of the modern Labrador."

Lorna, Countess Howe

Lorna, Countess Howe, one of the peerless names in Labrador history, has stated in her book, *The Popular Labrador Retriever*, the following theories on the origin of the Labrador:

> In the latter part of the eighteenth century a certain Lieutenant Cartwright, R.N., traveled extensively in Newfoundland. In his book on his travels, he writes 'Providence has even denied them (the aboriginal Indians) the pleasing services and companionship of the faithful dog.' From this statement, which is reliable, I think, we may suppose that there were no dogs in North America. If we accept this statement, it seems reasonable to assume that the Labrador Retriever was brought by Europeans to those parts when they began to settle there.
>
> Labrador is said to have been discovered in the year 1000, but it was not until 1498 that Englishmen first went there in search of fish. The English were followed one hundred and fifty (approximately) years later by men from other nations—Portugal, France and Spain. Reports were written of the inroads made by wolves, but the author adds that these were kept from camps by fires, dogs and other means. In the early days trade, mainly in fish, was carried on with the West Country. In England in those days the black hounds of St. Hubert were much prized and it is well within the bounds of possibility that some of these dogs found their way back to Labrador and that they were the ancestors of the modern Labrador. It is doubtful if the real origin of the breed will ever be decisively settled, but it is certain that as the fishing industry increased in Labrador a breed of dog was founded there that has become world famous.

Did Lady Howe mean Labrador or Newfoundland?

Commercial fishing on the banks of Newfoundland was a very big business in the early 1800s. Ships were busy going back and forth, coming into the port of Poole, laden with the bounteous crop of cod. Sometimes the dogs missed the boat and hung around the docks and streets just as they had in St. John's. Sometimes they were sold by the captain or member of the crew to knowledgeable men who had discovered their retrieving prowess. Word had gone around about the ability of these "little Newfoundlanders" and their reputation among shooting men was becoming widely known.

Some historians believe the dogs were taken to Newfoundland by fishermen from Portugal. Indeed, English author and breeder, Mary Roslin-Williams found a photograph of a dog in an old Italian book, *Le Razzi Canine* by Florenzo Fioroni, that may support this theory. It is of a dog that could possibly be the forerunner of our Labrador Retriever. The caption reads, "Cane di Castro Laboreiro," Castro Laboreiro being a village in Northern Portugal. There is a resemblance in head, coat texture and tail to an old type yellow Labrador. To quote Mrs. Roslin-Williams, "It seems to me that this breed of dog may have somehow found its way to the shores of Newfoundland with a sailor who hailed from Portugal, taking the self colour and the name with it, the dog becoming incorporated in the local breed and the name corrupted by usage into the well-known local name."

Dr. Michael J. Woods

Michael Woods is a Labrador Retriever breeder and owner, and a conformation and obedience judge. He was born and raised and presently lives in Newfoundland. As a Professor of English Literature at Memorial University, he is fortunate to have access to many old and rare books at the center for Newfoundland Studies that are not available to authors who usually write on the history of the breed. His Waterdog prefix can be found on many fine dogs. Here is his account on the origins of the Labrador Retriever:

> I have a rather different perspective on the history than most, since I believe that the breed not only originated in Newfoundland but was developed here. As you know, the popular belief is that the 'waterdog' originated here and was then taken to England where it was crossed with various breeds and the result was what we now call the Labrador Retriever. This popular misconception has existed for so long simply because it is convenient and no one disputed it. This concept is the same as the idea that the breed came from Labrador, an idea that is now generally recogized as false, as is the thought that the Labrador is some type of genetic deterioration of the Newfoundland dog. Genetically it is known that when dogs are allowed to breed indiscriminately the result is a tendency toward the medium so that giant breeds will tend to become smaller and toy breeds larger. Only judicious breeding will prevent this natural occurrence, so it is evident that the Newfoundland is probably a cross between the smooth-coated smaller indigenous dog and some large European breeds introduced into the island.
>
> It is my view that the English did not originate or develop the breed, rather they imported the breed into Britain, refined it, and preserved it. For this all Labrador breeders owe the English an eternal debt of gratitude. However, it must be recognized that the breed imported was essentially

the dog that we have today. This is not to say that there were not some crosses made into the breed, but the essential characteristics of the dog, although refined, remained unchanged. Saying this is the case is not, however, proving it.

Although uncertainty still remains about the breed's origins, recent historical and archaeological research have shed some light onto the mystery. Archaeological excavations in the small Newfoundland community of Port au Choix have discovered the remains of several dog skeletons. These skeletons are of dogs that weighed between 45 and 55 pounds, were well muscled but not necessarily traction animals, and were most likely kept for companionship and hunting. The dogs belonged to the Maritime Archaic Indians who inhabited Newfoundland, and the bones have been carbon dated from around 1937 B.C. James Tuck, the chief archaeologist, also concluded that these dogs were typical of the dogs owned by most North American Indians at the time and did not possess either the size or the morphology of today's Newfoundland dog.

The Beothucks, the native people of Newfoundland who were present when the first Europeans came to the island and who became extinct in the late nineteenth century, also possessed dogs that resembled the wolf-like dogs of the Maritime Archaic Indians. Richard Whitbourne in 1620 mentions his amazement that his mastiff dog began to play with these 'wolves' and disappeared with them into the countryside for some nine or ten days. The truth is that these 'wolves' were native dogs, and the mastiff who 'began to fawne and play with the other' was seduced away from his master by his reproductive urges. Since Whitbourne notes that in 1615 there were more than 250 ships from England, France, Spain, Holland, and Portugal engaged in fishing in Newfoundland, it is unlikely that his was the only European dog in the fleet or the only one that inter-bred with native dogs.

In later centuries after the European domination of the island, and after the Beothucks had been driven into abject poverty and were hunted and exterminated as if they were despised animals, Europeans noted that they did not possess dogs. James Howley commented:

'To complete their wretched condition, Providence has even denied them the pleasing services and companionship of the faithful dog. This affectionate and social creature is partner in the joyous chase, fellow-traveler, protector, and domestic attendant, to every race of mankind that history has brought to my knowledge, except to those most forlorn of all human beings.'

What is essential to remember about the history of the Labrador is that there were native Indian dogs in Newfoundland from pre-historic times. These native dogs then bred indiscriminately with whatever dogs were brought from Europe by fisherman, since dogs in Newfoundland were not confined and bred at will. These dogs were used for many purposes, including hunting and the all important work of pulling home the firewood needed to survive the harsh Newfoundland winters. That dogs increased and multiplied in the island is evident in the comments of W.R. Kennedy, who in 1881 complained of the 'packs of half-wild, half-starved curs that infest the country' and recommended 'before all, death to the dogs! or, at all events, to nine-tenths of them.'

Kennedy's suggestion and the complaints of others were not ignored. Two years later the Sheep Act of 1885 was passed which allowed the majority of electors in any district to prohibit dogs in their district. Some 137 districts passed the legislation; those that did not passed some restrictions such as higher taxes for bitches. Thousands of dogs were killed and the breeding population was decimated.

It is also noteworthy that into this chaotic mixture that formed the Labrador and the Newfoundland dogs might be genes from Viking dogs whose masters inhabited Newfoundland circa 1000 B.C. Other ancestors might have been dogs of the Basques who had a strong presence in the island from the 1540s to the early 1700s.

Hatton and Harvey recorded in a discussion of the Newfoundland dog that 'old settlers say that the ancient genuine breed consisted of a dog about twenty-six inches high, with black ticked body, gray muzzle, and gray or white stockinged legs, with dew claws behind.'

One of the earliest references from a person who was actually in Newfoundland and commented on a dog that was specific to Newfoundland was Joseph Banks in 1766:

> Almost Every Body has heard of the Newfoundland Dogs I myself was desird to Procure some of them and when I set out for the Countrey firmley beleivd that I should meet with a sort of Dogs different from any I had Seen whose Peculiar Excellence was taking the water Freely I was therefore the more surprizd when told that there was here no distinct Breed Those I met with were Mostly Curs with a Cross of the Mastiff in them Some took the water well others not at all The thing they are valued for here is strenght as they are employed in winter time to Draw in Sledges whatever is wanted from the woods.

Unfortunately, Banks does not give us any description of the dogs he found or of how he expected a Newfoundland dog to look. The problem with references to dogs in Newfoundland is that terms were used without a great deal of accuracy. We find references to Newfoundland dogs, Greater Newfoundland dogs, Lesser Newfoundland dogs, Labrador dogs, St. John's dogs, St. John's Labrador dogs, etc. Unless the person making the observation describes the dog involved one is not sure of exactly what dog is being referred to, since their terminology does not mean the same as ours.

An early description of a waterdog, later renamed the Labrador, is by W. E. Cormack in 1822 who describes 'dogs who are admirably trained as retrievers in fowling, and are otherwise useful. The smooth or short-haired dog is preferred because in frosty weather the long-haired kind become encumbered with ice on coming out of the water.' What we note here is that Cormack identifies two essential characteristics of the Labrador: retrieving ability and coat type. Burton, the editor of Cormack's journal, observes in 1927 that these dogs still existed in Newfoundland, that he had himself seen them, and that all Cormack had said about them was correct. In 1842, Jukes describes 'a thin, dog' that 'was very different from what we understand by the term Newfoundland dog in England.' These dogs were the most abundant dogs of the country and 'had a thin tapering snout, a long thin tail, and rather thin but powerful legs, with a lank body, the hair short and smooth.' Henri Herz, a Frenchman, stated that on his visit to Newfoundland, he learned there were 'two kinds of Newfoundland dogs, short-haired and long-haired. The long-haired are beyond doubt more beautiful than the short-haired, and are the only ones known generally in Europe; but the short-haired are more prized than the former in Newfoundland because they are more energetic and therefore more able to do what is asked of them. and they carry that out with eagerness and intelligence.' Another interesting observation by Herz is that the long-haired dogs were raised for sale and brought twelve or fifteen English shillings, a goodly sum in these times. This preference for long haired dogs was common among the more well to do in North America and Europe since these type of dogs were commonly associated with wealth and position. Even as late as 1911, the American writer, Stanley Duncan, believed that with 'the beautiful flat-coat as a rival, the Labrador can scarcely ever hope to secure the premier position among our gundogs.' This preference for long-hair might well explain why the Labrador was often viewed as a cur, a butcher's dog, or a mongrel both in Newfoundland and in England, and why the breed was seen as some type of deterioration of the larger hairy dog. It also explains why middle-class English shooters preferred their dogs being a cross between the imported Labrador and some long-haired breed. The aristocrats being aristocrats had no need to keep up with the fashionable desires to appear aristocratic and were more concerned with keeping their strains pure and outstanding working dogs. This association between long-hair and purebred is seen in the comment of Carroll in 1909: 'The smooth breed is not nearly extinct, as there are thousands of them around the island to-day, though they may not be pure bred. The description of the typical Newfoundland is not the one which most of us are familiar and which we have always fondly believed to be the type.'

What exactly is the 'true' type, the true Newfoundland dog, is open to debate. Is the true Newfoundland dog the Labrador and is the dog we today call the Newfoundland a creation at home and abroad of a fashionable dog? Certainly from very early times' visitors to the island deplored the lack of the 'true' type; recall Banks comments in 1766 that all he encountered were curs. Hawker notes that the real Newfoundland dog is not the 'curley haired heavy brute' but is 'quite black, with a long head, very fine action, and something of the otter skin.' Perhaps, the reality is that Europeans coming to the island found mainly the smaller short-haired dogs. There were probably some larger long-haired dogs also present, but these might have been genetic variations or the result of some cross between the smaller dog and some recent European imports. As the European presence increased, the local population realized that there was a market for the larger, hairy dog both among the wealthy on the island and in Europe. This would explain both why visitors to the island always complained about being unable to find true Newfoundland dogs and why the European idea of the Newfoundland dog became associated with the larger, hairy dog.

Eventually, as we know, some of the smaller dogs found their way to Britain through trade between Newfoundland and Poole. I agree with Mary Dalgarno's observation that these dogs came to England in two groups: prior to 1814 when they were used by the common people for wild fowling, and after 1860 when they became the domain of the aristocrats. The first group of dogs were bred indiscriminately with whatever other breeds were available and no effort was made to keep the strain pure. However, once the aristocrats began importing and buying these dogs, every effort was made to ensure that the dogs were bred very carefully within the strain. Scott and Middleton make constant reference to 'the pure strain,' 'purity of blood,' and 'the original strain.' They also quote the famous lines of the Third Earl of Malmesbury: 'We always call mine Labrador dogs, and I have kept the breed as pure as I could from the first I had from Poole.' Lorna, Countess Howe also emphasizes this purity: 'It is fortunate that the early breeders of the Labrador . . . went to such infinite trouble to keep their strains pure and the pedigrees of their dogs intact.' Countess Howe also quotes Lord Knutsford, one of the early breeders, as opposed to cross-breeding and he refers to the offspring of such unions as 'curiosities.' We can assume, then, that these early breeders were extremely concerned with preserving the purity of these imported dogs and that they did not engage in any cross-breeding unless it became absolutely unavoidable. There were undoubtedly some crosses made into these strains, as is evident in the pedigrees of early Labradors in the Scott and Middleton book. However, these breeders did everything in their power to maintain the integrity of the imported breed and it is from their lines that the Labrador of today descends. It is also interesting that in both Scott and Middleton, and in Howe, there is mention of the dominance of the Labrador blood. 'The Labrador strain must be a very strong one, for it nearly always impresses itself on its descendants even if they are not pure-bred.' Howe quotes Knutsford: 'That is one of the remarkable things about them, how strong the Labrador blood is.' This prepotency would indicate that the Labrador must have existed as an established breed long before it was imported into England.

If we accept the fact that these early breeders were indeed truthful and kept the breed as pure as possible, and were greatly concerned with the perpetuation of the breed they had imported, and were not stupid men, a fact that would seem to be supported by their success in worldly pursuits, then, we must assume that their later importation of dogs from Newfoundland was based on their sincere belief that these dogs belonged to the same breed they were concerned about and could add important new blood to the gene pool. These early breeders did go back to Newfoundland for new dogs! Indeed, as late as 1933, two Labradors were imported from Newfoundland, Cabot and Fanny, and are described in Scott/Middleton as 'the type sought for in size, colour of eye, shape and texture of coat, and were water-dogs.' These characteristics are certainly the essential qualities of the Labrador and they were present in dogs from Newfoundland as they were present in the dogs in England: dogs that were separated by nearly a hundred years of separate breeding, yet were essentially the same, because the early breeders in England kept their strains pure! These late importation's, decades after the Labrador was recognized by the Kennel

Club, were praised by H.T. Bowell, the Secretary of the Kennel Club, as 'reassuring' and he hoped that there would be more successful importation from the cradle of the breed. This would seem an extremely unusual attitude for the Secretary of the Kennel Club to take if he had any doubts about the dogs imported from Newfoundland not being exactly the same breed as the dogs in England. It is also interesting to note that the breeders in England seemed quite pleased with the progeny of these later imports. Several litters sired by Cabot are described by Scott as having 'every desirable quality both as retrievers and in appearance,' and Fanny's pups are said to 'show great promise.' In a letter dated December 11, 1938, Middleton wrote to his former personal secretary in Newfoundland that he had a grandson of Cabot's who 'is simply a delightful fellow,' is a wonderful retriever, and 'has got a fine thick undercoat like Cabot and this is what his grandmother and father . . . are lacking.' Middleton also asks his former secretary, Sir Leonard Outerbridge, to see if he can find a bitch like this dog in Newfoundland and offers to pay up to twenty-five dollars for her. All this evidence shows that in 1938 and before, the serious breeders from whose kennels the Labrador descends, as well as a high official of the Kennel Club, considered the Labrador in England and the waterdog in Newfoundland the same breed. This date was long after the breed was recogized by the Kennel Club and the Labrador was a recogized breed in the rest of North America. The myth that the waterdog from Newfoundland was somehow changed into the Labrador in England is, I think, of recent origin and is not supported by the evident facts. Scott and Middleton emphasize in their book that the pedigrees included 'show purity of line of descent' in the breed from the early imported dogs. It is about time that we as advocates of the breed looked at the facts not at the myths!

So it seems we are still a little in the dark about the origin of our beloved Labradors. Was there a black hound, a black pointer, a yellow Castro Laboreiro or some other ancient canine mixed with the Newfoundland? Or is the Labrador the older breed and the Newfoundland dog an offshoot? I'm sure we'll never know the answer, but the chance factors of evolution have given us a wonderful dog whose features must be carefully guarded by those who really care about the future of the Labrador.

Buccleuch Avon bred by the Third Earl of Malmesbury and owned by the Sixth Duke of Buccleuch. According to records, "Avon" was about 20 inches tall.

Chapter 2

Early England

Near the town of Poole was Hurn Court, the estate of the Second Earl of Malmesbury (1778-1841) who purchased a number of the "Little Newfoundlanders" from Colonel Hawker. He used them for retrieving game and kept them until his death. The Third Earl, his son, carried on with the "Labrador" dogs, importing more and breeding them.

It has been recorded that in about 1825 or 1830 others who brought in the smaller black dogs from Newfoundland were the Fifth Duke of Buccleuch; his brother Lord John Scott of Scotland, the Earl of Home; Mr. Montague Guest; Lord Wimbourne and Mr. C. J. Radclyffe (of Hyde, Wareham). Continuing the quote referred to by Dr. Michael Woods from a letter written in 1887 by the Third Earl of Malmesbury (1807-1889) to the Duke of Buccleuch:

> We always call mine Labrador dogs and I have kept the breed as pure as I could from the first I had from Poole. . . The real breed may be known by their having a close coat which turns the water off like oil and, above all, a tail like an otter.

Lord Malmesbury's dogs were described as: "Small, compact and very active; their coats were short, thick and smooth with sometimes a brown tinge at certain seasons, the eyes of most were in colour, something like burnt sugar. Their heads which were not big, were broad and the skull shapely and not long in muzzle. Their bright countenances denoted their sweet tempers and high courage."

From *The Stud Book of the Duke of Buccleuch's Labrador Retrievers*, we know that: "The Sixth Duke of Buccleuch and Twelveth Earl of Home spent some winters at Bournemouth in the early 1880s and were amazed, when shooting at Hurn Court at the work of Lord Malmesbury's dogs, especially in water." Lord Malmesbury gave them some of his breed. When the first dog, Ned, 1882 (Malmesbury Sweep ex Malmesbury Juno), arrived at Langholm Lodge, he proved himself of a different catagory to any of the other dogs there, whereas "Avon," 1885 (Malmesbury Tramp ex Malmesbury Juno), was even better than Ned. Ned was given to a good dog man for breaking, and impressed everyone with his retrieving ability. "He was a little compact dog of perfect shape, about 19 inches. When Avon arrived as a puppy from Lord Malmesbury, he too was trained and even outshone Ned. Avon was slightly larger, perhaps nearly 20 inches. All the Buccleuch breed trace back to these two dogs.

Thus the foundation of the modern Labrador Retriever consists of the following dogs:

From Lord Malmesbury—

	Sire	Dam
Ned, 1882	Lord Malmesbury's Sweep, 1877	His Juno, 1878
Avon, 1885	Lord Malmesbury's Tramp	His Juno, 1878
Nell, 1886	Lord Wimborne's dog 1882	Lord Malmesbury's Juno, 1882
Dinah, 1885	Lord Malmesbury's Nelson	His Nell
Juno Smut, 1885	Bred by Lord Malmesbury	
The Duke of Hamilton's Sam, 1884	Preston Hall Diver*	Hamilton's Fan (The Hamilton old Labrador breed)

* Preston Hall Diver was by a dog of Lord Malmesbury's; his dam, Lord Ruthven's Jet, about which he wrote that she was the last of the Labradors at Winton.

The Hon. M. Guest's Sankey	Mr. M. Guest's Sweep (from Lord Malmesbury)	Lord Wimborne's bitch

and last—

Kielder , 1872	Netherby Boatswain*	Netherby Nell*

* Netherby Boatswain was from the Eleventh Earl of Home
* Nell was from the Fifth Duke of Buccleuch.

In the year 1888, Lord George Scott, younger son of the Sixth Duke of Buccleuch became in charge of all the Labradors. In those days there were 60 or more gamekeepers on the different family estates, and each was supplied with one or more dogs. All matings were planned by Lord George, and although some were given to friends and relatives, none were ever sold. A description of coat colour by Lord George follows:

The coats of black pure-bred Labradors have always been inclined to show a slight tinge of brown colour at certain times of the year. About 1892 two whelps were born liver coloured, but such a thing has not happened for over four decades, at any rate in the Buccleuch Kennel where none have since been discarded.

In the 1880s, many areas of Newfoundland banned the keeping of dogs. Trade with England was coming to an end, so if it were not for the kennels of the Earls of Malmesbury, the Dukes of Buccleugh, Mr. C. J. Radelyffe and a few others, we may not have the Labrador of today. None of these dogs ever appeared in competition, but it is from these bloodlines that the purebred Labrador became established.

The above mentioned Mr. Radclyffe had a litter years later from black parents in which there were two yellow pups—the first yellows to be recorded. Of those two puppies, the male was named Hyde Ben, the first yellow registered Labrador in England.

Munden Sentry (Munden Sixty x Munden Scottie) was bred by Lord Knutsford.

A painting of Major Maurice Portal's FTC Flapper.

Chapter 3

Breed Development in England

Even though a number of the early breeders were trying to keep their stock pure, it is thought that some others were mating their Labradors with Pointers, Fox Hounds or other retriever breeds. Dogs of mixed retriever breeding could be registered by the Kennel Club under whatever breed the owner chose. Therefore some concerned breeders came together in London on April 5, 1916, to form The Labrador Retriever Club, to protect the interests of the breed and later to run its own field trials and shows.

The first elected Chairman was the Hon. Arthur Holland-Hibbert (later to become Lord Knutsford of the Munden prefix), Vice Chairman was Major Maurice Portal, D.S.O., and Mrs. Quintin Dick (later to become Lorna, Countess Howe) was elected as Secretary and Treasurer. A committee was formed including the remaining seven people attending. They were: Lord Chesterfield; Lord Lonsdale; Lord Vivian; Lord Harlech; Mr. Burdett-Coutts, M.P.; Mr. R. Heaton and Mr. A. Nichol who laid down the foundation for the modern Labrador They drew up a Breed Standard that was accepted by the Kennel Club and remained in usage until the revision in 1950. Members could join by invitation that first year, and there were 129.

Author's note: In 1990, The Labrador Retriever Club membership reached 2,000 with members from at least 25 countries. There are more than 400 members from overseas.

Munden

"Lord Knutsford, of the Munden Kennel, took office as the Club Chairman in 1916 (as the Hon. Arthur Holland-Hibbert) and continued at the helm until his death in 1935. Much credit must go to him for his diplomatic chairmanship during the formative years of the breed." Mrs. Jo Coulson wrote the above accolade for *A Celebration of 75 Years, The Labrador Retriever Club 1916-1991*. Labradors from Lord Knutsford's famous Munden Kennel were successful in the field and in the show ring. His first Labrador, Munden Sybil, was a granddaughter of Boatswain, imported from Newfoundland.

His main concern was for the advancement of the breed, and through his efforts, Labradors were recognized in The Kennel Club Stud Book in 1903, and subsequently classes were held at Cruft's Dog Show. The first Stud Book entries were Munden dogs: Sentry, Single and Sovereign. This kennel was based on the early Malmesbury and Buccleuch lines.

In 1900, the International Gun Dog League (IGL) was formed from Pointer and Setter groups, and the Spaniels and Retrievers. The Retriever

Society's first trial was held in 1900, and Rust, a brown Wavy Coated Retriever bitch, was the winner over 10 entries. The Hon. Arthur Holland-Hibbert's Munden Single was the first Labrador to place at a trial, and she did so four times through 1907. When she died, her body was mounted and placed in the British Museum where it remained for years, but is no longer there.

Vice Chairman of the Club, Maurice Portal, D.S.O., served in this office from 1916 until his death in 1947. He was a field trial man who owned the famous FTC Flapper (Barnett's Stag x Betsay) born in 1902. Flapper came directly from Malmesbury and Buccleuch lines, a great-grandson of Buccleuch Ned. Flat-Coated Retrievers dominated those early trials until Flapper and his progeny came along. Before he died in 1914, Flapper sired some 700 puppies, and he and his progeny won 22 firsts, eight seconds and eight thirds.

In 1910, six years before a Standard was set down by The Labrador Club, Major Portal gave his description of the Labrador in an article for *The Field*:

> Briefly in appearance the Labrador should be a compactly built dog. Straight legs, shortish and with plenty of muscle, a deep chest, rather short neck and well set on head which should be rather broad, not pointed at nose or very little. Eyes well set and full of expression and the colour of burnt sugar for choice. Ears set rather low and close to the head. The tail straight set rather low and short and rather broad at the base. The coat short, hard and thick and wiry, no waves or curl in it. The legs have no feather, the feet good and not splayed out.

In the same article, Major Portal states, "Several instances have occurred where the colour of the litter has varied, one or two puppies coming a brown color, light rusty brown, the make and shape of the puppies being true Labrador and the coat perfect. I can offer no solution for this, I know of one or two bitches which produce this colour in each litter, though they are quite black and their pedigrees show no outcross." So, since we know there were a few Buccleuch chocolates, the colour must be very old.

The next star to come along was Mr. Archibald Butter's FTC Peter of Faskally who had a super career and produced some important offspring: FTCs Patron of Faskally and Peter of Whitmore; Scandal of Glynn, sire of Dual Ch. Banchory Bolo. In 1911, Peter won the Retriever Champion Stake and his daughter, Gwendoline, was second. Mr. Butter and Peter were the first team to use whistles and hand signals emulating those used in sheep dog work.

Zelstone

As stated in the previous chapter, Major C. E. Radclyffe's early yellow, Hyde Ben, was born in a litter of blacks, from black parents in 1899, and proved to be the starting point for kennels interested in the yellow colour.

The Labrador Retriever Club's 31st field trial, November 1933. Left to right: Hon. Mrs. Hill-Wood with Ranger of Kentwood; Brig. Gen. R.L. Ricketts; Lorna, Countess Howe with Banchory Trump; Major Bonham Carter; and Mr. Tom Gaunt with Jock of Glastry. Photo—Sports & General.

Mrs. Audrey Radclyffe, Zelstone, with Zelstone Diver, Crisp and Misty "picking up" at a local shoot.

Ben was the first yellow registered Labrador from whom descend the kennels of Knaith, Zelstone, Folkingham, Boghurst, Hawksbury, Kettledean, Braeroy and others. Mr. Radclyffe's daughter-in-law, Mrs. Audrey Radclyffe, established the Zelstone kennel of yellows in 1929. She has bred, owned and trained both show champions and field champions: FTC Zelstone Darter, dam of Ch. Zelstone Leapyear Lass, winner of nine CCs and several field trial awards; Lass in turn was the dam of FTC Zelstone Moss. Mrs. Radclyffe, at age 87 (in 1993), said, "My greatest pleasure is going out, usually with three dogs for picking up. I seem to be in demand, booked up in advance for the shooting season." Every Thursday between April and September, she shares her 60 years of experience picking up and training gundogs with her Dorset neighbors.

Knaith

The Knaith kennel in Scotland was begun in 1910 by Major and Mrs. Arthur Wormald, who also kept only yellows. Of all their Labradors, Dual Ch. Knaith Banjo was the most famous, the last living dual champion in England, and the only one to have been bred, trained and handled at field trials by his owner, Mrs. Wormald. He also had an enviable show record of 12 CCs all won under different judges, four BOBs and seven Reserve BOBs. At field trials he collected 41 awards. The Wormalds started The Yellow Labrador Club in 1924, and Major Wormald was Hon. Secretary until his death in 1953, after which Mrs. Veronica Wormald took over the position until a year before she died in 1979, at which time she was almost 94.

During the first World War, from the years 1914 through 1918, dog activities, along with other pleasant pursuits, certainly took a back seat. However, with the formation of The Labrador Retriever Club in 1916, and the setting down of a Standard to be followed by all serious breeders, we come to the dedicated Lorna, Countess Howe (the Club's first Secretary, the former Mrs. Quinton Dick) and her Banchory kennel.

Banchory

It has been said of Lady Howe that she had a genius for bringing together dogs of different lines from all areas and consistently keeping a uniform type. She pursued the best and made a name for breeding and buying the best. For over three decades, with her gifted trainer, Mr. Tom Gaunt, and later the world-famous Mrs. Gwen Broadley as partner, Lady Howe claimed title to four Dual Champions, 29 Bench Champions, and seven Field Champions. Probably her most famous dog was Dual Ch. Banchory Bolo. Mr. Mackay Sanderson's tribute to Bolo in the British Stud Book contains the following passage:

> He came at a time when prestige both in a competitive and breeding sense was being put to rigorous tests. Behind the full story of remarkable expansion during the last period, lies the priceless contribution made by

A Ward Binks painting of Lorna, Countess Howe's famous Dual Ch. Banchory Bolo.

Bolo and his descendants. In the interval since Bolo caught the imagination of the public, one can discern certain events of change and significance, and the feats of this remarkable dog and his progeny give joy to the memory as one contemplates the advance which followed. The name and fame of Bolo will always be indissolubly bound up with the Banchory kennel of Lorna, Countess Howe, of which he was such a distinguished inmate.

To access the imprint of the descent from Malmesbury Tramp in its wholeness and right proportion, a separate feature has to be accorded in the line from FC Peter of Faskally through Scandal of Glynn which gained its fullest expression with the emergence of Dual Ch. Banchory Bolo. Between the period which had given birth to Tramp and the advent of Bolo some forty years later, no single figure had arisen which had exercised such a great and moulding influence on progress.

Other noted Banchory dogs were Dual Ch. Bramshaw Bob, winner of Best in Show at Crufts Dog Show, London in 1932 and 1933, and his sire, Ch. Ingleston Ben, FTCs Balmuto Jock and Balmuto Hewildo, Dual Ch. Peter the Painter and Ch. Ilderton Ben. The Labrador owes its prominent status in the gun dog world today in large measure to Lady Howe.

Liddly

The Liddly Kennels of Mr. and Mrs. H. A. Saunders began in 1922 with the acquisition of their foundation bitch, Toddy of Whitmore, and another bitch, Delyn of Liphook. Their first dog was Tar of Hamyax who became their first champion in 1927. "The foundation was for work and all Liddly stock are workers. When shown, they won well so we aimed only to breed to the standard and they have been continuously successful in the ring ever since." Some of the Liddlys were also winners at field trials and dual winners. Ch. Liddly Cornflower has a special place in Labrador Club history. She was one of a few to win Best in Show at the Club show two years running, 1967 and 1968. Also Cornflower is the model for the Club motif, and illustrates well what a really good Labrador should be. Cornflower is part of an unbroken Liddly line down from Ch. Tar of Hamyax to the last champion, Ch. Liddly Buddleia who was made up in 1970—43 years of breeding good working and good looking Labs. Along with his work over the years for The Labrador Club, Mr. Saunders served on the General Committee of The Kennel Club, and was Vice President of the International Gundog League Retriever Society, but first and foremost he enjoyed the country pursuits of shooting, with a good dog at his side, and river fly-fishing.

Hiwood

The Hiwood Kennel of Lady Hill-Wood began in the 1920s. Her mother was a Buccleuch, and her Uncle George pioneered Labrador breeding at the Buccleuch Kennels. Her first Labrador, by Titus of Whitmore, was acquired on her honeymoon from friends, and her interest just grew. Her favorite dog was FTC Hiwood Chance, born in 1928. After World War II, FTC Hiwood Gypsey was the dam of four field trial champions. FTC Hiwood Dipper won the Retriever Championship in 1960, and won a CC at Windsor. FTC Dacre Hiwood Frank, owned by Anne Hill-Wood, also won the Retriever Championship in 1964. Lady Hill-Wood has been Vice-Chairman of The Labrador Club 1960 through 1974, and President from 1974 to the present.

Holton

The Holton Kennels of Mr. Maurice Gilliat, and later his daughter, Mrs. Daphne Walter, have made quite a name over the years. In the early 1930s, Mr. Gilliat purchased two females of good breeding that became his foundation stock. One of them, Towyriver Bee, was the dam of his first champion, Holton Joyful, when mated with the Saunders' Ch. Liddly Jonquil. Mr. Gilliat always aimed to produce a dual-purpose dog, and maintained that good looks and brains must go together. Some other champions were Holton Pipit, Holton Lancelot and Holton Baron in England; Holton Tranquil and Holton Welkin in the U.S. and Holton Focus in Australia. The most famous of these was Ch. Holton Baron who won 25 CCs which was the record for many years. Mr. Gilliat has served as a member of several committees of The Kennel Club including The General Committee which is the Parliament of Dogdom. From 1936, he held different positions in The Labrador Club, and was Chairman from 1961 until 1980.

Sandylands

The world renowned Sandylands Kennel of Mrs. Gwen Broadley began in 1929 with her first Labrador, Juno of Sandylands, daughter of Darky Dan and Laund Linky, going back to Ch. Ilderton Ben and FTC Peter of Faskally. Later, from the Wilworth Kennels came Jerry of Sandylands who became

Mrs. Gwen Broadley on holiday with Eng. Ch. Sandylands Jerry and Eng. Ch. Sandylands Juno, 1933.

the first champion for Mrs. Broadley in Labradors in 1934. When these two were mated, the first homebred champion was Ch. June of Sandylands. "I started as a teenager, and remember how it feels to be a nervous beginner. Poor Jerry, it took five years to get his championship!"

Although Gwen Broadley has had champions in four other breeds—English Springer Spaniels, Cocker Spaniels, Pointers and Flat-Coated Retrievers—the Labradors won out. Since 1959, there have been only Labradors at Sandylands. "Every other breed I had was just taken over by a Labrador."

"About the time my first marriage to Cyril Broadley was coming apart, Lorna, Countess Howe told me she was going to have to give up her Labradors since her handler and trainer was retiring. Lady Howe suggested that we go together, and after giving it some thought, I agreed. So it was that we became partners and I took along five champions. I went to live on her estate, Hawkridge House, Hermitage, near Newbury in Berkshire. It was very interesting and I'm sure we both learned a lot. I greatly respected her and her fine sense of humor. The only thing we disagreed about was my driving! We went to all the trials, but that was Tom Gaunt's department. I did all the showing while I was with her which was about two years. Unfortunately Lady Howe had a serious accident. She was in her seventies and had broken her hip and so was using an electric wheelchair. One very sticky morning she went out into the garden and somehow got into a rut and tipped over with the wheelchair motor still running, and her other hip was broken. We parted very good friends, but it was the end of her days in Labradors. She continued for a while in Pugs. I cannot speak too highly of Lady Howe."

Gwen moved back to the Midlands, near Rugby, in the 1950s where she met and married Frank Truslove 34 years ago. "Coming from farming background he is invaluable with the dogs—whelping, exercising, etc., but

*Mrs. Gwen
Broadley,
Sandylands, with
Eng. Ch.
Sandylands Mark
at 11 years of
age, 1977.*
Photo © Fall.

he is not so interested in the showing side," says Gwen. At the time of her marriage to Frank, she was well established as a judge and changing her name from Broadley to Truslove was proving very difficult, so to the dog world, she has stayed as Gwen Broadley since.

Erica Smith came to help with the dogs when she was only a school girl, and continues today with Gwen. They are very good friends and travel together to shows. Erica handles the Sandylands dogs in the ring and is a Championship Show judge of Labradors.

In the 1960s, Mr. Garner Anthony from the U.S. wanted to buy Sh. Ch. Sandylands My Lad, but Gwen was reluctant to sell him, so it was decided that there would be a partnership. "It has worked well, and Mr. and Mrs. Anthony are wonderful friends," says Gwen.

For over 70 years, the Sandylands kennel has been going strong! There have been so many great dogs:

- **Ch. Sandylands Tweed of Blaircourt,** bred by Mr. and Mrs. Grant Cairns, and behind most of the Sandylands dogs, siring many champions in many parts of the world.
- **Ch. Sandylands Tan** who sired eight champions in two litters out of Sandylands Shadow before he went out to Australia where he sired 40 Australian champions.
- **Ch. Sandylands Tandy,** from the above mating of Tan and Shadow, produced a

remarkable number of top winners when mated with Tweed daughters. He is in many yellow pedigrees.

- **Ch. Sandylands Mark** (Ch. Reanacre Mallardhurn Thunder x Ch. Sandylands Truth). "He is the dog who has done the most for the breed and the kennel, and continued a line of prepotent stud dogs," states Gwen. He sired 29 British champions, an all time record in any breed in the U.K., and a great many elsewhere.
- **Eng./Am. Ch. Sandylands Midas,** littermate to Mark.
- **Ch. Sandylands Stormalong,** very sadly died at age three, but he was top stud dog for two years after his death.
- **Int./World Ch. Sandylands Rip Van Winkle,** gaining his title in France and America.
- **Ch. Sandylands Truth,** dam of Mark and Midas and her sister,
- **Ch. Sandylands Mercy**
- **Eng./Am. Ch. Sandylands Tanna**
- **Sh. Ch. Sandylands Midnight Magic,** and . . .
- **Sh. Ch. Sandylands Longley Come Rain,** both great brood bitches for the kennel.

Gwen Broadley awarded her first set of CCs in English Springers just after the war (WW II). During succeeding years she judged all over the world: "Norway and Sweden have particularly good dogs, but some of the best dogs I have judged have been in America," declares Gwen. She has retired from judging, her last engagement being The Yellow Labrador Club Championship Show in 1986. She has been a Committee Member of The Labrador Club since 1946, and Vice-Chairman since 1974. She has been a member of The Kennel Club for many years, serving on a number of committees, including the General Committee. Today she is an Honorary Member of The Kennel Club.

Some other kennels of note from those early 1900s were:

Adderley - Mr. Reginald Corbett
Balmuto - Mr. David Black
Brocklehirst - James Dinwoodie
Colwill - Mr. Collins
Drinkstone - Dr. Monro Home
Flodden - Lord Joicey
Hamyax - Mr. Whitworth
Hawlmark - Mr. Anderton
Kinpurnie - Sir C. Cayzer
Lochar - Tom Dinwoodie
Netherby - Sir Richard Graham
Orchardton - Mr. Carruthers
Pettistree - Mr. Kennard
Treesholme - Mr. Smith
Whitmore - Mr. Twyfor
Withington - Mr. Hulme

With the advent of World War II, dog breeding in England ceased. One breeder told me of cooking nettles to feed one or two dogs, another described the public disdain of having dogs rather than edible animals. A few breeders kept only a small nucleus.

*Mrs. Audrey James Field,
first president of The
Labrador Retriever Club,
Inc. in the United States.*

*Four imported kennelmates from the Wingan Kennel of Jay Carlisle, Long Island,
New York. Left to right: Orchardton Doris, Drinkstone Pons of Wingan, Bancstone
Ben, and Banchory Nightlight of Wingan, December 1934.*

Chapter 4

Breed Development in the United States

Authors's note: Mrs. Joan (Redmond) Read became involved with Labradors at a very young age. She lived in Oyster Bay, New York, a main flyway for migrating game birds and a residential area for affluent sportsmen and women. As a child she knew them all, and her help with the early history of the Labrador Retriever in America is greatly appreciated.

In the late 1920s, some very wealthy Americans patterned themselves after the British gentry. They went to Scotland for the shooting and fishing, and came back with gamekeepers, dog trainers and Labradors. Those early kennels were instrumental in establishing the popularity of the Labrador Retriever in the United States. During 1931, all Retrievers (except Chesapeake Bay Retrievers) were grouped and registered Retrievers, but in the latter part of the year, The Labrador Retriever Club, Inc. (LRC) was formed and Labradors were given separate status. In that year, 40 Labradors were registered, and in 1932 there were 58. The number grew steadily until 1941 and the beginning of the war when the annual registration reached 523.

Marshall Field's wife, Mrs. Audrey James Field, came from England, and was quite familiar with Labradors. She was instrumental in the formation of The Labrador Retriever Club, Inc. and served as its first President from 1931 through 1935. The Fields used the kennel name, Caumset. Robert Goelet (Glenmere) and Franklin B. Lord (Blake) both served as Vice Presidents, and Wilton Lloyd-Smith (Kenjockety) was Secretary-Treasurer. Directors were Marshall Field, William J. Hutchinson and Paul Pennoyer. Others who were very active and became officers and directors in 1935 were Charles L. Lawrence (Meadow Farm), Jay Carlisle (Wingan), Alfred Ely, Benjamin Moore and Mrs. E. Roland Harriman. The first Labrador Retriever Club, Inc. field trial was held at "Glenmere," the estate of Robert Goelet in Chester, N.Y. on December 21, 1931. The judges were David Wagstaff (Ledgelands) and Dr. Samuel Milbank (Earlsmoor). There were 29 starters in three stakes, and the winners were:

Puppy - **Drake**, W. Averell Harriman
American Bred - **Sam of Arden**, W. Averell Harriman
Open - **Carl of Boghurst**, Mrs. Marshall Field

The first Specialty show of the LRC was held in someone's garage in New York in 1933. The Superintendent was George F. Foley, the judge was

Mrs. Marshall Field and Best of Breed was Boli of Blake, a yellow owned by Franklin B. Lord.

Wingan, Chidley, West Island, Ledgelands

Jay F. Carlisle served as President of the LRC from 1935 through 1938, and gets the most credit for the rise in popularity of the Labrador in the United States. David Elliot came from Scotland to become kennel manager and trainer, and many dogs were imported from England. Dogs that came by ship from Lady Howe were Banchory Trump of Wingan and Banchory Jetsam. Other imports included Drinkstone Pons, Drinkstone Mars and Drinkstone Peg, imported in whelp to English Dual Champion Bramshaw Bob. The resulting litter was full of winners:

> Ch. Bancstone Ben of Wingan
> Ch. Bancstone Peggy of Wingan
> Ch. Bancstone Lorna of Wingan
> Ch. Bancstone Countess of Wingan

All were owned by Jay F. Carlisle. However, one was given to young Joan Redmond, Ch. Bancstone Bob of Wingan. Joan already had a firm interest in Labradors as her uncle had given her a puppy bitch in 1930 from his Scottish imports, Diver of Liphook and Ridgeland Black Diamond.

The Labrador Retriever Club Specialty Show, 1948. Left to right—BOB, Stowaway of Deer Creek owned by Mrs. Kathleen Poor and handled by Jim Cowie; LRC, Inc. president, Jay Gould Remick; judge, Dr. Samuel Milbank; and Joan Redmond with Chidley Spook, WB and BOS. Photo by Evelyn Shafer.

"Cinders" was her first and most favorite Labrador, and was later mated to Ch. Bancstone Ben of Wingan. That breeding produced Bender, sire of Ch. Star Lea Sunspeck, the forerunner of the Whygin Kennels of Mrs. Helen Ginnel. Another good dog of Joan's was Ch. Hugger Mugger (Ch. Bankstone Bob of Wingan x Marsh) who finished after W.W. ll and won Best in Show at the LRC, Inc. Specialty Show under judge Alva Rosenberg. Later his daughter, Ch. Chidley Spook did a lot of winning. Mrs. Read also owned the first American-bred yellow champion, Chidley Almond Crisp. Other notable early owners were financier J.P. Morgan who owned Banchory Snow, possibly the first yellow in this country, and his son, Junius, who along with his wife bred dual-purpose blacks at their West Island kennels. Mr. and Mrs. David Wagstaff of Ledgelands were also very involved with the breed. Dr. Samuel Millbank was given a dog from Scotland, Raffles of Earlsmoor, who became a champion very quickly and produced many good dogs—four from one litter were dual champions.

Arden

The most famous early kennel has to be Arden, the prefix of W. Averell Harriman, who imported several influencial Labradors. Tom Briggs, another Scotsman, came to serve as trainer and gamekeeper. Peggy of Shipton (Ronald of Candahar x Gehta) was an early import and she proved to be an excellent producer. Her first litter was sired by an English dog, Duke of Kirkmahoe. Mr. Harriman kept Sam of Arden from this litter, a good working dog. When Peggy was bred next to Mrs. Marshall Field's Odds On, she produced FTC Decoy of Arden and FTC Blind of Arden in 1933. Later Peggy was mated with English import Hiwood Risk (Hiwood D'Arcy x Hiwood Chance) bred by Lady Hill-Wood. From this union came the famous FTC Tar of Arden, who went to Paul Bakewell III of St. Louis, Missouri, and she became the basis of many great Deer Creek dogs.

Peggy's daughter, Decoy, broke the record! She was bred to Dr. Millbank's Ch. Raffles of Earlsmoor three different times. In the first litter in 1937, there were two dual champions—Dual Ch. Braes of Arden, owned by Mrs. J. R. McManus and Dual Ch. Gorse of Arden, owned by Mrs. Morgan Belmont.

Dr. Millbank kept Ch. Earlsmoor Moor of Arden who went on to win 40 BOBs, 12 Group Is, five Best in Show and retired two LRC, Inc. Challenge Cups. In all these wins, he was handled by Jim Cowie. This successful litter was repeated again in 1939. This was the famous "fish" litter from which came the remarkable Dual Ch. Shed of Arden and three-time National Field Trial Champion, who also belonged to Paul Bakewell III. There was another dual champion, Bengal of Arden (Good Hope Angus x Burma of Arden), owned by Mrs. A.P. Loening.

Sadly, Tom Briggs died in a car accident in 1940. This ended Mr. Harriman's interest in trials and shows, but not in Labradors.

FTC Tar of Arden bred by W. A. Harriman, Arden, and owned and trained by Paul Bakewell III.

Ch. Earlsmoor Moor of Arden, first Labrador Retriever to win Best in Show in the United States. Owned by Dr. and Mrs. Samuel Millbank, Earlsmoor.

Some others involved with Labradors in those early days were:

How Hi - Mr. & Mrs. Howes Burton, East Islip, L.I.,N.Y.
Kilsyth - Mr. & Mrs. Gerald M. Livingstone, Huntington, L.I.,N.Y.
Dunottar - Mr. & Mrs. Henry S. Morgan, Northport, L.I.,N.Y.
Marvadel - Mr. & Mrs. J. Gould Remick, N.Y.,N.Y.
Meadow Farm - Charles Lawrence, L.I.,N.Y.
Timber Town - Mrs. Kathleen B. Starr (later Mrs. K.B.Frederick)

Eng. Ch. Kupros Master Mariner owned and bred by Mr. and Mrs. Peter Hart, Kupros. Photo by H. Price Jessop.

Eng. Sh. Ch. Croftspa Hazelnut of Foxrush at seven years old, the winner of 45 CCs and 15 Res. CCs, bred by Mr. and Mrs. A. Chapman and owned by Mrs. J. Charlton. Photo by David Bull.

SECTION II
Definition of a Standard

■ **Chapter 1**

The English and the United States Standard

■ **Chapter 2**

Form Follows Function

Ch. Liddly Cornflower, model for the English Labrador Retriever Club logo, described as "a true Labrador example." Photo © Fall.

Ashlyn's Sea Jetty, owned and bred by Wendy Brehm, Ashlyn, a good American example Photo by Ashbey.

Chapter 1

The English Standard and the
United States Standard for Labrador Retrievers

A Standard is a picture in words of what an ideal Labrador Retriever should be—a pattern or criterion of the perfect Labrador. Of course there is no perfect dog or horse or person, but a written "standard" is established for use as a basis of comparison in judging quality.

The British Breed Standard

The mother of all breed standards for the Labrador Retriever is the British Kennel Club Breed Standard. I would like to quote a few lines from a recent book on the breed, *Labrador Retrievers Today*, by Mrs. Carole Coode: "In most countries of the world the British Kennel Club Breed Standard is in use; Britain is considered to be the Labrador's country of origin. The FCI (Federation Cynologique Internationale), with all its aligned countries, also uses the British Standard." In surveying other countries, I found that their Standards were either exactly that of the British Kennel Club or as close a translation as possible. Therefore it is presented here, with the kind permission of The Kennel Club.

British Breed Standard—1986
Labrador Retrievers

GENERAL APPEARANCE   Strongly built, short-coupled, very active; broad in skull; broad and deep through chest and ribs; broad and strong over loins and hindquarters.

CHARACTERISTICS   Good tempered, very agile. Excellent nose, soft mouth; keen love of water. Adaptable, devoted companion.

TEMPERAMENT   Intelligent, keen and biddable, with a strong will to please. Kindly nature, with no trace of aggression, or undue shyness.

HEAD AND SKULL   Skull broad with defined stop; clean-cut without fleshy cheeks. Jaws of medium length, powerful, not snipey. Nose wide, nostrils well-developed.

EYES   Medium size, expressing intelligence and good temper, brown or hazel.

EARS   Not large or heavy, hanging close to head and set rather far back.

MOUTH   Jaws and teeth strong, with perfect, regular and complete scissor bite, i.e., the upper teeth closely overlapping the lower teeth and set square to the jaws.

NECK   Clean, strong, powerful, set into well-placed shoulders.

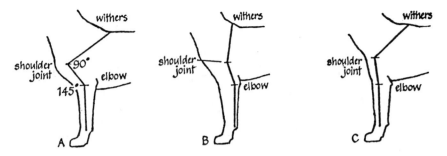

Shoulder Angulation
Drawings by Pat Woollaston, New Zealand, 1986.
A. Correct—90 degree angle at shoulder, 145 degree at elbow, shoulder-blade back.
B. Wrong—Angles at shoulder and elbow almost straight, shoulder-blade straight up.
C. Wrong—Open angle at shoulder. No elbow-angle, shoulder-blade laid back

FOREQUARTERS Shoulders long and sloping. Forelegs well boned and straight from elbow to ground when viewed from either front or side.
BODY Chest of good width and depth, with well-sprung barrel ribs. Level topline. Loins wide, short-coupled and strong.
HINDQUARTERS Well-developed not sloping to tail; well turned stifle. Hocks well let down, cow hocks highly undesirable.
FEET Round, compact; well-arched toes and well-developed pads.
TAIL Distinctive feature, very thick towards base, gradually tapering towards tip, medium length, free from feathering, but clothed thickly all round with short, thick, dense coat, thus giving 'rounded' appearance described as 'otter' tail. May be carried gaily, but should not curl over back.
GAIT/MOVEMENT Free, covering adequate ground; straight and true front and rear.
COAT Distinctive feature, short dense without wave or feathering, giving fairly hard feel to the touch; weather-resistant undercoat.
COLOUR Wholly black, yellow or liver/chocolate. Yellows range from light cream to red fox. Small white spot on chest permissible.
SIZE Ideal height at withers: Dogs 56-57 cm (22 inches.- 22 1/2 inches) Bitches 54-56 cm (21 1/2 inches - 22 inches.)
FAULTS Any departure from the foregoing points should be considered a fault and the seriousness with which the fault should be regarded should be in exact proportion to its degree.
NOTE Male animals should have two apparently normal testicles fully descended into the scrotum.

The U.S. Breed Standard

The current U.S. Standard for the Labrador Retriever contains considerably more text than the English version, as well as five disqualifications including one for height. When the first Standard was written in the United States it was the same as the English Standard, word-for-word, the only difference being the English spelling of the word "colour" versus the

American spelling, "color." There was no mention of desired height. The original Standard was short and to the point, and early breeders in America saw no reason to change anything.

However, with each revision, there have been more and more differences between the English and American Standards for the breed. In the 1950s, revisions were made in both countries and, although there were similarities, several deviations appeared which certainly changed the picture. I list some of them here:

	English	American
Stop	Pronounced	Slight
Jaws	Medium length	Long
Teeth	Lower teeth just behind, but touching the upper	Level mouth
Eyes	Brown or hazel	Brown, yellow or black, but brown or black preferred
Coat	Short, dense, without wave with weather resisting undercoat and should give a fairly hard feeling to the hand	Short, dense, without wave and should give a fairly hard feeling to the hand
Weight	(nothing mentioned)	Dogs: 60 to 75 lbs. Bitches: 55 to 70 lbs.
Size	Desired height Dogs: 22-22 1/2 inches Bitches: 21 1/2-22 inches	Height at Shoulder Dogs: 22 1/2-24 1/2 inches Bitches: 21 1/2-23 1/2 inches
Faults	Under or overshot mouth; No undercoat, bad action, feathering, snipiness on the head; large or heavy ears; cow-hocked; tail curled over back.	(none mentioned)

Please note the wide variance in height allowed. American Labrador dogs could be two inches taller than the English dogs, but not allowed to be one-half inch shorter, and American Labrador bitches could be one and a half inches taller than their British counterparts. This size difference posed a real dilemma because in every other part of the world Labradors were not supposed to be as tall as the American Standard specified.

The contemporary British Standard for Labrador Retrievers, as presented at the beginning of this chapter, was the product of a third revision in 1986. About that time, The American Kennel Club, Inc. asked each breed club in the U.S. to put its Standard into a format that would be used by all the breeds. This brings us to the present predicament in America. The American Kennel Club, Inc. approved a Standard revision for the Labrador Retriever effective March 31, 1994. The Standard revision proposed by the parent club, The Labrador Retriever Club, Inc., proved to be highly controversial because of its length, redundancy and, in particular, the disqualifications. It is presented here.

American Breed Standard
APPROVED STANDARD FOR THE LABRADOR RETRIEVER
March 31, 1994

General Appearance

The Labrador Retriever is a strongly built, medium-sized, short-coupled, dog possessing a sound, athletic, well-balanced conformation that enables it to function as a retrieving gun dog; the substance and soundness to hunt waterfowl or upland game for long hours under difficult conditions; the character and quality to win in the show ring; and the temperament to be a family companion. Physical features and mental characteristics should denote a dog bred to perform as an efficient Retriever of game with a stable temperament suitable for a variety of pursuits beyond the hunting environment.

The most distinguishing characteristics of the Labrador Retriever are its short, dense, weather resistant coat; an "otter" tail; a clean-cut head with broad back-skull and moderate stop; powerful jaws; and its "kind," friendly eyes, expressing character, intelligence and good temperament.

Above all, the Labrador Retriever must be well balanced, enabling it to move in the show ring or work in the field with little or no effort. The typical Labrador possesses style and quality without over refinement, and substance without lumber or cloddiness. The Labrador is bred primarily as a working gun dog; structure and soundness are of great importance.

Size, Proportion, and Substance

Size—The height at the withers for a dog is 22 1/2 to 24 1/2 inches; for a bitch 21 1/2 inches to 23 1/2 inches. Any variation greater than 1/2 inch above or below these heights is a disqualification. Approximate weight of dogs and bitches in working condition: dogs 65 to 80 pounds; bitches 55 to 70 pounds.

The minimum height ranges set forth in the paragraph above shall not apply to dogs or bitches under twelve months of age.

Proportion—Short-coupled; length from the point of the shoulder to the point of the rump is equal to or slightly longer than the distance from the withers to the ground. Distance from the elbow to the ground should be equal to one half of the height at the withers. The brisket should extend to the elbows, but not perceptibly deeper. The body must be of sufficient length to permit a straight, free and efficient stride; but the dog should

never appear low and long or tall and leggy in outline. *Substance*—
Substance and bone proportionate to the overall dog. Light, "weedy"
individuals are definitely incorrect; equally objectionable are cloddy lumbering specimens. Labrador Retrievers shall be shown in working condition, well-muscled and without excess fat.

Head

Skull—The skull should be wide; well-developed, but without exaggeration. The skull and foreface should be on parallel planes and of approximately equal length. There should be a moderate stop—the brow slightly pronounced so that the skull is not absolutely in a straight line with the nose. The brow ridges aid in defining the stop. The head should be clean-cut and free from fleshy cheeks; the bony structure of the skull chiseled beneath the eye with no prominence in the cheek. The skull may show some median line; the occipital bone is not conspicuous in mature dogs. Lips should not be squared off or pendulous, but fall away in a curve toward the throat. A wedge-shaped head, or a head long and narrow in muzzle and back skull is incorrect as are massive, cheeky heads. The jaws are powerful and free from snippiness—the muzzle neither long and narrow nor short and stubby. *Nose*—The nose should be wide and the nostrils well-developed. The nose should be black on black or yellow dogs, and brown on chocolates. Nose color fading to a lighter shade is not a fault. A thoroughly pink nose or one lacking in any pigment is a disqualification. *Teeth*—The teeth should be strong and regular with a scissors bite; the lower teeth just behind, but touching the inner side of the upper incisors. A level bite is acceptable, but not desirable. Undershot, overshot, or misaligned teeth are serious faults. Full dentition is preferred. Missing molars or pre-molars are serious faults. *Ears*—The ears should hang moderately close to the head, set rather far back, and somewhat low on the skull; slightly above eye level. Ears should not be large and heavy, but in proportion with the skull and reach to the inside of the eye when pulled forward. *Eyes*—Kind, friendly eyes imparting good temperament, intelligence and alertness are a hallmark of the breed. They should be of medium size, set well apart, and neither protruding nor deep set. Eye color should be brown in black and yellow Labradors, and brown or hazel in chocolates. Black or yellow eyes give a harsh expression and are undesirable. Small eyes, set close together or round prominent eyes are not typical of the breed. Eye rims are black in black and yellow Labradors; and brown in chocolates. Eye rims without pigmentation is a disqualification.

Neck, Topline and Body

Neck—The neck should be of proper length to allow the dog to retrieve game easily. It should be muscular and free from throatiness. The neck should rise strongly from the shoulders with a moderate arch. A short, thick neck or a "ewe" neck is incorrect. *Topline*—The back is strong and the topline is level from the withers to the croup when standing or moving. However, the loin should show evidence of flexibility for athletic endeavor. *Body*—The Labrador should be short-coupled, with good spring of ribs tapering to a moderately wide chest. The Labrador should not be narrow chested; giving the appearance of hollowness between the front

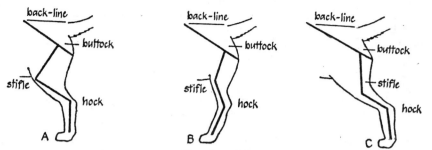

Rear Angulation
Drawings by Pat Woollaston, New Zealand, 1986.
A. Correct. B. Wrong—Stifle straight, sickle hocks. Dog tends to stand on its heels with hind-legs under body, back often humped and hind-legs straight. C. Wrong—All angles too open; hind-legs stretched behind dog with sloping topline.

Shoulder Movement
Drawings by Pat Woollaston, New Zealand, 1986.
Ideally the shoulder blade should slope 45 degrees to meet the ground. Ideal pelvic slope meets the ground at 30 degrees. The reason these angles are considered "ideal" for a Labrador is because they allow the maximum forward movement to balance maximum length of stride. When gaiting both shoulder and humerus move.

Movement
Drawings by Pat Woollaston, New Zealand, 1986.
Shaded areas indicate extent of muscular attachment to skeletal structure. This is a very simplified diagram indicating the greater reach achieved with correct shoulder and hip angulation. Dog "B" will have to take more steps and work much harder to cover the same distance as dog "A."

legs, nor should it have a wide spreading, bulldog-like front. Correct chest conformation will result in tapering between the front legs that allows unrestricted forelimb movement. Chest breadth that is either too wide or too narrow for efficient movement and stamina is incorrect. Slab-sided individuals are not typical of the breed; equally objectionable are rotund or barrel chested specimens. The underline is almost straight, with little or no tuck-up in mature animals. Loins should be short, wide and strong, extending to well developed, powerful hindquarters. When viewed from the side, the Labrador Retriever shows a well-developed, but not exaggerated forechest. *Tail*—The tail is a distinguishing feature of the breed. It should be very thick at the base, gradually tapering toward the tip, of medium length, and extending no longer than to the hock. The tail should be free from feathering and clothed thickly all around with the Labrador's short, dense coat thus having that peculiar rounded appearance that has been described as the "otter" tail. The tail should follow the topline in repose or when in motion. It may be carried gaily, but should not curl over the back. Extremely short tails or long thin tails are serious faults. The tail completes the balance of the Labrador by giving it a flowing line from the top of the head to the tip of the tail. Docking or otherwise altering the length or natural carriage of the tail is a disqualification.

Forequarters

Forequarters should be muscular, well coordinated and balanced with the hindquarters. *Shoulders*– The shoulders are well laid-back, long and sloping, forming an angle with the upper arm of approximately 90 degrees that permits the dog to move his forelegs in an easy manner with strong forward reach. Ideally, the length of the shoulder blade should equal the length of the upper arm. Straight shoulder blades, short upper arms or heavily muscled or loaded shoulders, all restricting free movement, are incorrect. *Front Legs*—When viewed from the front, the legs should be straight with good strong bone. Too much bone is as undesirable as too little bone, and short legged heavy boned individuals are not typical of the breed. Viewed from the side, the elbows should be directly under the withers, and the front legs should be perpendicular to the ground and well under the body. The elbows should be close to the ribs without looseness. Tied-in elbows or being "out-at-the-elbows" interfere with free movement and are serious faults. Pasterns should be strong and short and should slope slightly from the perpendicular line of the leg. Feet are strong and compact with well-arched toes and well-developed pads. Dew claws may be removed. Splayed feet, hare feet, knuckling over, or feet turning in or out are serious faults.

Hindquarters

The Labrador's hindquarters are broad, muscular and well-developed from the hip to the hock, with well-turned stifles and strong short hocks. Viewed from the rear, the hind legs are straight and parallel. Viewed from the side, the angulation of the rear legs is in balance with the front. The hind legs are strongly boned, muscled with moderate angulation at the stifle, and powerful, clearly defined thighs. The stifle is strong and there is no slippage of the patellae while in motion or when standing. The hock joints are strong, well let down and do not slip or hyper-extend while in motion or when standing. Angulation of both stifle and hock joint is such as to achieve the optimal balance of drive and traction. When standing, the rear toes are only slightly behind the point of the rump. Over angulation produces a sloping topline not typical of the breed. Feet are strong and compact, with well-arched toes and well-developed pads. Cow-hocks, spread hocks, sickle hocks and over-angulation are serious structural defects and are to be faulted.

Coat
The coat is a distinctive feature of the Labrador Retriever. It should be short, straight, and very dense, giving a fairly hard feeling to the hand. The Labrador should have a soft, weather-resistant undercoat that provides protection from water, cold and all types of ground cover. A slight wave down the back is permissible. Woolly coats, soft silky coats, and sparse slick coats are not typical of the breed, and should be severely penalized.

Color
The Labrador Retriever coat colors are black, yellow and chocolate. Any other color or combination of colors is a disqualification. A small white spot on the chest is permissible, but not desirable. White hairs from aging or scarring are not to be misinterpreted as brindling. *Black*—Blacks are all black. A black with brindle markings or a black with tan markings is a disqualification. *Yellow*—Yellows may range in color from fox-red to light cream with variations in shading on the ears, back, and underparts of the dog. *Chocolate*—Chocolates can vary in shade from light to dark chocolate. Chocolate with brindle or tan markings is a disqualification.

Movement
Movement of the Labrador Retriever should be free and effortless. When watching a dog move toward oneself, there should be no sign of elbows out. Rather, the elbows should be held neatly to the body with the legs not too close together. Moving straight forward without pacing or weaving, the legs should form straight lines, with all parts moving in the same plane. Upon viewing the dog from the rear, one should have the impression that the hind legs move as nearly as possible in a parallel line with the front legs. The hocks should do their full share of the work, flexing well, giving the appearance of power and strength. When viewed from the side, the shoulders should move freely and effortlessly, and the foreleg should reach forward close to the ground with extension. A short, choppy movement or high knee action indicates a straight shoulder; paddling indicates long, weak pasterns; and a short, stilted rear gait indicates a straight rear assembly; all are serious faults. Movement faults interfering with performance including weaving; side-winding; crossing over; high knee action; paddling; and short, choppy movement, should be severely penalized.

Temperament
True Labrador Retriever temperament is as much a hallmark of the breed as the "otter" tail. The ideal disposition is one of a kindly, outgoing, tractable nature; eager to please and non-aggressive towards man or

animal. The Labrador has much that appeals to people; his gentle ways, intelligence and adaptability make him an ideal dog. Aggressiveness towards humans or other animals, or any evidence of shyness in an adult should be severely penalized.

Disqualifications
1. Any deviation from the height prescribed in the Standard.
2. A thoroughly pink nose or one lacking in any pigment.
3. Eye rims without pigment.
4. Docking or otherwise altering the length or natural carriage of the tail.
5. Any other color or a combination of colors other than black, yellow or chocolate as described in the Standard.

I feel that some parts of this Standard are very good, but as a member of the parent club I voted against it for several reasons. It is very long, and I think it should be edited down to retain the pertinent points, striking out passages that are either unnecessary or redundant. One highly respected English authority has said, "That Standard is horrific! What are they trying to do—write a book?" In comparing the British and American Standards, the former is short and to the point, covering everything briefly and concisely, and it is recognized by Labrador clubs and breeders throughout the world as the Standard for the breed. It is unclear to me why our American Standard should be different from virtually all the other countries in the world. Dissimilar hunting conditions have been cited as an explanation for allowing a much taller dog in the U.S., but what about Australia, South Africa, Sweden or Finland? Surely they do not have the same hunting conditions as the U.K., but each of those countries retains the Standard of the country that developed the breed. Does anyone seriously think that a Labrador that stands 24 1/2 inches can retrieve better than one that is 22 inches or succeed better in the show ring? From my Webster's *New World Dictionary*, a "standard" is something established for use as a rule or basis of comparison in measuring or judging capacity, quantity, content, extent, value, quality, etc. I believe the Labrador Retriever should be the same worldwide, and there should be a standardization of the Standards.

Brian Yeowart and his Labrador Retrievers Langshott Crusader (black), Langshott Sable Princess and Langshott Charm of Tina "walking up" in Delnabo, Scotland, October 1992.

Chapter 2

Form Follows Function

The originators of the Labrador Retriever had in mind certain features that allowed the dog the ability to what they wanted from him. He was bred for a purpose to perform certain tasks. To explain the concept of form follows function we will use the continental gun dogs of Europe as an example.

Editor Tony Jackson and his collaborators state in their book, *Hunter Pointer Retriever* (HPR):

> The sporting nobility of Europe, with their vast estates and extensive variety of game required an all-purpose dog, one which could cope with differing terrain and game. Such dogs would be required to quarter the ground or close according to prevailing conditions, find game, staunchly point and on order flush, mark the fall and retrieve on command from land or water. The dogs would work not only game and wildfowl but also boar and deer. Such breeds or types of dogs, the Hunters-Pointers-Retrievers, were thus developed with enormous skill and care.
>
> Continuing in this vein, each of the dogs (six in number) who make up the Continental Gun Dog family of HPR dogs has its own characteristics and that each is unique in appearance, conformation, color, type, style and method of working. Each has its own standard set in its country of origin, and as it has been imported into this country it has been registered and classified by the American Kennel Club. There is no reason at all why the structure of these breeds should be altered and it is essential to understand that one and the same dog can fulfill the necessary requirements for bench and field.
>
> You must take heed of the standard, without prejudice, since it is the blueprint based on the original prototype; those who know and understand how to read a pedigree will be all too aware of the hazards of breeding the wrong type. For example, the correct coat is essential in a Gundog. No silky, thin, soft coat will stand up to punishing cover,

a winter's day with the north wind biting or rain driving in sheets across the plain.

If you have ever designed anything with functional parts, you will know that structural design implies more than bare bones of anatomy. You know that a good design takes into account all factors that will help the structure serve its purpose. Similarly, the structural design of a dog must provide for all the needs of its owner.

In keeping with the principles of good architectural design, organic structure must take into account the specific properties that the animal uses in his work. These materials must be able to withstand the stresses implicit in the design. Therefore, no breeder of a dog designed to hunt game would think of placing a thin unprotected skin where a tough layer of subcutaneous muscle and bristly coat should go. Here again, the inter-relationship of structure and function is obvious—the two go together. One of the most important things in designing and working with any breed is to always keep in mind the inseparability of structure and function. That is, the form of the animal must be designed for the function for which it had been originally bred.

The function for which dogs were originally bred is not necessarily the function for which they are utilized today. Many Labradors are kept in houses or apartments as family pets and seldom have the opportunity to perform their specific skills. Many dogs are placed in groups today where they are not required to perform any specific function.

Organic Engineering

You can get a better understanding of the functional aspects of a breed of dog if you think of them in terms of engineering. Consider, for example, the role of the early breeders in England. They had two kinds of jobs. First, they tried to design a useful product, that is a dog who could go after upland birds, stay close to the hunter, have a good nose, be steady and have the ability to go all day long in the field. Don't forget, originally they had to put food on the table. Only later were they used to hunt for sport. Then these early breeders had to find a way to manufacture these products. In bringing a new product into being, an engineer first lays out a method of operation. He might even design and build a new tool just for making this one product. With the breeder, he might bring in another breed and cross it and re-cross it and introduce others until he got the correct mixture.

The breeder might have to go through dozens of developmental stages before turning out a satisfactory replica of the designed product. But no matter how many steps you must take, a good product engineer (breeder) never departs from the intent of the basic design. He recognizes that the design has a special purpose that his efforts must serve. The farmer in England who had to protect his livestock and fowl against the incursion of foxes who holed up in dens in rocky lairs, invented a sturdy little dog to take care of that problem. This dog had to get along with the pack hounds who were used to run the fox to ground. Added to the design was the necessity of having a skull and rib cage that were flat enough to allow him to squeeze into any crevice the fox could. And finally, to have punishing jaws to dispatch the fox and haul him out. This little dog was called the Lakeland Terrier.

Whether we are talking about a dog breeder or an engineer, each designs his products or devises techniques to make use of certain basic designs. For example, an engineer must use only those geometrical figures that would yield desired structural strength. He must also use shapes that will conserve on materials and yet provide for the greatest efficiency. Furthermore, he must also concern himself with simplicity of design. Therefore, whenever possible he must construct simple machines (levers, pulleys, and inclined planes) as such, rather than intricate combinations of these machines.

A dog, or any living organism, is its own engineer. Throughout its life, it constantly refers to a basic design and manufactures the product it needs. In so doing, it makes use of the same mechanical principles that underlie the operation of man-made devices. Consider, for example, the transmission of force. When an animal moves its moveable parts, it transmits force in much the same way that machines do. In so doing, the animal uses its built-in simple machines. You can see this quite clearly in locomotor structures and that is why judging the gait of a dog in terms of its ability to perform its function is so very important in the overall approach to judging dogs.

Movement

For many years physiologists and even the vast majority of dog people believed that animals running at higher speeds would exact a higher "cost" in terms of energy burned. It didn't turn out that way! Recent studies have shown that animals use up energy at a uniform, predictable rate as the speed of movement increases.

As if that shattering piece of information wasn't enough, they found out that for any given animal, the amount of energy expended in getting from point A to point B was the same regardless of how fast the trip was taken. A Cheetah running 100 yards at a top speed of 60 miles per hour uses the same amount of energy as it would walking the same distance. The running is more exhausting because the calories are used up more quickly.

Size, however, does make a difference. Small dogs require much more energy per unit of weight to perform at top speed than Great Danes would. Small dogs appear to have higher "idling" speeds. The cost of maintaining muscular tension and of stretching and shortening the muscles are higher in small animals.

These same series of studies suggest that as much as 77 percent of the energy used in walking comes, not from the operation of the muscles themselves, but from a continual interplay between gravity and kinetic energy. From an engineering standpoint, it seems that the body tends to rotate about a center of mass, somewhat like an egg rolling end-on-end or the swing of an inverted pendulum. The 30 percent of effort supplied by the muscles is imported through the limbs to the ground to keep the animal's center of mass moving forward.

During running or trotting, the built-in springs for propulsion are the muscles and tendons of the limbs. When the animal has the need to move even faster, he has the ability to use an even bigger spring. As dogs shift from the fast trot to a gallop they tend to use their bodies as large springs to store more energy. They do not change the frequency of their strides, rather they increase the length of them.

Simple Bio-Machines

Let us consider how the dog compares with man-made machines. The dog can be compared to combinations of simple machines and other mechanical systems you might find in any factory. A few familiar examples will quickly clarify this analogy. The dog's legs for example could be diagrammed as levers. The appendages of all animals, in fact, serve as levers. If laid out side by side, they present a rather special array of "machines." As we have seen, dogs from the Chihuahua to the Great Dane, present a wide variety of angles and levers.

You would expect this, for their owners have widely different ways of life. Modifications in such bio-levers reflect the animal's way of life. So you would expect the Saluki's leg to be the kind of lever that gives the advantage of speed and distance; by the same token you would expect the design of the front legs of the Dachshund, "a burrowing animal," to provide for the multiplication of force, rather than the advantage of distance or speed.

Another simple machine that is easy to detect in nature is the pulley. You will find the living counterpart of the pulley wherever you find a muscle tendon joint apparatus. Whenever a tendon moves over a joint, it behaves like a pulley. Such mechanisms enable the dog to change the direction of force. A notable example of an application of the pulley principle is the action of the tendons and muscles in the dog's neck. When the handler "strings the dog up" on a tight lead, the ability of the dog to use that pulley correctly is gone.

Inclined planes are prevalent in all living things, but their presence is not always obvious. They frequently appear as wedges, which are made up of two inclined planes arranged back-to-back. The incisors of the dog, for example, are wedges. The cutting action of these teeth is an application of the wedge principle in nature. Another illustration is when a standard calls for a sloping topline in movement. The sloping plane from withers to tail is designed to harness the thrust or drive from the rear quarters and move the dog along a straight line with power.

Hydraulics and Life

Any person who has tried to dam up a creek or in some way tried to manage moving water has had experience with hydraulics, which involves the application of energy to practical uses. Frequently, therefore, hydraulics deals with the transfer of mechanical energy of moving fluids to the powering of machinery. It also deals with the use of pressure created by fluids (hydraulic pressure). All this finds an application in biology, wherein fluid is of paramount importance. Applications of hydraulic pressure are evident in dogs.

Certainly the pumping action of the heart to move blood through the circulatory system is an appropriate example. A standard asking for a deep chest and the front wide enough for adequate heart and lung space is telling us we need room for a pump big enough to keep the dog going under pressure all day long. This pump exerts pressure, directly or indirectly, on all body fluids. As you know, when the heart is in need of repair or is worn out, the blood pressure of the animal varies abnormally. When this happens, the animal finds it hard to maintain a proper fluid balance of its tissues and organs. The final result is interference with the movement of the materials of life.

Death can occur if the equipment designed to maintain hydraulic pressure fails in its function. As you may recall from your school studies of anatomy, it takes more than the pumping of the heart to maintain normal fluid pressure in an animal. The condition of the arteries and the veins is equally important. If these circulatory structures do not have the proper strength or elasticity, this condition could cause abnormal variation in the hydraulic pressure of the body. The arteries and veins are fluid conduits. Therefore, they must have a structural design that will enable them to withstand and adjust to sudden changes in hydraulic pressure.

As you may recall how effectively the design met the need, the walls of the arteries are designed to have heavier muscular construction than the veins. That's because the blood being pumped under great pressure from the heart goes out through the arteries and returns under less pressure through the veins. Thus, the arteries can withstand greater pressure than the veins can tolerate. The arteries tend to be more elastic than the veins so they can react more quickly to changes in pressure and so regulate the movement of fluid to compensate for the change in the situation.

Organic Architecture

The shape of a building usually reflects its function. The design of its various parts (roof, doors, ventilators) also relates to special functions, and so it is with the shape of the dog. In a large dog, the design often calls for a shape that will provide the necessary strength, compactness and capability to perform certain functions. For example, dogs such as the Rottweiler were used to haul heavy loads. They were designed with a shoulder construction and balanced size that would enable them to perform this function. On the other hand, for example, a long and slender shape characterizes the coursing type of dog (Afghan, Greyhound, Russian Wolfhound and Saluki). This shape facilitates the faster movement of energy from place to place. The Labrador with his coat and build is an ideal field dog.

Structure, Shape and Symmetry

As we have noted, overall body shape has a definite relationship to a dog's way of life. It relates, for example, to the use of energy. It also has to do with the animal's ability to relate to its environment and to perform the function for which it was originally bred. As you continue to study dogs, you will see more and more

---

how the shape of things facilitates their functions. Take the opportunity to see how the smooth functioning of an animal, or of its parts, relates to its survival.

As you look at your Labrador in the yard at home, in the show ring or out in the field working birds, look for the features of its design that might account for its survival and popularity. Look for the relationship of structural design to vital function. Ask yourself: "How is the shape of this animal related to the environment in which it has to live?" In searching for answers, go beyond the obvious facts and look for subtle relationships.

Ch. Winterset Magic Marker U.D., JH bred, owned and trained by Enid Bloome, Winterset.

SECTION III
The Versatile Labrador

- **Chapter 1**

  The Labrador as a Field Dog

- **Chapter 2**

  The Labrador as a Show Dog

- **Chapter 3**

  The Labrador in Obedience and Tracking

- **Chapter 4**

  The Labrador as a Service Dog

Two time winner of the Field and Stream Trophy and the National Championship title, 1952-1953 NFC King Buck, owner—John Olin, Nilo Kennels, Illinois.

Dual Ch. Burham Buff was the first yellow female Labrador Retriever to earn this title, owner—J.P. McGee.

Chapter 1

Labradors In The Field

In the realm of field work, the Labrador is **King**. There isn't another retrieving breed that can come close to his achievements. He has dominated American retriever field trials—hands down!

Field Trials and Hunting Retriever Tests

Field trials have been a part of the retriever scene since the early 1930s. However, in the early 1980s, because some retriever owners felt that field trials had evolved into tests that no longer resembled actual hunting situations, The North American Hunting Retriever Association (NAHRA) was formed as an organization independent of The American Kennel Club (AKC). The purpose of this club was to develop non-competitive tests for retrievers in scenarios that more closely resembled actual hunting conditions, thus providing information for a working retriever stud book for the hunter. Shortly thereafter, The AKC began its Hunting Retriever Tests based on many of the same ideas, and the popularity of this program has mushroomed. Mrs. Martha Lee Voshell, who has been successful in just about all areas of Labrador training, has written the following description of the differences between AKC field trials and the hunting retriever tests:

> Labradors are a wonderfully versatile animal with adaptability that far exceeds most other breeds. They are called upon to perform a variety of tasks, many that are easily handled. Some jobs require a bit more training, but all can be accomplished to some degree with proper instruction.
>
> The Lab is a first class family member. It loves people, is superior with children, loves to run and play games, or sit by the fire on a chilly evening. Probably one of the Labrador's most energetic pastimes is retrieving, or it should be! If a puppy is introduced to this game early in life, generally it loves to retrieve. This also holds true with retrieving birds. If started early in life, hunting becomes a favorite activity.
>
> Hunting is not always possible for everyone; therefore, trials and tests for hunting dogs have become extremely popular. Field trials for retrievers were started many years ago. As the years rolled by, conditions and circumstances for these events changed and the need for something different—a sport where more people could participate—prompted a new type of testing for retrievers. Approximately ten years ago the AKC Hunting Retriever Tests were developed. At the present time we have retriever field trials and hunting retriever tests, both licensed by The American Kennel Club. How do these two types of retriever activities differ?

Let us look at field trials first—over the years trials have become more oriented toward professional handlers, and precise and demanding. They are certainly the most difficult type of activity for the average retriever and handler to participate in and be successful. Field trials are composed of four types of stakes:

The DERBY STAKE is for dogs under two years of age. (Six months of age is the minimum for all licensed AKC functions.) The Derby consists of only 'marked falls' where a dog must see and remember the fall of a bird—a test of memory. There are no blind retrieves in the Derby, i.e., the dog does not see a bird fall, but a bird is planted and the dog must be directed to the bird—a test of control. The marks may be singles, doubles or, on occasion, a triple fall. These marks are run on land as well as water. The dog must be steady, under control, and deliver to hand.

The next stake is the QUALIFYING STAKE. This is for dogs of any age who have not won two Qualifying Stakes. Multiple marks, as well as blind retrieves, are utilized in this stake, both on land and in the water. Dogs must honor (sit at heel) while the birds go down and another dog is sent to work. Breaking (leaving the handler's side before commanded to do so) is grounds for disqualification in any field trial stake, but may be accepted in the Derby if the dog can be stopped or controlled immediately. This is usually a judge's decision. The Qualifying Stake is somewhat of a stepping stone to the Open Stake. Dogs that have graduated from the Derby, but may not be quite experienced enough for the Open Stake, are usually run in the Qualifying Stake. Generally the tests are not quite as difficult as those in the Open Stake. Judges may be a tiny bit more lenient!

The two remaining stakes are the AMATEUR and the OPEN (Special All-Age, Limited) stakes. The Amateur Stake is for dogs who must be run or handled by a bonafide amateur. The handler does not have to own the dog, unless it is an Owner-Amateur Stake. In such a stake, the owner must handle the dog. Retrievers competing successfully in this stake earn points toward an Amateur Field Champion title.

The OPEN is the stake in which points are awarded for the first four places toward a field championship title. Anyone may run a dog in the

Martha Lee Voshell and OTCh. Broad Reach Kiss 'N Tell, MH (left) and Broad Reach Whisker Pole U.D., SH (right).

Open—professionals, amateurs, any age. The tests in this stake are the most demanding. In both the Open and Amateur the tests may include such things as: single, double, triple or delayed quadruple marks; retired guns (after shooting the bird, the gunners and bird throwers move out of sight); double blinds; marks with an indented bird; over-and-under marks; and any of these may be on land or in water.

Most of the retrieves in any field trial stake will be considerably longer than in the hunting retriever tests. The dog work in field trials is much more precise and exacting. Blind retrieves require much straighter lines, fewer whistles and exact response to hand signals. Handlers and throwers in field trials wear white jackets so that dogs can mark and identify their positions more easily. In the Open Stake a dog must be honed down to the finest degree. From this stake emerge the qualifiers for the National Retriever Championship Trial, held each November to determine one National Champion for that year. The National Championship Trial runs for one week with dogs competing each day until they are eliminated. The field is usually narrowed to about 10 dogs by the last series at the end of the week. To qualify for the National, a dog must win an Open Stake and acquire seven (7) additional points during the current year. Placements for first through fourth in Open stakes earn the following points: 5, 3, 1-1/2 and 1/2 points. Only 93 retrievers in the entire U.S. qualified for the 1992 National Trial!

A National Amateur Retriever Championship is held in early summer each year. The format for the trial is similar to the Open Championship and qualifications require an amatuer handler, a win and two additional points.

An alternative performance event for retrievers is the AKC Hunting Retriever Tests. These tests are geared more for the average duck hunter who has a good hunting dog. He would like to prove the dog's ability, but the owner may not be up to field trials. The precision and distance for blind work and marks, along with the expense and training demands, make field trials out of reach for most retriever lovers.

Hunting retriever tests have shorter retrieves, no more than 100 yards—more like real hunting situations. The bird throwers, gunners and handlers wear camouflage or dark attire, and many gunners and throwers are out of sight, sometimes with only a duck or goose call to identify their position. The typical HRT scenario includes some kind of bird call and then a bird is thrown and shot. The more advanced tests may include diversionary shots or thrown birds when a dog is retrieving another bird. Sometimes birds are thrown as marks, but the dog must first pick up a blind retrieve before being sent for the birds he has just seen go down. Sometimes dogs are positioned outside a holding blind while the handler is inside the blind during a test scenario. In the hunting retriever tests, walk ups are required with the handler shouldering an unloaded gun, however handlers are not allowed to shoot. This is not done in present day field trials. However, like field trials, dogs must honor another working dog.

There are three levels of testing for the hunting retriever: Junior, Senior and Master. Dogs must be steady in the two more advanced tests, the Senior and Master. AKC licensed field trials are competitive with dogs vying for four placements in each stake. The AKC hunting retriever tests

Nancy Martin with three Junior Hunters (left to right), Ch. Ayr's Real McCoy C.D.X., JH (co-owned with Joanne Summers), Ayr's Lollapalooza, JH and Ayr's Real Humdinger, JH. Photo by Larry Hickey.

are not competitive—you and your dog either pass or fail a set of standards.

The JUNIOR HUNTER Test consists of all single retrieves, two on land and two in the water. Dogs must deliver to hand, but do not have to be steady. A dog must pass in four hunting tests to become a Junior Hunter.

The next level is SENIOR HUNTER. This test consists of double marks and a blind retrieve both on land and in the water. Shouldering a gun, a walk-up and diversionary shot birds are also part of the test. Dogs must be steady, deliver to hand, and honor. If a dog has a Junior Hunter title, he must qualify in four trials for a Senior Hunter. If the dog has no JH title, he must qualify in five tests for the title SH.

The MASTER HUNTER Test is the most advanced. It consists of multiple land and water marks as well as land and water blinds. There must be at least three series or tests. Diversion birds or shots must be used at least once. Dogs must be steady, deliver to hand and honor. If a dog breaks, it is automatically disqualified.

In 1991, the hunting retriever clubs formed the Master National Club and a Master National Hunt Test was initiated. Bernadette Brown's yellow Labrador qualified for the Master National in 1992. She shares her thoughts and feelings about this event in the following narrative:

Many hours of training had finally reaped a benefit—Solberg's Giddeon by Choice C.D., MH,' A.K.A. 'Giddeon' and I had made it to the 1992 Master National Hunting Tests held in LaVergne, Tennessee. To be eligible to run in the Master National, a retriever must earn four Master test qualifications during the year prior to the event. Master National judges are chosen each year representing a cross-section of the country. Their judging assignment in the 1992 Master National included several days of pre-test set up, and the testing of over one hundred fifty dogs that began on a Monday and ran straight through until Saturday. Pre-National training for Master qualifiers was allowed on grounds provided by the Middle Tennessee Amateur Retriever Club. After several days of serious training with some very special friends, I felt Giddeon and I were ready to work as a team.

On Monday morning the handlers were called to line to watch the test dog run the first scenario. From the start there was a sense of camaraderie and support among the handlers that could not go unnoticed. They shared running tips with each other, including handling techniques and marking keys. Even the judges, after their test scenario, stated that they wanted all the handlers to do well and qualify. It has been my experience that this type of unifying atmosphere goes unmatched at any other AKC retrieving event. Monday progressed and finally my number, one hundred two, was called. As I walked to the line, my knees knocked and my stomach churned in a rhythmical flip. This walk to line was unlike all others, for it brought my dreams to reality. Giddeon and I were to challenge a double mark with a retired gun and a double blind. The guns went off and Giddeon was sent. We worked well together and completed this first series with great style. As I thanked the judges and walked off line, I felt excited and exhausted at the same time. I knew if I was fortunate, I would be allowed to experience this same emotional turmoil at least five more times! As the week progressed, so did the tests. There were triple marks, double diversions, delayed flyer triples, poison birds and multiple blinds given in true hunting scenarios to test the dogs' abilities. Throughout the week, the caring and support from friends, both old and new, blossomed. We were disheartened when dogs were eliminated, for we truly wanted everyone to succeed.

Saturday, the day when the judges would make their final decision on the dogs completing the test, arrived with a delayed flyer triple the challenge. The weather was humid and rainy. This time my walk to line included prayers as well as nerves, for the final result was only three retrieves away. The guns went off and Giddeon left knowing exactly where his birds had landed. When I took the last bird from his mouth, I heard clapping from the gallery. As I turned toward the judges, each wearing a big smile, one of them jumped up and yelled, 'YES!' Tears instantly ran

Solberg's Giddeon by Choice
C.D., MH, A.K.A. "Giddeon"
and his owner/trainer
Bernadette Brown.

from my eyes. I felt so happy, so fulfilled, to have reached my goal. Finally, I could relax and deep breathe.

The closing event, the awards ceremony, followed shortly after the last series. The awards included a large orange qualifying rosette, and a pewter plate engraved with 'Master National' around the edge and the National logo engraved in the center. The display of awards was just beautiful. Approximately one-third of the starters qualified for these awards. During the awards ceremony, as I accepted my rosette and plate, I was cheered on by great friends and supporters. It was obvious that no handler was alone. We had become a family.

As I headed home, I realized that the Master National was indeed a test of endurance for both dog and handler. To have endured and succeeded was a phenomenal sensation, but there was more. I left not only with a qualifying rosette and pewter plate, but with a sense of brotherhood. Yes, unforgotten camaraderie, caring and support were also coming home with me. I reached down and gave Giddeon a hug and kiss as he was eating his well earned T-Bone. Little did he know how much richer a person his 'mom' was for running the 1992 Master National!

The first National Master Hunting Test was held in Delaware in 1991. There were 98 retrievers qualified, and of these, 26 finished all the series successfully. In 1992, the Master was held in Tennessee. One hundred thirty-six retrievers started the week-long tests and 46 completed all series. The 1993 Master National was hosted by the Kansas City Retriever Club and held in Missouri. There were 157 dogs entered and 41 completed the tests.

The National Retriever Championship

Field trials, as opposed to hunting retriever tests, are very competitive. There are always very large entries with lots of talent, and the series in each stake have to be very difficult to help judges determine placements. As mentioned previously, many of the successful handlers at the Open Stake level are professionals hired by a dog's owner to train and handle it in the trials. All handlers in Open, amateur or professional, seek placements for their dogs to qualify them for the National Championship Stake—the stepping stone to retriever fame.

Back in 1935, the *Field and Stream* magazine donated a trophy to be awarded annually to the "Outstanding Retriever of the Year." Points toward the trophy were awarded in all open championship stakes on the following basis: five (5) for a First; three (3) for a Second; two (2) for a Third; and one (1) for a Fourth.

After a few years a number of experienced retriever men decided to have one great championship stake to be held annually at the conclusion of the regular season, in which proven dogs would be eligible to compete. Thus the National Retriever Field Trial Club, Inc. was formed in 1941. The members and founders were: Messrs. Morgan Belmont, Henry Bixby, Alfred Ely, Thomas W. Merritt Jr. and Walter Roesler. The winner of the new Club's trial was to be awarded the title, "National Retriever Champion of 19—."

Consequently, in 1941, confusion existed between the Field and Stream Trophy Award and the award to the winner of the National Club's first trial. Each award went to different dogs. However, beginning in 1942, the winner of the National Trial was given both awards through 1953 when the Field and Stream trophy was retired.

The early winners of the Field and Stream Trophy were:

1935 - **FC Blind of Arden** (Labrador), owner—Mr. W.A. Harriman
1936 - **FC Dilwyne Montauk Pilot** (Chesapeake Bay), owner—Mr. R.R.M. Carpenter, Jr.
1937 - **FC Banchory Night Light** (Labrador), owner—Mr. J.F. Carlisle
1938 - **FC Nigger of Barrington** (Labrador), owner—Mr. Gordon P. Kelly
1939 - **FC Rip** (Golden), owner/handler—Paul Bakewell III
1940 - **FC Rip** (Golden), owner/handler—Paul Bakewell III
1941 - **FC Tar of Arden** (Labrador), owner—Paul Bakewell III

To attain the title National Field Trial Champion is a great achievement. Martha Lee Voshell has explained how a dog can qualify for this trial, and I list here all the National winners since the club was formed. Please note that some dogs have won the title more than once, and that several owners have won with different dogs. It is also clear that Labradors have stolen the show.

Winners of the National Retriever Championship Stake

The Retriever Field Trial News has allowed me to print its statistics that prove the paramount status of the Labrador in the field. The photos of National winners are reproduced with the permission of *The Retriever Field Trial News*.

1941　**FC KING MIDAS OF WOODEND**, Gold. M.
Mr. E.N. Dodge, Minnesota

1942　**DUAL CH. SHED OF ARDEN**, L.M.
Mr. Paul Bakewell III, Missouri

1943　**'42 NFC/DUAL CH. SHED OF ARDEN**, L.M.
Mr. Paul Bakewell III, Missouri

1944　**FC SHELTER COVE BEAUTY**, Gold. F.
L.M. Evans,M.D., Minnesota

1945　**BLACK MAGIC OF AUDLON**, L.F.
Mr. Mahlon B. Wallace, Jr., Missouri

1946　**'42 & '43 NFC/DUAL CH. SHED OF ARDEN**, L.M.
Mr. Paul Bakewell, III, Missouri

1947　**DUAL CH BRACKEN'S SWEEP**, L.M.
Mr. Daniel E. Pomeroy, New Jersey

1948　**FC BRIGNALL'S GRINGO**, L.M.
Mr. Clifford N. Brignall, California

1949　**FC MARVADEL BLACK GUM**, L.M.
Mr. and Mrs. Paul Bakewell III, Missouri

1950　**FC BEAUTYWOOD TAMARACK**, Gold. M.
L.M. Evans,M.D., Minnesota

1951　**FC READY ALWAYS OF MARIANHILL**, Gold. M.
Mr. Mahlon B. Wallace, Jr., Missouri

1952　**FC KING BUCK**, L.M.
Nilo Kennels, Illinois

1953　**'52 NFC KING BUCK**, L.M.
Nilo Kennels, Illinois

1954　**FC MAJOR VI**, L.M.
Mrs. Fraser M. Horn, New York

1955　**FC CORK OF OAKWOOD LANE**, L.M.
A. Harold Mork, M.D., Minnesota

1956　**FC MASSIE'S SASSY BOOTS**, L.M.
Mr. William T. Cline, Illinois

1957　**FC SPIRIT LAKE DUKE**, L.M.
Mrs. George Murnane, New York

1958　**DUAL CH. NILO POSSIBILITY**, L.M.
Mr. K.K. Williams, Wisconsin

1959　**'57 NFC SPIRIT LAKE DUKE**, L.M.
Mrs. George Murnane, New York

1960　**FC/AFC DOLOBRAN'S SMOKE TAIL**, L.M.
Mr. Richard H. Hecker, Arizona

1961　**FC DEL-TONE COLVIN**, L.M.
Mr. Louis J. Snoeyenbos, Wisconsin

1962　**FC/AFC BIGSTONE HOPE**, L.F.
Mr. and Mrs. Bing Grunwald, Nebraska

1963　**'61 NFC/AFC DEL-TONE COLVIN**, L.M.
Mr. Louis J. Snoeyenbos, Wisconsin

1964　**FC RIPCO'S V.C. MORGAN**, L.F.
Mr. J. D. Ott, Washington

1965　**FC MARTEN'S LITTLE SMOKEY**, L.M.
Mr. John M. Olin, Illinois

Louise and August Belmont with NFC/NAFC Super Chief. Super Chief won the National Championship Stake in 1968 and the National Amateur Championship stake twice, in 1967 and 1968.

1966   **FC WHYGIN CORKS COOT**, L.M.
Mrs. George Murnane, N.Y.

1967   **FC/AFC BUTTE BLUE MOON**, L.M.
Mr. and Mrs. Bing Grunwald, Nebraska

1968   **FC '67 & '68 NAFC SUPER CHIEF**, L.M.
Mr. August Belmont, Maryland

1969   **'66 NFC WHYGIN CORKS COOT**, L.M.
Mrs. George Murnane, New York

1970   **FC/AFC CREOLE SISTER**, L.F.
Mrs. George Murnane, New York

1971   **FC MI-CRIS SAILOR**, L.M.
Mrs. George Murnane, New York

1972   **FC/AFC ROYAL'S MOOSE'S MOE**, L.M.
Mr. William D. Connor, Colorado

1973   **FC/AFC BAIRD'S CENTERVILLE SAM**, L.M.
Mr. and Mrs. Mahlon B. Wallace, Missouri

1974   **FC/AFC HAPPY PLAYBOY'S PEARL**, L.F.
Mr. and Mrs. David Crow, Louisianna

1975   **FC/AFC WANAPUM DART'S DANDY**, L.F.
Mr. Charles L. Hill, Washington

1976   **FC/AFC SAN JOAQUIN HONCHO**, L.M.
Judith S. Weikel, California

1977   **FC/AFC EUROCLYDON**, L.F.
Mr. Don Strait, Georgia

1978   **FC/AFC SHADOW OF OTTER CREEK**, L.M.
Mr. Bob Kennon, Louisianna

1979   **FC/AFC MCGUFFY**, L.M.
T. J. and Debbie Lindbloom, Oregon

National Retriever Champions

 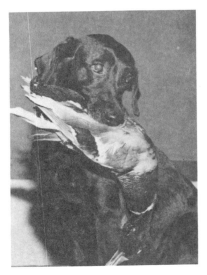

Upper left, 1983 NFC/AFC Trieven Butch of Big Jake, owners—Joe and Gloria Boatright, California. Handled by Joe Boatright.

Upper right, 1984 NFC/AFC Wanapum's Lucyana Girl, owner/handler—Mr. John Parrott, Louisianna.

Lower left, 1986 NFC/AFC Jubilashus T.C. Malarky, owner— Mr. John Larkin, Texas.

Lower right, 1987 NFC/AFC/CFC/CAFC Yankee Independence, owner—Mr. Gunther Rahnefeld, Manitoba, Canada. Handler—Bill Eckett.

1971 NFC Mi-Cris Sailor,
owner—Mrs. George Murnane,
New York.

1980 **FC/AFC RISKY BUSINESS RUBY**, L.F.
Gary and Denise Thompson, Minnesota

1981 **FC/AFC ORION'S SKY**, L.M.
Mr. John Martin, Ohio

1982 **FC WESTWINDS SUPERNOVA CHIEF**, L.M.
D.J. and Nancy Esposito, Virginia

1983 **FC/AFC TRIEVEN BUTCH OF BIG JAKE**, L.M
Joe and Gloria Boatright, California

1984 **FC/AFC WANAPUM'S LUCYANA GIRL**, L.F.
Mr. John Parrott, Louisianna

1985 **FC/AFC DYNAMITE DUKE IV**, L.M .
Marshall and Linden Dunaway, Georgia

1986 **FC/AFC JUBILASHUS T.C. MALARKY**, L.M.
Mr. John Larkin, Texas

1987 **FC/AFC/CFC/CAFC YANKEE INDEPENDENCE**, L.F.
Mr. Gunther Rahnefeld, Manitoba, Canada

1988 **FC/AFC PP'S LUCKY SUPER TOBY**, L.M.
Fred Kampo and Charles Hays, Minnesota

1989 **FC/AFC OTUS OF REDFERN**, L.M.
Aurelia Rice, Texas

1990 **FC/AFC CANDLEWOOD'S TANKS A LOT**, L.F.
Mary Howley and Randy Kuehl, Wisconsin

1991 **'90 NFC CANDLEWOOD'S TANKS A LOT**, L.F.
Mary Howley and Randy Kuehl, Wisconsin

1992 **NAFC/FC CANDLEWOOD'S SUPER TANKER**, L.M.
Joyce Williams, Wisconsin

1993 **'90 & '91 NFC CANDLEWOOD'S TANKS A LOT**, L.F.
Mary Howley and Randy Kuehl, Wisconsin

1988 NFC/AFC PP'S Lucky Super Toby, owners—Fred Kampo and Charles Hays, Minnesota.

In 1942, 1943 and 1946, the National Retriever Championship Stakes were won by NFC/Dual Ch. Shed of Arden, a black Labrador male. This record of three wins remained unbroken and untied for 47 years until "Lottie," a black Labrador female, came along to tie it with her wins in 1990, 1991 and 1993. "Lottie" was bred by Mary Howley's Candlewood Kennel, and is owned by Mary and Randy Kuehl. Mike Lardy is the successful trainer and handler for this most talented bitch. The 1992 National Champion, NFC/NAFC Candlewood's Super Tanker (also bred by Mary) is "Lottie's" sire. So Mary Howley has had four years of wonderful wins, and I'm sure she's saying, "Tanks a Lot!"

Mary was in high school when she and her Dad got their first Labradors in 1957. She joined the Madison Retriever Club for training assistance. It is a club with about 100 members. They put on two field trials and two hunting retriever tests every year, and own 78 acres with water, land and a nice clubhouse. There are plenty of different sites for training, and there are usually experienced members around to help. Mary trained every day after school. "I bought a few puppies, and after they were well trained, sold them." Now retriever breeding has become a way of life and a profession for her, and she certainly has turned out some great winners, as well as wonderful pets.

Mary has used a professional trainer for her dogs since the mid-eighties. Although training is very enjoyable, it is a full time job to do it yourself and do it right. Because of her business, Mary does not have that time. Her trainer is Mike Lardy who lives about an hour away, so Mary can jump in her car to join him for training sessions. She likes to run her dogs when she can get to the trials, but Mike has done superlative things with the Candlewood Labradors.

Mary is a bug on pedigrees. "I love to see one that is just full of good proven or titled dogs. Many of my winners are out of titled bitches which you don't find too often." She has all three colors in her breeding stock, and

'90,'91,'93 NFC/AFC Candlewoods Tanks A Lot, owner—Mary Howley & Randy Kuehl, breeder—Mary Howley. "Lottie" was also the 1989 National Derby Champion accumulating 108 points.

'92 NFC, '90 NAFC Candlewood's Super Tanker, owner—Joyce Williams, handler—Mike Lardy. Super Tanker is "Lottie's" sire.

one of her yellows, Candlewood's Nifty Nick, epitomizes her idea of how a Labrador should look. He isn't titled, but has an excellent field pedigree, and has produced some good looking pups, as well as seven FCs and AFCs.

Mary Howley has made "Candlewood" a very special name in the field trial world, and lots of onlookers wish her and "Lottie" the best.

Mary remarks about Lottie's pedigree:

> I owned most of the bitches and some of the dogs in her pedigree which goes back 25 years when I bought Shamrock Acres Duck Soup from Sally McCarthy. Her sire is Super Chief, so Super Deal is closely line-bred on Super Chief. I also bred Mad Mouse, one of the top performing yellows in the breed.

FC/AFC Trumarc's Raider

'76 NFC/AFC San Joaquin Honcho

Doxie Gypsy Taurus

'92 NFC/'90 NAFC Candlewood's Super Tanker

NAFC/FC River Oaks Rascal

Candlewood's Delta Dash

FC/AFC Candlewood's Nellie-B-Good

'90/'91/'93 NFC/AFC Candlewoods Tanks A Lot

'68 NFC/'67, '68 NAFC Super Chief

FC Candlewood's Super Deal

Candlewood's Liffey

Candlewood's Liffey

'74 NAFC/FC Ray's Rascal

Blackfoot Tiz Too

FC/AFC Washington Tizzy Lizzy

1954 NFC/NAFC Major VI, owner—Mrs. Fraser M. Horn, New York. This retriever was also the first National Amateur Championship winner in 1957 at the age of nine years.

Lottie has, from her first litter by FC/AFC Trumarc's Ziparoo, one titled son—FC/AFC Trumarc's Lota Zip, three others with Open wins, and one with an Amateur win. She has had two more litters, and there are great ones from each breeding with Qualifying wins, Open placements and youngsters on the Derby List. It just goes to show, a bitch can still perform, be bred, have pups and then come back and tie the record for National Championship wins—and have her offspring be great, too!

The National Amateur Retriever Championship

The National Amateur Retriever Championship Stake is held every year in the early summer, and as the name denotes, this is a competition for amateur handlers only. On the following list of National Amateur Championship winners you will see many dogs that have also won the National Open title as well:

1957 **NFC/AFC MAJOR VI**,L.M.
Mrs. Fraser M. Horn, New York
1958 **FC/AFC BOLEY'S TAR BABY**, L.M.
Bing Grunwald, Nebraska
1959 **FC/AFC BRACKEN'S HIGH FLYER**, L.M.
George L. Dudek, Oregon
1960 **FC/AFC QUEENIE OF REDDING**, L.F.
Rolland Watt, California
1961 **FC/AFC ACE'S SHEBA OF ARDYN**, L.F.
Dr. B.L. Finlayson, Washington
1962 **FC/AFC CARR-LAB HILLTOP**, L.M.
Glen B. Bump, California

National Ameteur Retriever Champions

Top left, 1983 NAFC/FC Beorn's Blazing Hydropsyche, owners—Dr. William and Cynthia Howard, Washington, handler—Breck Howard.

Top right, 1986 NAFC/FC Winsom Cargo, owner/handler—Cal Cadmus, D.V.M., California.

Bottom left, 1987 NAFC/FC/CFC/CAFC Westwind Jemima Super Cake, owner/handler—Eva Proby, Washington.

Bottom right, 1991 NAFC/FC Cody's R. Dee, owner/handler—Larry Bergmann, Idaho.

1963	**FC/AFC PEPPER'S JIGGS**, L.M.
	Bob Pepper, Washington
1964	**AFC DUTCHMOOR'S BLACK MOOD**, L.M.
	A. Nelson Sills, Delaware
1965	**FC/AFC REBEL CHIEF OF HEBER**, L.M.
	Gus Rathert, California
1966	**FC/AFC/CFC CAPTAIN OF LOMAC**, L.M.
	Rudy R. Deering, B.C. Canada
1967	**FC/AFC SUPER CHIEF**, L.M.
	August Belmont, Maryland
1968	**'67 NAFC-FC SUPER CHIEF**, L.M.
	August Belmont, Maryland
1969	**FC/AFC GUY'S BITTERROOT LUCKY**,L.M.
	Guy P. Burnett, Montana
1970	**FC/AFC ANDY'S PARTNER PETE**, L.M.
	Mrs. Clifford B. Brokaw,Jr.New York
1971	**FC/AFC DEE'S DANDY DUDE**, L.M.
	Michael Paterno, New York
1972	**FC/AFC/CNFC RIVER OAKS CORKY**,L.M.
	Michael R. Flannery, Colorado
1973	**'71 NAFC/FC DEE'S DANDY DUDE**,L.M.
	Michael Paterno, New York
1974	**FC/AFC RAY'S RASCAL**, L.M.
	Raymond & Dorothea Goodrich, California
1975	**'72 NAFC/FC/CNFC RIVER OAKS CORKY**,L.M.
	Michael R. Flannery, Colorado
1976	**'75 NFC/AFC/CNFC WANAPUM DART'S DANDY**,L.F.
	Charles Hill, Washington
1977	**FC/AFC RIVER OAKS RASCAL**, L.M.
	Joseph M. Pilar, Illinois
1978	**FC/AFC KANNONBALL KATE**, L.M.
	Peter Lane, California
1979	**FC/AFC LAWHORN'S CADILLAC MACK**, L.M.
	Dennis Bath, Illinois and Gerald Lawhorn, Georgia
1980	**'79 NAFC-FC LAWHORN'S CADILLAC MACK**,L.M.
	Dennis Bath, Illinois and Gerald Lawhorn, Georgia
1981	**FC/AFC DUDE'S DOUBLE OR NOTHIN'**,L.M.
	Delma Hazzard, South Carolina
1982	**FC/AFC/CFC/CAFC PIPER'S PACER**,L.M.
	Roy & Jo McFall, Alaska
1983	**FC/AFC BEORN'S BLAZING HYDROPSYCHE**,L.M.
	Dr. William & Cynthia Howard, Washington
1984	**FC/AFC TRUMARC'S ZIP CODE**,L.M.
	Judith Aycock, Texas
1985	**FC/AFC TOPBRASS COTTON**, Gold.M.
	Jeff & Bev Finely & Jackie Mertens, Illinois
1986	**FC/AFC WINSOM CARGO**,L.M.
	Cal Cadmus, D.V.M., California
1987	**FC/AFC/CFC/CAFC WESTWIND JEMIMA SUPER CAKE**,L.F.
	Eva Proby, Washington
1988	**FC/AFC HONKY TONK HERO**, L.M.
	Jerry Wickliffe, Texas
1989	**FC/AFC THE LITTLE DUKE OF FARGO**,L.M.
	Dean Troyer, Kansas
1990	**FC/AFC CANDLEWOODS SUPER TANKER**, L.M.
	Joyce Williams, Wisconsin

Top left, 1989 NAFC/FC The Little Duke of Fargo, owner/handler—Dean Troyer, Kansas.

Top right, 1988 NAFC/FC Honky Tonk Hero, owner/handler—Jerry Wickliffe, Texas.

Bottom left, 1992 NAFC/FC Gusto's Last Control, owner/handler Lynne Dubose.

Bottom right, 1993 NAFC/FC M.D's Cotton Pickin Cropper, owners—Newt Cropper and Karen Rabeau, Maryland, handler—Newt Cropper.

1991   FC/AFC CODY'S R. DEE,L.M.
       Larry Bergmann, Idaho
1992   FC/AFC GUSTO'S LAST CONTROL, L.M.
       J.M. & L.K. DuBose, North Carolina
1993   FC/AFC MD'S COTTON PICK'N CROPPER, L.M.
       Newt Cropper & Karen Rabeau, Maryland

Dual Champion Labrador Retrievers

There have been thirty-five Labrador Retrievers that have achieved the coveted title of Dual Champion. The following is a list of the dogs who earned this HIGHEST accomplishment:

DUAL CH. MICHAEL OF GLENMERE, L.M.
DUAL CH. GORSE OF ARDEN, L.F.
DUAL CH. BRAES OF ARDEN, L.F.
DUAL CH. SHED OF ARDEN, L.M.
DUAL CH. LITTLE PIERRE OF DEER CREEK, L.M.
DUAL CH. YODEL OF MOREXPENSE, L.M.
DUAL CH. BRACKEN'S SWEEP, L.M.
DUAL CH. MATCHMAKER FOR DEER CREEK, L.M.
DUAL CH. GRANGEMEAD PRECOCIOUS, L.M.
DUAL CH. HELLO JOE OF ROCHELTREE, L.M.
DUAL CH. CHEROKEE BUCK, L.M.
DUAL CH. BENGAL OF ARDEN, L.M.
DUAL CH. TREVEILYR SWIFT, L.M. (IMPORT)
DUAL CH. DELA-WINN'S TAR OF CRAIGNOOK, L.M.
DUAL CH. BOLEY'S TAR BABY, L.M.
DUAL CH. NILO POSSIBILITY, L.M.
DUAL CH. BEAU BRUMMEL OF WYNDALE, L.M.
DUAL CH. PENNY OAKS CORKY, L.M.
DUAL CH. KINGSWERE BLACK EBONY, L.M.
DUAL CH. ALPINE CHEROKEE ROCKET, L.M.
DUAL CH. MARKWELL'S RAMBLIN' REBEL, L.M.
DUAL CH. KROOKED KREEK KNIGHT, L.M.
DUAL CH. BURNHAM BUFF, L.F. (YEL.)
DUAL CH. PROBLEM BOY DUKE OF WAKE, L.M.
DUAL CH. DANNY'S COLE BLACK SLATE, L.M.
DUAL CH. CALYPSO CLIPPER, L.M.
DUAL CH. RIDGEWOOD PLAYBOY, L.M.
DUAL CH. TORQUE OF DANGERFIELD, L.M. (YEL.)
DUAL CH. SHERWOOD'S MAID MARION, L.F. (YEL.)
DUAL CH. HAPPY PLAYBOY, L.M.
DUAL CH. PETITE ROUGE, L.M.
DUAL CH. SHAMROCK ACRES SUPER DRIVE, L.M.
DUAL CH. ROYAL OAKES JILL OF BURGUNDY, L.F.
DUAL CH. WARPATH MACHO, L.M.
DUAL CH. HIWOOD SHADOW, L.M

Will there be another one? I certainly hope so! In the meantime, there are show champions with Master Hunter Titles, and that's a super achievement. As long as there are people dedicated to trying for excellence in each area, our breed will be just fine.

Dual Ch. and three-time National Field Trial Champion Shed of Arden was probably the most acclaimed Labrador in American history. Bred by William Averall Harriman, Arden, Shed was owned and trained by Paul Bakewell III of St. Louis, Missouri.

Am./Can. Dual Ch. Happy Playboy (Castlemore Shamus x Susie) was owned by Mrs. Grace Lambert, Harrowby.

Dual Ch. Grangemead Precocious (Dual Ch. Shed of Arden x Huron Lady) and three famous sons, Dual Ch. Cherokee Buck, FC Cherokee Medicine Man and FC Freehaven Muscles. All three were from a litter whelped by Grangemead Sharon. Dual Ch. Grangemead Precocious is also the grandsire of Dual Ch. Alpine Cherokee Rocket.

Dual Ch. Warpath Macho with handler John Dahl, Oak Hill Kennels; owners—Carol & Bob Lilenfeld, New Jersey.

Chapter 2

The Labrador as a Show Dog

Showing dogs is a very old sport. It began with breeders who wanted to bring out their youngsters and breeding stock to show to their peers, or perhaps to sell a dog to a spectator, or to be judged by an authority of their breed. All dog shows are sponsored by either all-breed clubs made up of owners of various breeds of dogs, or by specialty clubs made up of owners of only one breed of dog. Today there are several kinds of dog shows. At the informal level is the Match Show, which is a good place to learn for both you and your puppy or dog. The basic match show classes for young dogs of either sex are: Puppy 3-6 months; Puppy 6-9 months; and Puppy 9-12 months. Adult classes are usually Novice and Open. The Puppy Dog classes are judged first, then the Puppy Bitch classes. The judge will chose the Best of Breed Puppy from the winners of each class. The adult classes are then judged, and a Best of Breed Adult is picked from the class winners. Ribbons are given out, but no championship points are awarded at matches. Additional classes may be offered at a specialty club match.

At AKC licensed all-breed shows and specialty shows the classes for young dogs of both sexes are: Puppy 6-12 months (sometimes divided 6-9 months and 9-12 months). For older dogs a 12-18 months class may be offered at specialty shows, as well as Novice, Bred-by-Exhibitor, American-bred and Open Classes. At almost all specialty shows, the Open Classes are divided by color—black, chocolate and yellow. The winners of each of the classes compete for Winners Dog (WD) and Winners bitch (WB). The dog and the bitch selected as Winners Dog and Winners Bitch are awarded points toward their championship depending on the number of dogs in competition. The point schedule ranges from one (1) through five (5), and the points awarded vary according to the number of dogs in that breed shown in each of the dog show divisions across the U.S. If a dog wins three or more points, that is considered a "major" win. Fifteen points are needed for a champion title with at least two "major" wins under two different judges. The Winners Dog and Winners Bitch then compete against champions for the Best of Breed (BOB) and Best of Opposite Sex (BOS) win. At an all-breed show the winner of Best of Breed advances to competition in the Sporting Group which includes all the other gun dog breeds. The winner of the Sporting Group advances to compete for Best in Show (BIS).

The Labrador is generally not a showy dog. His medium size and sturdy build serve him well in the field, as he may be required to spend the entire day retrieving birds shot by his master. He is built for stamina and strength

---

Gene Czerwinski gaits chocolate dog, Sir Peter Kent of Greenwood, owned by Mrs. Judy Groves—note the level topline and tail carriage.

Ch. Driftwood's Midnight Madness (Ch. Anderscroft Mijan's Bravo x Ch. Driftwood's Limited Edition) owned and bred by Pam Kelsey, Driftwood Kennels, was "baited" into this pose.

rather than for speed and flash, which typify some of the other sporting or gundog breeds that are very successful in the show ring. It is discouraging to many Labrador exhibitors when the judge expects the Labrador to fly around the ring as do the pointers, setters, spaniels and several others in the Sporting Group. There have been a few Labradors that have been trained to race around and, in general, these dogs place more often in the Group. However, as the Labrador is, and should be, a more laid-back, easy-going dog, he just isn't going to win over the dash and flash of other breeds unless the judge happens to be either a breeder/judge or a very knowledgable multi-breed judge. The judge is supposed to know these things about each individual breed that he or she evaluates. If a dog has been highly publicized as a winner, he'll probably get a look, perhaps a placement in the Group, but most people in Labradors care far more about how well their dog stacks up against other Labradors. It seems to me, despite the high registration numbers making the Labrador Retriever the #1 dog in America, Labrador entries at all-breed shows have fallen off quite a bit. It has become more and more difficult to find a show in which there are enough Labs entered to make it a "major" win. On the other hand, Labrador specialty shows which employ breeder/judges have enjoyed large entries most of the time. We do have quite a few breeder/judges in the United States, but in other countries, almost all of the judges are breeders.

Ch. Borador's Ridgeway Reflection, owned and handled by Sally Bell, Borador Kennels, has been formally "stacked" for his win picture with the judge.

To prepare your Labrador for a show one of the easist things to do is take him for a swim. In this photo the "gang" at Carol Heidl's Tabatha Kennel is going for their daily swim.

The characteristics that set the Labrador apart from other breeds as described in the breed Standard in Section II are his head, his coat and his distinctive tail. These three elements are of prime importance in conformation evaluation, and are necessary in a good Lab; however, there is more to look for. The Labrador must have a strong natural retrieving instinct; he must be willing and able to mark well the downed bird, and to go through heavy cover, over fences and through icy water to retrieve it. To do all this, he must have proper structure and a coat with undercoat, and be a picture of strength.

Even though you have a good-looking dog, a bit of time in training is helpful. A young puppy can be taught a few basic things, keeping his lessons short, sweet and happy. Most areas in our country now have Puppy Kindergarten Classes. As soon as puppy has received all his innoculations, you and he can go to school. This is usually run by an obedience club or trainer, and is an excellent way to socialize a puppy. I particularly like the summer outdoor classes. Pups are passed around from person-to-person, and are encouraged to meet and greet the other babies. They learn to walk on a leash and some are taught to sit (I usually skip this part because you don't want your dog sitting in the show ring). In the class I attend, the youngsters are taught to retrieve toys or puppy dummies. If you want to learn to pose or stack your puppy, you can, but a little of this goes a long way and Lab puppies become bored with this part quickly. Most Labrador

An example of the Labrador's water-resistance coat and otter tail are shown in this photo of Ch. Braemar Anchor Bay, WC just after a swim. This dog was a shooting companion for Jay and Jane Borders, Braemar, for nine seasons.

exhibitors nowadays are not "stacking" their dogs, but prefer to show them by "free baiting" or free standing. As a judge, I would far rather see them standing free. I believe that a Labrador looks better when its tail is not held up. This practice came from the professional handlers who, in other breeds, do hold up a lot of tails. I also object to people stringing up their dog—the poor creature looks as though he's being strangled. It is very wise to teach your puppy to trot at your side on a loose lead because many judges will expect him to do that when he's grown.

The main thing to remember when training a puppy is to keep the lessons short, to make each practice time a happy experience, to use a lot of praise and some healthy treats, to remain patient when puppy doesn't want to cooperate and to end on a happy note with lots of pats and hugs.

In many places today there are show handling classes. If a young dog needs more practice within a class of other dogs, or if a handler is a novice and needs some guidance and confidence building, these classes can be a great help. Labradors can be rambunctious and difficult to manage because they are very active and strong, so it is wise to attend to their training when they are quite young. Besides, they love to go and do things with you as long as you're both having fun.

There is one wonderful aspect of showing a Labrador—very little grooming. The Lab is truly a "wash and wear" dog, but please don't bathe your Lab just before a show. If the show is on Saturday, Wednesday would be all right. A bath right before a show softens the coat, and a Lab's coat should feel hard to the touch. I find the best and easist thing to do is to take him for a swim, and he'll love you for it too. When he comes out of the water for the last time, rub him down thoroughly with a thick towel and, presto, he's clean.

There was a day when people felt they had to do some trimming. I think this started when the professional handlers felt they had to "tidy" up any dog they took into the ring, no matter what breed. So whiskers were chopped off and backsides scissored. However, to the great relief of Labradors in most areas, this seems to be a thing of the past. Since whiskers are a part of the sensory system, it seems a very cruel thing indeed to cut them off. The only trimming needed these days is the removal of the twizzle on the end of the Lab's tail—not a blunt cut, just a bit of shaping. But if you didn't do his tail, probably no one would notice. Any dog's toenails should be cut regularly so that his feet remain compact. Long, curving nails can spoil a dog's foot, making it open or splayed.

That's all there is to it! A Labrador is a NATURAL dog and should be shown in as natural way as possible.

Chapter 3

The Labrador in Obedience and Tracking

Author's note: The introduction to this chapter has been written by my friend, Joanne Summers, who teaches obedience classes and competes with her dogs in American Kennel Club Obedience Trials.

TO THE NEW LABRADOR RETRIEVER PUPPY OWNER:

Welcome to the wonderful world of canine companionship! At least that is what it should be if you follow one important rule, obedience train your dog. You have before you the world's greatest opportunist—your puppy. He is a pack animal, and will be looking for leadership as soon as you bring him home. He will test you whenever possible. While he was part of a litter, the puppy's mother was in charge of his every move, and now it is your turn.

You may have purchased your puppy to be the family pet, a breed champion, an obedience competitor, a hunting companion, a guard dog or one to work in agility, tracking, drug detection, search and rescue or as a service dog—whatever your aspirations, basic work in obedience is a must. You need to teach your puppy acceptable behavior. You should be persistent in directing his energy to productive activities, and you will need the patience to calmly pursue these activities, and, above all, to praise your puppy when he's doing things right. This is what obedience training is all about.

There is a saying among obedience people that dog owners get the dog they deserve. If you are willing to put productive teaching time into your puppy, you deserve to have a wonderful canine companion.

Obedience Degrees

For those who may be interested in showing a Labrador in AKC Obedience Trials, the obedience degrees in ascending order are:

C.D.	Companion Dog
C.D.X.	Companion Dog Excellent
U.D.	Utility Dog
U.D.X.	Utility Dog Excellent

To earn each of the obedience degrees, a dog must score more than 50 per cent of the available points in each exercise with a final score of 170 or more points (out of a possible 200), under three different judges, in at least three different shows. Obedience Classes are divided into A and B categories.

NOVICE CLASS—to qualify for a C.D. title a dog must pass the following exercises:

Heel on leash	40 points
Stand for Examination (off leash)	30 points
Heel Free (off leash)	40 points
Recall (off leash)	30 points
Long Sit (group exercise)	30 points
Long Down (group exercise)	30 points

The Novice A Class is for dogs that have not won the title of C.D. and for a person who has never handled nor trained a dog that has won a C.D. No person may handle more than one dog in Novice A.

The Novice B Class is also for dogs that have not won the title of C.D., but dogs in this class may be handled by anyone. After a handler has obtained a C.D. on a dog, he must show all future dogs in this class. A person may show more than one dog in the Novice B class.

OPEN CLASS— all exercises are off lead. To qualify for C.D.X. title a dog must pass the following exercises:

Heel Free	40 points
Drop on Recall	30 points
Retrieve on Flat	20 points
Retrieve over High Jump	30 points
Broad Jump	20 points
Long Sit (group-handler out of sight)	30 points
Long Down (group-handler out of sight)	30 points

The Open A Class is for dogs that have won the C.D. title, but have not as yet won their C.D.X. Degree. Each dog must be handled by its owner or by a member of the immediate family.

The Open B Class is for dogs that have won the C.D. title or C.D.X. A dog may continue to compete in this class even after it has won the U.D. title. Dogs in this class may be

Ernie Heidorn accepts a qualifying score ribbon in Novice with his dog, Ch. Northwood Squaw of Caldorn C.D., owned by Pam and Ernie Heidorn.
Photo by Wm. P. Gilbert.

Ch. Beechcroft Wren of Shadow Glen U.D., JH owned, trained and handled by Margart Wilson is shown working the Open B Figure Eight Heeling Pattern.

handled by the owner or another handler. No dog may be entered in both Open A and Open B classes at any one trial.

UTILITY CLASS—to qualify for Utility title a dog must pass the following exercises:

Signal exercise	40 points
Scent discrimination (article 1)	30 points
Scent discrimination (article 2)	30 points
Directed Retrieve	30 points
Directed Jumping	40 points
Group Examination	30 points

Utility may be divided into A and B Classes. The A Class will be for dogs that have won the C.D.X. title, but haven't earned the U.D. title. The B Class will be for dogs that have earned the C.D.X. and the U.D. titles (these dogs may also compete in Open B).

In 1977, the Obedience Trial Champion title, was approved by the AKC. Championship points are recorded and any dog that has been awarded the title of Obedience Trial Champion may preface their name with OTCh. Four Labrador Retriever completed the title in 1993.

OBEDIENCE TRIAL CHAMPION requirements are as follows:
1. The dog must have won 100 points.
2. The dog must have a First place in Utility (at least three dogs competing).
3. The dog must have won a First place in Open B (at least six dogs competing).

Chocolate Labrador, Am. Ch./Can. OTCh. Northfields Double Dutch U.D.T.X., WC owned by E. Crisafulli of Eagle River, Alaska executes the bar jump in Utility.

Ch. Attaboy Harmony Sunshine U.D.X., JH owned and trained by Leslie Boucher retrieves a dumbell during the Utility Scent Discrimination Exercise. Photo by Alan Boucher.

4. The dog must have won a third First place under conditions 2 or 3 above.
5. The dog must have won these three First places under three different judges.

The points available are determined by the number of dogs competing in both the Open B and Utility classes.

The UTILITY DOG EXCELLENT (U.D.X.) is a new title approved by the AKC in 1993. The title can be recorded only to those dogs that have already acquired a C.D.X. and U.D. degree. The requirements are as follows:

1. The dog shalll have earned at ten separate events qualifying scores in both Open B and Utility B Classes.

2. The dog shall have earned these qualifying scores at ten licensed or member obedience trials or dog shows, providing the sum total of dogs that actually competed in the Open B Class was not less than six, and not less than three in the Utility Class. An exception is made regarding the number of competing dogs for breed club specialties and trials in Puerto Rico, Hawaii or Alaska—qualifying scores will be recored if the sum total of dogs that actually compete in all classes is not less than six.

Some obedience trials offer Non-regular Classes. They can be any of the following: Graduate Novice, Brace, Veterans, Team and Versatility. No titles may be earned by competing in these classes. Scent Hurdle races and Fly-Ball competitions, team sports requiring several obedience skills, may also be demonstrated at a fun match or a show, but they are not an AKC-recognized event.

Tracking Degrees

The purpose of the Tracking Test is to demonstrate the dog's ability to recognize and follow human scent and to use this skill in the service of mankind (from AKC Tracking Regulations). The Regulations require that each track be designed to test dog and handler with a variety of terrain and scent-

This black Labrador is a member of a Fly-Ball Team trained by Debbie Kay in Virginia. Note the series of hurdles and the Fly-Ball box that ejects a tennis ball when the dog presses the lever.
Photo by Pet Portaits.

Three generations of Labrador Retriever Obedience Trial Champions, the first in the breed's history according to their breeder. Left to right—OTCh. Winfield's High Expectations, JH owned and trianed by Sandy Barbour; OTCh. Winfield's High Hopes Casey, SH, owned and trained by Sue DeAgular; and OTCh. Winfield's Stand By Me, JH. All three were bred by Sandy Barbour.

Winroc's Yaqui de Oro U.D.T., bred, owned and trained by Sue Luebbert of San Leandro, California displays confidence in following his T.D. track. Photo by Callea.

ing conditions. The dog need not find the track layer, but he must overcome a series of typical scenting problems and locate objects dropped by the track layer. Before a dog can be entered in a test, he must be certified by an AKC-Approved Tracking judge that he is considered to be ready for a Tracking Test. This certification must be within six months of the date of the test.

For those who may be interested in entering a Labrador in AKC Tracking Tests, the tracking degrees in ascending order are:

T.D.	Tracking Dog
T.D.X.	Tracking Dog Excellent

The obedience and tracking degrees above can be in combination as a part of the suffix of a dog's official name (example—U.D.T., Utility Dog Tracking Dog or U.D.T.X., Utility Dog Tracking Dog Excellent).

TRACKING DOG

To qualify for the Tracking Dog title a dog must complete the following: An elementary track is laid by a stranger. The track must be from one half to two hours old, and 440-500 yards in length. It must consist of at least four right-angle turns, but never comes to within 75 yards of itself. At the start there are two flags, one indicating the start of the track and another, about 30 yards away, indicating the direction of the first leg. At the end of the track, the dog is to identify an article dropped by the track layer. The dog must work in harness at the end of a long line. The handler should be 20 to 40 yards behind the dog.

TRACKING DOG EXCELLENT

The Tracking Dog Excellent track is quite a bit longer—800 to 1,000 yards, and must be from three to five hours old. The track itself crosses over part of the original track, and there is only a track layer scented article at the starting stake to give the dog the scent.

In 1993, only 27 Labrador Retrievers completed the T.D. title, and four the T.D.X. title.

Agility Trials

The AKC has approved regulations for an intriguing new performance event—Agility Trials. Effective August 1, 1994, Agility Trials, according to the Regulations, will "afford owners the opportunity to demonstrate a dog's willingness to work with its handler under a variety of conditions. The program begins with basic entry level Agility, and progresses to more complex levels that require dogs to demonstrate higher levels of training and interaction with their handlers."

Classes are divided into Novice, Open and Agility Excellent. The equivalent titles are: Novice Agility Dog (NAD), Open Utility Dog (OAD) and Agility Dog Excellent (ADX). Each level will require three separate qualifying scores for a title.

An Agility Class will consist of a "course" that is made up of 12 to 20 obstacles or jumps (depending upon the level of competition). Dogs must complete the course within a prescribed time limit for the maximum number of points (100). Point deductions will be made for every second over course time. Point deductions for obstacle refusal are allowed in Novice and Open, but not permitted at the advanced level. Following is a list of the types of obstcles:

1. A-Frame
2. Dog Walk
3. See Saw
4. Pause Table
5. Open Tunnel
6. Closed Tunnel
7. Weave Poles
8. Crawl Tunnel
9. Sway bridge
10. Jumps
    —Circle/Tire and Window Jump
    —Broad Jump
    —Double Oxer Jump
    —Triple Bar Jump
    —Other jumps suitable for the class

All jumps and obstacles must be constructed according to specifications in the Regulations.

Am./Can. OTCH. Millgrove's Special Amie, WC (Ch. Heatheredge Mariner x Haverhills Merry Martha C.D.) owned and trained by Vicky Creamer of Belquest Labrador Retrievers was the Number One Obedience Dog in the country all breeds in 1979, Shurman System. According to her owner, "Amie" is the only Labrador to ever be awarded this honor.

Three Champion, Utility Dog, Tracking Dog Labrador Retrievers owned and trained by Martha Lee Voshell, Broad Reach. Left to right—Ch. Zipper's Hustlin' Wahoo U.D.T.; Ch. Broad Reach's English Muffin U.D.T.; and Ch. Yarrow's Broad Reach Psaphire U.D.T. In addition, all three qualified for an LRC, Inc. Working Certificate.

If you are going to have a dog, first have a good dog; second, train it to be useful. It takes a little trouble to train a dog, maybe, but you will find that it more than pays in the end. It will give you a broader sympathy with the animal world, and that includes your fellow man.

—Harry J. Mooney

"Bentley" (Ch. Bold Aron C.D., WC x Ch. Valleywood's Romany Riannon C.D.X, WC), a Labrador donated for guide work by Sandra Wasson-Stanley, Romany Labradors, graduates as a guide dog.

Am. Ch. Westwind Winchester, JH, Can. C.D., TDI with a patient at Eastern Maine Medical Center. Photo courtesy of Nancy Brandow, Bradford, Maine.

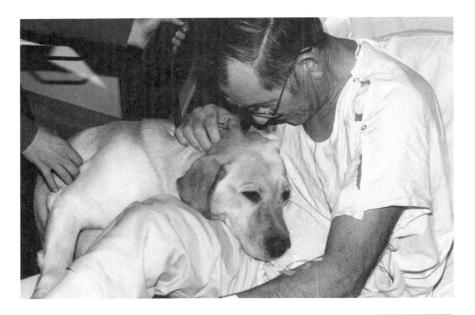

Chapter 4

The Labrador as a Service Dog

The Labrador Retriever is truly a "jack of all trades," and a master of many. The breed has performed so well as a guide dog for the blind in so many lands, that it is now used in this work more than any other breed. The Labrador can be easily trained, and has the right kind of temperament to be gentle and calm, as well as bold enough to handle stressful situations. I have donated several puppies to different organizations training guide dogs, and have been very proud when they passed the tough training and went on to be successful in their jobs. One chocolate fellow, Trusty, traveled each day with his master on the "wild and woolly" subways of Manhattan. Following is a partial list of organizations that train Labradors and their blind owners: The Seeing Eye, Inc. in New Jersey; The Guide Dog Foundation for the Blind in New York; Guide Dogs for the Blind, Inc. in California; Leader Dogs for the Blind in Michigan; International Guiding Eyes, Inc. in Southern California; and The Guiding Eyes for the Blind in New York.

There are other groups that train Labradors to help the handicapped and the hearing impaired. Canine Companions For Independence in Santa Rosa, California; Support Dogs in St. Louis, Missouri; and New England Assistance Dog Service are only a few of the organizations making use of this versatile breed. Labradors have proved to be especially helpful for handicapped with wheelchairs as they have the strength and can be trained to assist with the chair, as well as learn a number of useful tasks such as turning on and off lights and retrieving dropped objects.

Therapy Dog is another form of service performed by the Labrador. Therapy

This Labrador is a therapy dog for handicapped children, owner Charlotte Veneziano, New York.

Dogs International (TDI) was formed several years ago to develop a test to determine dogs suitable for visiting nursing homes and other rehabilitation facilities. TDI-certified dogs have been tested for appropriate behavior and disposition. Regular visits to nursing homes or rehabilitation facilities have been a labor of love for many owners and their dogs.

For several years my friend Christine Watt and I took our Labradors on a regular basis to a local psychiatric clinic where we visited patients of all ages. Many of the older patients missed their own dogs, and were very happy to see our Labs. The clinic also treated children from ages six to early teens, and this group especially looked forward to the dog's visits. They would hug them and walk them around on lead, usually arguing about who would lead whom. Several "rescue" Labradors have been adopted by nursing homes, and are living happy lives enjoying many friends and masters.

Debby Kay is the president of International Detector Dogs, Ltd. in Virginia, and is the author of the training book: *The Complete Guide to Accelerent Detection Dog Training.* She has sent me the following information on a number of different services performed by Labradors:

If a measure of a breed's versatility is the widespread use of that breed in dozens of jobs requiring many different skills, then the Labrador has to

Debby Kay, head trainer for International Detector Dogs, Ltd., with a yellow Labrador during a training exercise showing the use of the scent wheel.

An arson dog, "Nikki," works a fire scene for evidence of accelerants. This dog was trained by Debby Kay, IDD, Ltd., for the Loudon County Fire Marshall's Office, Leesburg, VA.

be near the top of the list as one of the truly versatile breeds. The Lab's stable temperament, willing nature and athletic abilities make him suitable for a large number of working jobs. In addition, the outstanding scenting ability bred into the Labrador for bird hunting has served him well as a detector dog.

Many breeds of dogs were used during World War II, and Labradors were among them. They served primarily as messenger dogs and Red Cross aides. In today's military, the Lab is used as a mine detection dog or a narcotics detection aide. The escalation of the drug problem in the 60's necessitated a quick and reliable method of detecting concealed drugs. For the Labrador it was an easy transition from searching for birds to searching for dope. Drug dogs are trained using the play retrieve method, so a love of retrieving is necessary. Simplified, this method involves the introduction of the target narcotic odor with the dog's retrieve toy—a tennis ball or a scented rolled up towel. The game of getting to the toy is made progressively difficult until finally the dog, using only his nose, must find the location of the hidden toy. When he locates it, he will try to dig the toy out of its hiding spot. At this time, the handler will throw down another toy for the dog—his reward for finding drugs. In reality the dog is looking for his toy, not for drugs. He doesn't 'think' the suitcase is hiding cocaine, he 'thinks' it is where his toy is, because he always gets a toy when he smells that smell. At no time is the dog allowed to inhale directly, ingest or make contact with the narcotics.

Sharlos Sea Biscuit is a bomb sniffer for Prince George's County, Maryland Sheriff's Department. She was bred and donated by Shari Capps.

Killingworth's Tristan, a chocolate Labrador Retriever bred by Lorraine Taylor, is an evidence recovery dog for the State of Connecticut, Department of Environmental Protection. His job involves tracking for poacher evidence, such as deer killed illegally and out-of-season.

Can. OTCh. Ramapo's Medicine Man Am./Can. U.D., AAD, AGI & II, TT, TDI owned and trained by Marietta Huber, Ramapo Retrievers is shown at a "shoot" for a Vogue Magazine layout in 1991.

The U.S. Customs Service established a detector dog program in 1970. Dogs are assigned to customs agents mainly at ports of entry into the U.S., and the breed used most often is the Labrador. Labradors have also been trained as bomb detection dogs. The New York Police Department has used Labs for many years in their bomb squad with success, and from work with this group came the idea of using dogs to aid in arson investigations. The Labrador was chosen for this job because of his past performance at other detector jobs. Arson dogs are assigned the difficult task of sniffing through the remains of buildings and vehicles that are suspected of being deliberately set afire by arsonists. In most arson cases, some type of flammable liquid, known as an accelerant, is used to start the fire. As incredible as it seems, even after a fire has burned and has been extinguished, a trained dog can sniff through the ashes and find the material remains that have been soaked with the accelerants. It is possible for a trained accelerant dog to track an arsonist by the odor of the accelerant on his clothes.

Another territory where Labradors have broken new ground is in the area of locating buried toxic waste. This type of work is similar to oil or gas pipeline leak detection in which the Lab has also been successful, thus helping the environment. The scenting ability of the Labrador has also been put to good use by the American search and rescue dog organizations.

Sirius Lad of Ayr C.D.X., owned and trained by June Oswald uses the scent discrimination exercise to "spell" CAT at a Cub Scout demonstration. "Laddy" also visited nursing homes.

These groups train teams to find people trapped in earthquakes, floods, avalanches or other catastrophes. Labs also have been trained to find cadavers. The world record for the oldest cadaver find is held by a chocolate Labrador, 'Candy,' owned and trained by Bill Tolhurst of New York. Candy located a grave that was 147 years old. Even after all those years, enough scent material remained to key the dog. Though grueling work at times, cadaver work can be most challenging especially when looking for victims at the bottom of a river or lake. For this type of water search, the dog rides in a low fishing-type boat, and is piloted in a zig-zag fashion over the victim's PLS (point last seen). When the dog locates cadaver scent, he will bark at the spot in the water. Divers then check in that area. Many factors come into play in determining success of water searches such as temperature, humidity, water salinity, depth, cause of death and currents. Trained cadaver dogs can save valuable time and make the job of finding missing persons easier.

DOG HERO OF THE YEAR 1992 Chicago—Sparky, a loyal and lovable 130-pound yellow Labrador Retriever from Tullahoma, Tennessee, is the

"Sparky" recipient of the Ken-L-Ration Dog Hero of the year award 1992, and his owner, John "Bo" Culbertson.

39th winner of the annual Ken-L-Ration Dog Hero of the year award. When Sparky's owner, John "Bo" Culbertson, suffered a heart attack in January 1992, Sparky saved his life by dragging him home where his wife discovered him unconscious at the front door. Today, Culbertson refers to Sparky as a "million dollar dog." "He saved my life and he's worth millions to me. I've had Sparky for six years now, and will never, never part with him."

You can also find Labradors modeling, in films and on the stage, and just having fun dressed up. (Hey, you can't work all the time!)

* * * * * *

Each of the chapters in this Section has demonstrated examples of the multiple uses of the Labrador Retriever. Not all Labrador Retriever owners participate in more than one activity, but many do cross-over to other areas. Multiple interests and the adaptability of the breed have encouraged three regional clubs to try to develop programs for versatile, all-around retrievers. The first to do so was the Waterland Retriever Club in Pennsylvania. This club was founded in 1965 by a few Labrador breeders who were showing their dogs, but wanted to learn about field work, too. Club membership is open to all retriever owners, and for many years the club has put on an annual Fun Day (now expanded to two days) of field tests, obedience trials and conformation classes. Dogs that qualify and place in all three areas of competition are given All Around Retriever Certificates. At the end of the year, challenge trophies are awarded to the top All Around and Dual Purpose Dogs.

In 1990, The Labrador Retriever Club of Southern California held its first Dual Challenge Labrador Retriever Day at which each Labrador was awarded points for every level successfully completed in the field. After the four field series are scored, the same Labs are judged in conformation with points given for each placement won. At the very end, the dog with the highest score in both areas is the winner of the Dual Challenge, but there are also four more runner-up awards determined by score. I was privileged to to judge the conformation part of this Dual Day in 1991 and it's interesting to me that the same dog won both years—Ch. Hawkett's Major Impression, JH a yellow dog owned by Diane and Craig Matsuura.

Not to be outdone, a group in Northern California, Labs Are Us (a part of the Golden Gate LRC), started the Do-It-All Challenge in 1991. This is a two-day event with conformation and obedience judging the first day, followed by judging of field events and a pot-luck supper the second day. The retriever accumulating the greatest number of points in all three areas is awarded the Do-It-All Challenge Trophy.

An unique group photograph of some of England's top breeders. *Standing, left to right: Mrs. Marjorie Satterthwaite (Lawnwood); Mr. Jeff Robinson (Mallardhurn); Mrs. Heather Wiles (Heatherbourne); Mrs. "Didi" Hepworth (Poolstead). Seated, left to right: Mrs. Dorothy Gardner (Novacroft); Mrs. Mary Roslin-Williams (Mansergh); Mrs. Gwen Broadley (Sandylands); Mrs. Margot Woolley (Follytower); and Mrs. Peggy Rae (Cornlands).* Reproduced with kind permission of The Midlands Counties Labrador Retriever Club from their 1990 Yearbook. Photo by Mr. David Bull.

SECTION IV
Breeders and Kennels

Her Majesty The Queen and "Garry" (Sandringham), 1993. Photo by kind permission of Martin Deeley.

Chapter 1

Breeders and Kennels in England

The Working Side

Author's note: Mr. Bill Meldrum, Gundog Trainer and Handler for the Sandringham Kennel of Her Majesty, Queen Elizabeth II, has sent the following information about the kennel. I'm very grateful to Martin Deeley for his lovely photograph of H.M. the Queen.

The Kennels at Sandringham are situated on the southern boundary of the grounds of Sandringham House, and they surround the Kennel House, which is occupied by H.M. The Queen's Dog Handler. H.M. Queen Alexandra possessed many breeds of dogs including the Sandringham strain of black Labradors founded in 1911. After her death in 1925, H.M. King George V changed the Royal Prefix at the Kennel Club from Wolferton to Sandringham. He also re-introduced the Clumber breed of Spaniels, originally started by King Edward VII at Sandringham, which were favoured by The King because of their rough shooting ability. They also won several prizes at dog shows including two firsts at Crufts. During the short reign of H.M. King Edward VIII (Duke of Windsor), the kennels were closed and there were no dogs at Sandringham. When H.M. King George VI came to the throne in 1936, he re-established the Kennels in a small way with six to eight yellow Labradors which he used for shooting only. In 1949 it was decided that the famous Labrador dog called Windsor Bob should be brought to Sandringham for breeding to build up the Sandringham strain once again. Her Majesty Queen Elizabeth II takes a very great interest in the Sandringham Kennels. Since her accession to the throne in 1952, the breeding program has gone from strength-to-strength culminating in the training of four field trial champions, namely, Sandringham Ranger, Sandringham Slipper, Sherry of Biteabout and Sandringham Sydney. The most recent, FTC Sandringham Sydney, has become very well-known and popular in the field trial world. In 1977 a television film was made called Sandringham Sydney & Co. which shows Sydney at field trials and during training sessions. Usually the Kennels house approximately 25 fully grown dogs of varying ages from the older and more experienced gun dogs, used by members of the Royal Family during the shooting season, to the younger dogs under training as gun dogs. In addition to providing dogs for the Royal Family, the estate gamekeepers are kept supplied with working Labradors. At certain times of the year, usually in the spring and early summer, there are often as many as forty puppies in the Kennels born to the four or five best bitches which are used for breeding. One or two puppies from each litter are kept at the Kennels for training, but the majority are sold at eight weeks old to be trained by other people. All the puppies born at Sandringham are given a name by Her Majesty the Queen and are registered at The Kennel Club with the prefix Sandringham. It is the policy of the Sandringham Kennels to attain the highest standard of trained dog possible and to achieve this end, a great deal of time is spent training the better dogs up to field trial standard. During the summer and autumn, the [Kennel] dog handler attends several working tests and field trials throughout the country in an attempt to create field trial champions and to keep Sandringham dogs at the top of the breed.

*Author's note: Quite a few field trials, including the International Gundog League Retriever Championship have been held at the Sandringham Estate, and H.M. the Queen has always taken a keen interest. One such held in 1992 has been described by Graham Cox in his article, "Great Expectations." Since it is an excellent description that will help the reader to understand how an English Field Trial is run, I give a very big thank you to Mr. Cox and to the **Retriever Field Trial News** for permission to reprint this portion of it and for the photo of Mr. John Halstead with his famous FTC Breeze of Drakeshead, three-time winner of The Retriever Championship.*

Asked recently if he had any advice to offer aspiring competitors, Roger Clarke, Britain's leading rally driver, pondered long and hard. Finally, after what seemed like an interminable silence, he uttered just seven words: 'All the prizes are at the end.'

Few sportsmen and women would feel the force of that truism more keenly than field trialers. Trialing can often seem to be more about survival than anything else, and the dog which continues to bring birds to hand whilst others are struggling and failing, imposes itself inexorably on the assessments of the judges. The Retriever Championship, held at Sandringham Estate, Norfolk, on December 8 and 9, 1992 by gracious permission of Her Majesty the Queen, proved a taxing contest in which reversals of fortune were frequent and dramatic. So much so that, at the close, only first and second could be awarded.

The result, a win for John Halstead with his five year old yellow Labrador, FTC Raughlin Pete of Drakeshead, again recast the record books. 'Again' because John Halstead has made the activity his own special preserve in recent years. Having already achieved the singular distinction of winning in three successive years with FTC Breeze of Drakeshead, he has now emphatically etched his name at the head of the roll of honour with a fourth win. There is simply nothing to compare it with.

To say that expectations for this seventieth Championship Stake were of the highest is simply to state the obvious. Sandringham, a wild bird shoot since 1939, is a very special venue in many ways. Her Majesty's enthusiasm for the best in British gun dog work is never more evident than in her commitment to the Retriever Championship. There is no hint of a token involvement: she is in line from start-to-finish, and her keen attention to everything that happens invariably has its own impact on the outcome, as well as giving the Stake a special distinction. For instance, the partridge that she alone marked down in 1987 did much to secure John Halstead his record breaking third win.

Consistency and quality were evident in equal and appropriate measure. Of the eleven bitches and nineteen dogs running—twenty two black Labradors, five yellows and three Golden Retrievers—no fewer than nineteen had already attained their field trial champion title. Eight of the previous year's qualifiers were back to challenge again with the eventual winner, Alan Thornton's 1990 Champion FTC Tasco Dancing Brave Of Willowyck and David Garbutt's 1991 Champion FTC Pocklea Remus were both running in their fourth successive Championship Stake. Tess Lawrence had the distinction of having qualified two . . .

[The final day of the trial.] . . . Altogether milder and, for the most part, extraordinarily still, the second day proved no more accommodating when it came to runners. The mist which shrouded the early work lifted by eleven and, with birds rising well-ahead of the line, a forward gun, last year's host, Richard Parker, was providing some testing marked birds on the right. Jim Blair was eyewiped by Aidan Carr, leaving Scottish hopes with Graham Gibson—though the work was not especially convincing. But shortly after the line had moved through to an area of self-sown corn, Black Purdey of Keswick came behind Alan Thornton's Brave and Tess Lawrence's FTC Cottismore Accord to pick a hen which had tucked up deep in the dense cover at the base of the towering Scots Pines which bounded the ground. The cheers for handler Nigel Mann from Norwich were predictably rousing. Another local, Frank Holman from the Woodhall Estate near Downham Market, was raising hopes as well, and there was applause for the retrieve of a live bird from amongst the pines. His other work was often noisy though. John Halstead, meanwhile, made light work of a bird which fell amongst trees to the right of a huge straw bale-ringed field of sugar beet. No handling was needed despite a vehicle reversing out of the path of Pete's outrun. It was impressive work.

After the line had turned ninety degrees, Tess Lawrence's FTC Willowyck Favour, who had been working consistently, gave a superb display of controlled hunting second down on a bird which was not found. The first dog failure on a hen dropped near an open boundary gate which followed was a cruel blow, for Favour came closest to owning and holding a line. Then the only remaining Golden challenge faded as Sarah Olner's Littlemarston Nutmeg failed first down on a bird which dropped in some very thick cover across a ditch. Again the line turned and, almost immediately, two birds were shot on the right. Sent for the first, Nigel Mann's bitch picked the second whilst hunting so she was sent again for the original bird. But a long hunt produced no really positive indication. The judges, however, completed an eyewipe in what must have been atrocious scenting conditions. As IGL President Basil Death remarked, 'there have been some great crashes.'

However, John Halstead was continuing to pick his birds with a minimum of fuss and Frank Holman's dog took another live hen to sustain a challenge which had great local support behind it. But after the drive at Park Pool it was FTC Raughlin Pete of Drakeshead who was sent first and, as if to emphasize the qualities that had propelled him to prominence, his water work was the most positive of the eight whom were tested.

FTC Breeze of Drakeshead delivers a strong cock runner to handler John Halstead at the 1985 Retriever Championship. Judges for the event were Mrs. J. Atkinson, Miss A. Hill-Wood, Capt. C.P. Hazelhurst and Mr. M. Patterson. John Halstead and FTC Breeze of Drakeshead achieved the singular distinction of winning England's Retriever Championship for three successive years. Photo courtesy of Graham Cox.

Tasco Thyme of Staindrop owned and trained by Mrs. Joan Hayes, Staindrop Kennel Gundogs.

At the close of a trial, whose pace had often seemed pedestrian on the first day, often underrated qualities had prevailed in conditions which were never easy. Pete's marking had been virtually flawless. That he handles with a willing readiness goes without saying, but the circumstances of this premier stake meant that John Halstead had little need to draw upon such skills. As others fell he survived and the manner of his survival made him as worthy a winner as you could hope to set before The Queen. Basil Death's call for three cheers was met with a heartfelt response. History had once again been made at Sandringham.

Results:
1. John Halstead's Labrador dog, **FTC Raughlin Pete Of Drakeshead**
2. Frank Holman's Labrador dog, **Birdbrook Trooper**

Diplomas of Merit to:
—Nigel Mann's Labrador bitch, **Black Purdey Of Keswick**
—Graham Gibson's Labrador bitch **Levendell Lorelie**
—Alan Fryer's Labrador dog, **FTC Kilnbeck Arrow**
—Tess Lawrence's Labrador bitch, **FTC Willowyck Favour**
—Sarah Olner's Golden Retriever bitch, **Littlemarston Nutmeg**
—Aidan Carr's Labrador dog, **FTC Clencar Captain**

Staindrop

The Staindrop Gundogs of Mr. Edgar Winter have been famous for many years. Established in 1929, the kennel was composed of Labradors, English Springer Spaniels and a few Cocker Spaniels. After WW II, a young yellow dog was purchased from J. J. Murray Dewar. He was by Glenhead Jimmy ex Our Lil (great-grandson of Dual Ch. Bramshaw Bob). In 1947 he was to become Dual Champion Staindrop Saighdear, the first yellow Dual Champion. His name appears in the pedigree of many modern dogs. The Staindrop kennel has been run for years by Edgar Winter's daughter, now Mrs. Joan Hayes, who has written some comments about her Labradors and about field trials today. Until just recently, Joan Hayes had served as Field Trial Secretary for more than 20 years for the Midland Counties Labrador Retriever Club.

"My halcyon days in field trials were in the 1960s."

Author's note: There were some excellent FT Champions for Joan—FTC Staindrop Woodstain Tern, FTC Staindrop Doune and her two daughters FTC Staindrop Sapphire and FTC Staindrop Trim. Recently her young bitch, Tasco Thyme of Staindrop has been doing very well. She was bred by Mary Roundtree of Northern Ireland out of her FTC Holdgate Bebe by Int. FTC Leacross Rinkals, owned and handled by Mary's husband Alan. When Thyme was mated to John and Sandra Halstead's FTC Haretor Shadow of Drakeshead, the Halsteads opted to keep a dog puppy who, in

October 1993 at just two years old, became FTC Staindrop Mint of Drakeshead.

... All credit to John Halstead. His abilities as a trainer and handler are certainly a 'Legend in his Lifetime'— a truly wonderful sportsman too, the same whether he wins or loses (and that's not often). John is a member of The Kennel Club Field Trial Committee, and Vice Chairman of the Kennel Club.

His wife Sandra is also a good handler, having won the 1979 Retriever Championship with FTC Westead Shot of Drakeshead. She and John are both judges in shows as well as field trials.

I asked if field trials had changed over the years, and Joan replied:

Yes, they most certainly have! The Retriever trials are oversubscribed. For one stake this season 115 members applied for a 12 dog Novice Stake. Very often there are over a hundred applicants for Open Stakes. Stakes do clash, which does enable more people to have a run, but it can be a nightmare for field trial secretaries. The Kennel Club has a sub-committee looking into the problem, but the solution is not easy. Conditions are ruled by the number of natural shooting grounds available and generous hosts and syndicates willing to offer days' shooting for our sport of field trials.

Competition is tough with the top dogs stretched to a limit. Other than the top, say 30 dogs in the country, I sometimes wonder if the overuse of the whistle, especially by the less experienced handlers who don't understand natural game finding ability, has eroded many of the dogs' natural ability to find game—that is, after all, the prime reason to have a gun dog! I must mention some other very well-known owners and handlers:

David Garbutt, a fellow Yorkshireman, is no doubt brilliant. He won the Retriever Championship in 1991 with FTC Pocklea Remus; in 1988 handling Mr. David Benson's FTC Pocklea Tide of Middlegate; and in 1981 with his own FTC Pocklington Glen. All these winners were bred by David. He is sought after as a fair and firm judge, and is judging the 1993 Retriever Championship, as indeed is Alan Thornton whom I mention next.

Alan is well-known as a trainer of people as well as dogs. His patience is immense and his efforts endless whenever he has a dog or handler with problems—again, a wonderful sportsman, come win or lose. His partner, Tess Lawrence, a comparative newcomer to the trial scene, has done very well with an ability and determination to win one seldom sees. Her wonderful yellow bitch, FTC Willowyck Favour has consistently run well in the Retriever Championship, particularly in 1992. Favour's natural game finding ability is unsurpassed.

There are, of course, many other handlers and owners who run very well and are a credit to the British working Labrador. We are proud of our working Labradors! All right, some couldn't win in the show ring, but overall, the majority are good types with wonderful temperaments.

I have heard from a few others in Great Britain who are interested in field work. Brief resumes of their kennels follow:

Manymills Drake C.D.Ex.owned and trained by Susan Scales is the winner of a two day field trial Open Stake and championship show prizes.

Left to right, FTC Abbotsleigh Nimrod, FTC Abbotsleigh Lynx, and FTC Abbotsleigh Kossack. Owners—Mrs. P.C. Hales and Mrs. Sarah Coomber, Abbotsleigh.

Mary Priestly of the well-known Cissbury Labradors with two of her dogs—left, Cissbury Marmaduke (liver) and, right, Cissbury Zachariah (black). Both dogs are used regularly for "picking up."

Manymills

Susan Scales, has been involved with field, working trials and obedience for many years. Although no longer doing the latter two, she has achieved numerous titles with her versatile dogs in the past: Manymills Lucky Charm WDEx UDEx CDEx and her daughter, W.T.Ch. Manymills Tanne TDEx WDE UDE CDE; Manymills Drake C.D.Ex.—firsts in field trials and championship shows (Drake is the sire of Ch. Abbeystead Herons Court owned by Mrs. Lynne Minchella); FTC Manymills Milady, first in championship shows. All the modern Manymills stock goes back to FTC Holdgate Willie, a good-looking Labrador. Susan is a judge in Britain of CCs, field trials, championship working trials, working tests and obedience.

Abbotsleigh

Trish Hales of the Abbotsleigh Kennels writes: "Our kennel aims to produce good-looking dogs whose temperament is as sound as their physique, and whose hunting ability has not been blunted by domestication nor brains dulled by lives of mere imprisonment. I only hope that pet breeders do not turn a working breed into an unable-to-work breed."

Her daughter, Mrs. Sarah Coomber, starting as a complete novice, has trained three dog pups and made-up all into field trial champions: Abbotsleigh Kossack, Lynx and Nimrod. She is now an "A" Panel Kennel Club Field Trial Judge. Mrs. Hales has been Field Trial Secretary for the South Eastern Gundog Society and is now President of the Kent, Surrey & Sussex Labrador Retriever Club.

Cissbury

Mrs. Mary Priestly of the well-known Cissbury Labradors does a lot of working her dogs on a shoot, and has sent a description: "Here in Britain the shooting of game birds is divided into two types, i.e., where game is driven over the guns who are stationary (formal shooting) and what is generally known as rough shooting where the sportsman walks up his own game, flushing it with the help of his dog. In formal shooting the guns stand with their own dogs, if any, at heel while others known as 'pickers up' (such as myself) stand with dogs at strategic points to gather birds that fall farther away, usually in woodland."

Meadowmill

The Meadowmill Labradors of Mrs. Eileen Ayling are versatile. She has written, "My aim is to produce a dual purpose Labrador, capable of winning at the top level of competition in the show ring and have the working ability to win a field trial. All my Labradors work a full shooting season picking up on the Duke of Norfolk estate at Arundel in Sussex. I try to keep as much field trial breeding in my pedigrees without a loss of type and quality, which keeps the working ability, as well as the angulation and athletic ability of the

Meadowmill Tap On Wood, owned and bred by Mrs. Eileen Ayling, had a reserve CC and won a Novice Dog/ Handler field trial. He was a wonderful shooting dog and greatly improved the stock of the field trial bitches on which he was used.

field-trial bred Labrador. Meadowmill Tap On Wood had a reserve CC and won a Novice dog/handler field trial. He was a wonderful shooting dog and greatly improved the stock of the field trial bitches on which he was used." Perkin Flump at Meadowmill, a great-grandson of Tap on Wood, and Yours for the Asking at Meadowmill, the last son of Tap on Wood, are also successful in both fields.

Leospring

Mrs. Joy Venturi of Leospring Kennels has told me: "I was greatly inspired by Mary Roslin-Williams' book, *The Dual Purpose Labrador,* and formed the opinion that I would like to pursue the ideal of trying to maintain both looks and working ability in equal amounts. The best dual purpose dogs have been the litter brothers Treherne Game Fall at Leospring and Treherne Fairly Game at Leospring (Manymills Drake x Buttsash Pollyflinders of Leospring, a Ch. Squire of Ballyduff daughter). Both won Novice Stake and Open Stake field trial awards, as well as awards in breed classes at Championship shows. Their half-brother, Leospring Mars Marine, sired by Pluto of Abbotsleigh, has won a two day Open Stake, an All-aged Stake and a Novice Stake, and awards in breed classes at championship shows. His son, Leospring Marmaduke (only two years old) was awarded Best Puppy in Show at a breed club championship show and gained a field trial award in his first season.

"To pursue the genuine dual purpose route one has to be single minded in the pursuit of an elusive ideal. Break all the normal rules about not mixing work and show lines in your breeding program. Rise above the fact that show breeders disregard you as a 'working person' and field trialers think you are a 'show person.' Get your 'highs' from watching your good-looking Labs working their hearts out for you, and ordinary people complimenting your 'good-looking old fashioned Labradors.' Never stop believing that

Joy Venturi's Treherne Game Fall of Leospring returns with a strong cock bird runner.
Photo by Jan West Photography.

you may one day produce another Dual Champion because even if you don't, you will own some lovely Labs and have a lot of fun on the way."

Joy Venturi is the Field Trial Secretary of the Kent, Surrey & Sussex Labrador Retriever Club. Its team won first place at Castle Howard two-day event in Yorkshire in 1989. Joy was the Captain.

Langshott

Mr. Brian Yeowart sent some super photographs. I wish I could use them all. His dogs are worked regularly in England and in Scotland, and they have won a number of field trial and working trial awards.

The Show Ring

To continue the history of the Labrador Retriever in England after World War II, one must review the accomplishments of some special breeders. Many of these important Labrador kennels have been written about numerous times, so readers with a long-term interest in the breed will be familiar with the following breeders and their dogs. They continue to have a strong impact on present day Labradors.

Sandylands

I am really happy to say that the Sandylands Kennel of Mrs. Gwen Broadley and her partner, Mr. Garner Anthony is still going strong. They are breeding top class dogs for themselves and for others as they've always done, although Gwen no longer judges. Ch. Sandylands Royal Escort comes to mind as does Ch. Sandylands My Guy and the very beautiful Ch. Sandylands Bliss. I was so lucky to have Am. Ch. Sandylands Morningcloud, a wonderful old girl who lived until age sixteen. But the best part has been

Eng. Sh. Ch. Sandylands Bliss, owned and bred by Gwen Broadley and Mr. Garner Anthony, Sandylands Kennels.
Photo © Anne Roslin-Williams.

knowing Gwen, a very special lady, and her husband Frank and her friend and helper, Erica Smith—just a great bunch.

Blaircourt

The Blaircourt Kennel of Grant and Margie Cairns in Scotland has had a number of good dogs, but the most famous was Ch. Ruler of Blaircourt. He was the winner of 22 CCs, and Best Gundog and Reserve Best in Show at Crufts. Another great black was Eng./Am. Ch. Sam of Blaircourt who came to America and was a terrific influence. Margie is a very popular judge in many countries, and a charming lady.

Ballyduff

The Ballyduff Kennel of Dr. Acheson and his wife Bridget were famous the world over. They had some outstanding field and show dogs. Some of their early Labradors were Ch. Whatstandwell Ballyduff Rowena and Ch. Ballyduff Holly-branch of Keithray and later, Ch. Ballyduff Seaman, Ch. Ballyduff Marketeer and Ch. Squire of Ballyduff. Bridget was a wonderful lady, and an astute dog breeder. The

Margie Cairns and her constant companion, a chocolate bitch "Coco," Blaircourt Kennels, Scotland.
Photo by Price Jessop.

Sh. Ch. Ballyduff Dawn of Bannowbridge, bred by Mrs. Sheelin Cuthbert and owned by Vic and Janet Cole.

Ballyduff name is being carried on by her daughter, Mrs. Sheelin Cuthbert and her son, Dr. Cavan Acheson in Canada. I was also the fortunate owner of Ballyduff Sparkler who is behind all my dogs.

Mansergh

Mary Roslin-Williams' Mansergh black Labradors have certainly made their mark also. Fondly known as "Black Mary," she is an extremely clever lady who has written some very important books, *The Dual Purpose Labrador, All About The Labrador* and *Advanced Labrador Breeding.* I've read the first one at least four times, and the third one twice, and could savor all of them again.

Six Mansergh champions—left to right: Mansergh Antonia, Mansergh Moleskin, Groucho of Mansergh, Damson of Mansergh; and the Borders, Mansergh Aprilmist and Mansergh Barn Owl. Photo © Anne Roslin-Williams.

Mrs. Joan Macan with Timspring Rarity at the veterinary surgery of Dr. Jane Wighton. "Rarity" is owned in the U.S. by Lisa McClain and Philip J. Palumbo. Photo by Philip J. Palumbo.

She is famous, too, for her weekly column in *Dog World* (England) on all kinds of doggy topics. Some of her important Labs were Ch. Midnight of Mansergh and five direct generations of champions from him: Ch. Mansergh Midnight, Ch. Bumblikite of Mansergh, Ch. Damson of Mansergh, Ch. Mansergh Antonia, Ch. Mansergh Ooh La La. Mary enjoyed field work for many years. She is no longer judging, but is still showing her lovely bitches.

Timspring

Mrs. Joan Macan was the victim of a cruel attack that caused her death in 1988. She was a dear lady who was interested in the working Labrador and the show Labrador, and she began a study of the statistics on hip dysplasia, publishing a book of all the hip reports for Labradors. This project is being carried on today by The Labrador Club. Joan's Timspring Labradors Retrievers are in the pedigrees of many Labradors today.

Poolstead

The Poolstead Kennels of Didi and Bob Hepworth began in 1959 with the purchase of two yellow bitch puppies from Mrs. Ann Wynyard— Braeduke Juniper and Braeduke Julia who were litter mates to Braeduke Joyful. A bit later Poolstead Kinley Willow was bought from Fred Wrigley and she became their first champion and the dam of Poolstead Pussy Willow, who in turn was the dam of the famous Eng. Sh. Ch. Poolstead Problem. Problem has been a tremendous influence, with all the present Poolsteads going back to him. His son, Eng. Sh. Ch. Poolstead Preferential, is certainly producing well. And his son, Eng. Sh. Ch. Poolstead Pipe Dreamer was BOB at Crufts 1991, BIS at the Labrador Club Championship Show 1991 and BOS at the Scottish Labrador Championship Show the same year. Many of the Poolsteads have gone abroad to different countries, and most of these have done well for their respective owners, gaining their titles and influencing breeding stock.

Four generations of Poolstead Labrador Retrievers—left to right: Eng. Sh. Ch. Poolstead Problem, Eng. Sh. Ch. Poolstead Pictorial, Eng. Sh. Ch. Poolstead Postal Vote, Poolstead Piccadilly, Poolstead Puskas, Eng. Sh. Ch. Pegg, Eng. Sh. Ch. Poolstead Preface, Eng. Sh. Ch. Poolstead Preferential, Poolstead Prelude (lying down), and Poolstead Pussy Willow (lying down). Photo © Anne Roslin-Williams.

Mention must be made of some other notable kennels: Mr. Dick Burton's Brackenbank Kennel of field trial champions; Mrs. Ann Wynyard's Braedukes; Mrs. May MacPherson's dual purpose Braeroys; Leo and Mim Kinsella's Brentchase Kennel; Mrs. Louise Wilson-Jones Diant's; the multipurpose Foxhanger Labs of Lady Simpson; the Garshangan Labradors of Lt. Col. and Mrs. M. Hill; the Heatheredge Kennel of Mrs. M. Ward; the Kinley Labradors of Mr. and Mrs. Fred Wrigley; the Rookwoods of Mrs. Marian Saffell; the Wendovers of Mr. and Mrs. L.C. James; and the Whatstandwell Kennel of Mr. and Mrs. Horace Taylor.

A gallery of photographs representing a cross-section of current English breeders appears on the following pages—

Insley Issa, a chocolate bitch owned and bred by Mrs. Diane Harris, Insley. Photo © Anne Roslin-Williams.

Right to left, Cornlands Landy, Cornlands My Fair Lady, Cornlands Kimvalley Crofter and Cornlands Highlight owned and bred by Mrs. Peggy Rae, Cornlands.

Eng. Sh. Ch. Heatherbourne Statesman owned and bred by Mrs. Heather Wiles-Fone, Heatherbourne.
Photo © Thompson.

Eng. Ch. Charway Ballywillwill owned and bred by Janice Pritchard, Charway.
Photo by H. Price Jessop.

Eng. Sh. Newinn Oasis owned and bred by Rosemary Hewitt, Newinn.

Eng. Sh. Ch. Balrion King Frost owned and bred by Mr. and Mrs. J. Crook, Balrion.

Eng. Ch. Carpenny Chevalier winning Res. BIS Hampshire Gun Dog Show— judge, Marilyn Reynolds; BIS judge, James Cudworth; owned and bred by Penny Carpanini.
Photo by Gibbs.

Eng. Sh. Ch. Kimvalley Legend owned and bred by Diana Beckett, Kimvalley.

This photo of Eng. Sh. Ch. Follytower Merrybrook Black Stormer was taken on his 12th birthday. "Stormer" was owned and bred by Mrs. M. Woolley, Follytower. Photo © Anne Roslin-Williams.

Eng. Sh. Ch. Bradking Cassidy owned and bred by Mr. and Mrs. A.D. Kelly, Bradking.

*Eng. Ch.
Fabracken
Comedy Star
owned and
bred by
Anne Taylor,
Fabracken.*

*Eng. Sh. Ch. Mardas
Corndilly owned and bred by
Marlene and David Hepper.*
Photo by David Bull.

*Balnova
Muffin Man
owned and
bred by Sheila
and Keith
Wallington,
Balnova.*

*Eng. Sh. Ch. Jayncourt
Star Appeal owned and
bred by Jane and Peter
Palmer, Jayncourt.*

*Eng. Sh. Ch. Blondella
Balalai'ka owned and
bred by Mr. and Mrs. H.
Burton, Blondella
Labradors.*
Photo by David Bull.

*Eng. Sh. Ch. Rocheby
Popcorn, 1992 BOB
Crufts, owned and bred by
David and Marion
Hopkinson, Rocheby.*

Eng. Sh. Ch. Bradking Music Maker at Kingstream, owned by Mr. and Mrs. J. Banner, Kingstream; bred by Mr. and Mrs. A.D. Kelly, Bradking. Photo © David Dalton.

Eng. Ch. Lawnwood's Free 'N' Easy owned and bred by Mr. and Mrs. G. Satterthwaite, Lawnwood. Photo © David Dalton.

Eng. Sh. Ch. Ardmargha Mad Hatter, behind quite a few present day winners, owned and bred by Mr. & Mrs. H. W. Clayton, Ardmargha. Photo © Anne Roslin-Williams.

Eng. Ch. Crosscroyde Cotton on Quick, BOB Crufts 1993 and 1994 owned and bred by Mr. and Mrs. R.J. Lavelle.
Photo © David Dalton.

Eng. Ch. Abbystead Herons Court owned by Lynne Michella. "Harry" has four field trial awards, 12 awards in working tests and 5 CCs.
Photo © David Dalton.

Maj. and Mrs. R.C. Aikenhead with four Powhatan Labradors.

Eng. Sh. Ch. Boothgates Kountry Kurio, a chocolate owned and bred by Marilyn and David Nightingale, Boothgate.

Eng. Ch. Warringah's Flinders, owned and bred by D. and C. Coode, Warringah. Photo © Anne Roslin-Williams.

Eng. Sh. Ch. Lindall Rachelle, owner M. Pfeifle and A. R. Porter, bred by Mr. and Mrs. A.R. Porter, Lindall. Photo by David Bull.

Eng. Sh. Ch. Linershwood Sentinal, owned and bred by Mrs. D.H. Coulson, Linershwood.
Photo © Anne Roslin-Williams.

Eng. Sh. Ch. Cambremer Madonna owned and bred by Mr. and Mrs. L. Brabben, Cambremer, was the top winning Labrador in the U.K. in 1993 with 8 CCs.
Photo by David Bull.

Davricard Bobby Shafto, 1 CC, owned by David Craig.
Photo © Anne Roslin-Williams.

Dorothy Howe and a litter of Rupert puppies, 1974.

Eng./Am. Ch. Sandylands Midas was bred and shown in England by Gwen Broadley and imported by Mrs. Gerald Lambert, Harrowby. Midas was handled exclusively in the U.S. by Ken Golden.

Chapter 2

Breeders and Kennels in the United States

Chidley, Aldenholme, Rupert, Chebacco, Scrimshaw, Whygin

After the end of World War II, the next fifty years brought about a growth in popularity for the breed that was undreamed of. America kennels in the northeast spearheaded the development and came forth with some good winning Labradors. The Chidley's of Joan Read continued to do well. Mrs. Barty-King's Aldenholme Kennel had some famous Labs: Ch. Ashur Deacon, Ch. Chidley Robber and Ch. Chidley Racketeer. Dorothy Howe of Rupert Kennel fame bred some influential dogs. In her first litter were three champions Rupert Dahomey, Rupert Daphne and Rupert Desdemona. Dahomey is behind both the Whygin and Shamrock Acres lines as well as some of Grace Lambert's Harrowby Labradors. Mrs. Howe also imported several dogs from England.

Mary Swan became interested in the breed in the late 1940s, and bred some wonderful Labs under the Chebacco prefix at her kennel in Massachusetts. Mary and Joan Read have wonderful scrapbooks and photos that document the growth of the Labrador, and these two friends have been a great help to me.

In New Hampshire Barbara Barfield began her Scrimshaw Kennel, and she is still producing some very special Labradors. In New York, Helen Ginnel began to set the lines for her Whygin Kennel. Whygin Labradors have had a great influence on the breed, in the field as well as the show ring. Ch. Whygin Poppitt and Ch. Whygin Gold Bullion were both grandsires of the famous Ch. Shamrock Acres Light Brigade. Poppitt was also the grandsire of 1966 and 1969 National Field Trial Champion Whygin Cork's Coot.

Franklin

The Franklin Kennel of Mr. and Mrs. Bernard Ziessow began in 1950 in Michigan, and they bred or owned some big winners, particularly Am./Can. Ch. Dark Star of Franklin who held the record of most Best in Shows (8) until Eng./Am. Ch. Sam of Blaircourt bested (9). FC/AFC Discovery of Franklin was a half brother of Dark Star, and another good dog was Am./Can. Ch. Troublemaker of Franklin.

Harrowby

Mrs. Grace Lambert's Harrowby Kennel in New Jersey had some early winners from her friend, Dorothy Howe. All Mrs. Lambert's dogs were

FC/AFC Discovery of Franklin owned by John Olin, Nilo Kennels; handled by T.W. Pershall: bred by Mr. and Mrs. B. Ziessow, Franklin.

shown by her kennel manager, Ken Golden. In 1955 Golden Chance of Franklin was purchased from the Ziessows, and in 1958 she won BOB at the LRC Specialty Show. In 1959 the previously mentioned Sam of Blaircourt was imported from Mrs. Gwen Broadley and quickly gained his American and Canadian title. Sam was a Top Producer as was another dog that was to come from Mrs. Broadley, Eng. Ch. Sandylands Midas, a lovely yellow dog. Mrs. Lambert also acquired the entire English Loughderg Kennel of eleven Labs from Mrs. Pamela Sim. In addition, she also had ten field trial champions that were trained by Billy Wunderlich, and *three* dual champions: Dual Ch. Markwell's Rambling Rebel, Dual Ch. Danny's Cole Black Slate, and Am./Can. Dual Ch. Happy Playboy.

Mrs. Lambert was a

Ch. Franklin's Champagne, a recent Group winning male owned and bred by Mr. and Mrs. B. Ziessow, Franklin.
Booth Photo by Ritter.

Ch. Lockerbie Sandylands Tarquin, an influential sire, was owned and handled by Helen Warwick, Lockerbie, and bred in England by Gwen Broadley. He is shown in this photograph handled by Helen (right) with his lovely daughter, Ch. Spenrock Banner (left), owned and handled by Janet Churchill, Spenrock. Photo by Evelyn Shafer.

lovely lady, and Ken Golden was a good friend of mine. (Billy Wunderlich is still going strong, having won many accolades over the years.)

Lockerbie

Helen and Jim Warwick had several Labradors as well loved pets in the early '50s. When they became interested in showing, the Warwicks went to Gould Remick, then President of the Labrador Retriever Club, Inc., to find a good female. He sent them to Mrs. Joan Read, and that is how they acquired Chidley Hocus Pokus, their first champion. Throughout their lives, the Warwicks and Joan Read remained good friends. Through a helper of Percy Roberts, they imported Ballyduff Candy, a good yellow bitch from Dr. Acheson and his wife Bridget. At about the same time, Mrs. S. Hallock duPont had brought over Ballyduff Treesholme Terry Boy for her son, Donald Ross, and Ballyduff Reilly for herself. When Ballyduff Candy was mated with Ballyduff Treesholme Terry Boy, there were three excellent males kept by Helen and Jim: Lockerbie Blackfella, Lockerbie Lancer and Lockerbie Spanker. In 1961, two black puppies were imported from Mrs. Gwen Broadley. They were Lockerbie Sandylands Tarquin and his sister, Lockerbie Sandylands Tidy. Tarquin became a champion and a great stud force of the sixties, and he can be found in many good pedigrees today. Tidy became the dam of the handsome yellow, Ch. Lockerbie Kismet. As time went on, quite a few other good dogs were brought over from England: Lockerbie Scwarlodge Brigadier, Lockerbie Lowna Neptune, Lockerbie

Ch. Sandylands Markwell of Lockerbie was bred in England by Gwen Broadley and owned in the U.S. by Helen Warwick and Diane B. Jones, Jollymuff.

Goldentone Jensen, Lockerbie Pebblestreet Dinah, Lockerbie Stanwood Granada, Sandylands Markwell and Margie of Lockerbie all of whom contributed to the quality of stock in this country. Helen and Jim were both popular judges in America and abroad, and were very well liked. Helen was the author of the excellent book, *The New Complete Labrador Retriever*, which is owned by breeders the world over. There were many new to the breed, including me, who were guided and helped by the Warwicks. They always had time to give the new person advice and confidence.

Shamrock Acres

In Madison, Wisconsin, Sally McCarthy and her family bought their first Labrador in 1955, and developed an interest in obedience and field work. In 1959 the McCarthys bought two puppies from Helen Ginnel's Whygin Kennels. The female was to become Am./Can. Ch. Whygin Campaign Promise, a Top Producing dam of 17 champions, and the dog was Am./Can. Ch. Whygin Royal Rocket C.D. Sally later acquired her favorite, Whygin Gentle Julia of Avec, and Whygin Busy Belinda. Both bitches became champions and were Top Producers. Although Sally doesn't usually handle her Labs, she did enjoy showing the good black dog, Am./Can. Ch Shamrock Acres Sonic Boom. The most famous dog for the kennel was the Top Producer, Ch. Shamrock Acres Light Brigade. When campaigned by Dick Cooper, he won 12 Bests in Show and 75 Group placements. He was the recipient of the Ken-L-Ration Sporting Group Award in 1968. Some

Am./Can. Ch. Whygin Campaign Promise, owned by Mr. and Mrs. James McCarthy, Shamrock Acres, and bred by Helen Ginnel, Whygin, handled by Ruth Williams, is shown winning at Westminster, 1961—judge, William Kendrick.

other notables bred by Sally are: Ch. Shamrock Acres Donnybrook C.D., Ch. Royal Oaks VIP of Shamrock Acres, and Ch. Shamrock Acres Benjamin C.D.

This kennel has always had an interest in field trials. The National Field Champion in 1979 was bred by Sally—NFC McGuffy, whose owner neglected to use her prefix. In addition, Dual Ch. Shamrock Acres Super Drive and Ch./AFC Shamrock Acres Simmer Down were both bred by her. Sally feels that Labradors should be "top-notch workers in the field, beautiful to look at and easy to live with."

Springfield

Springfield Kennels of Middleburg, Virginia, is owned by Mrs. R.V. Clark Jr., known to many in the dog world as "Liz." Her first Labrador, a black, was a dearly loved pet, and in the early 60s she became interested in one for showing. Her long time friend, Mrs. Connie Barton purchased a seven month old yellow female from Mr. and Mrs. Beckett in England. Her name was Kimvalley Cinderella, called "Barky," and she became one of Liz's favorites. Also high on her favorite list was Ch. Springfield's Miss Willing.

The top winning Labrador in '69, '71 and '72, Ch. Hillsboro Wizard of Oz, a two-time National Specialty winner, was owned by Springfield Farm. In 1974, Liz had the top Labrador in the beautiful black bitch, Ch. Kimvalley Picklewitch. For a number of years Mrs. Connie Barton was in charge of the kennel and principal handler. When she took a job as an AKC Field Representative in the early '70s, Mrs. Diana Beckett came from England to manage Springfield. Later, Susan Peters served in the same capacity in the '80s. Mr. Roy Holloway was a popular handler for some of the Springfield

*Am./Eng. Sh. Ch.
Kimvalley
Picklewitch owned by
Mrs. R.V. Clark, Jr.,
Springfield Kennels,
and bred in England
by Diana Beckett,
Kimvalley.*
Photo © Anne Roslin-
Williams.

Four generations of Springfield bitches—left to right: Ch. Kimvalley's Swingin Lizzie, Ch. Springfield's Buttercup, Ch. Springfield's Butter Cream, and Ch. Springfield's Barley Bree with handler Susan Peters. Photo by Charles Tatham.

dogs. Liz was a founding member of the Labrador Retriever Club of the Potomac and served as Vice President for many years. I have some very pleasant memories of puppy matches and parties held at Springfield Farm over the years. Liz and her Scottish friend, Edith Young, do a great deal of traveling around the world, and now it seems that dog shows for them are a thing of the past. However, they are both real animal lovers, and there are still dogs, cats, horses and other creatures at the beautiful farm. Liz told me that Margaret Woolf has been with her for many years and "She is like the 'pied piper,' they follow her everywhere. She has been the kennel keeper since 1966, looking after all the animals. Margaret is wonderful with the animals, a truly devoted person." Springfield brought over numerous imports from various English kennels over the years, and many Labradors were bred at Springfield that have certainly had an impact on the breed.

Briary

The Briary Kennel of Ceylon and Marjorie Brainard began in Atascadero, California, midway up the coast between Los Angeles and San Francisco. Their first Labrador was a female from hunting stock, Caledonia, who was shown and achieved her championship. Having "gotten the bug," they went to friends, the Warwicks, for another bitch who became Ch. Lockerbie Shillelagh, and a year or so later for a puppy dog who became the famous Ch. Lockerbie Brian Boru. When a daughter of Caledonia was mated to

Ch. Briary Bonnie Briana, owned by Jean Prior and bred by Cy and Marjorie Brainard, Briary, is the dam of three champions. She was the top show bitch in 1972. Photo taken at nine years by Debby Kay.

Ch. Briary Allegra bred and owned by Cy and Marjorie Brainard, Briary.

Brian, a good yellow was produced, Ch. Barnaby O'Brian. This dog did well in the show ring, winning an LRC Specialty under Mrs. Gwen Broadley, and it was he who made Brian's reputation. After that, Brian was in great demand, and had some very good bitches in for breeding. There are too many champions to mention here, but when Brian and Shillelagh were mated, some of their successful offspring were: Ch. Briary Trace of Brian C.D., Ch. Briary Barley and Ch. Briary Brendon of Rainell. When Ch. Briary Floradora was bred to Ch. Spenrock Anthony Adverse, there were two very special yellows, Ch. Briary Allegra and Ch. Briary Abbey Road. The Brainards also brought over two very good bitches from Mrs. Margot Woolley in England, Ch. Follytower Cressida and Ch. Follytower Sally. Marjorie has written, "We had a great time with the wonderful dogs Helen and Jim [Warwick] sent to us. First of all was the delightful temperament that they were able to pass on to their descendants, second their essential soundness. Where would I be without them [the Warwicks]?" Indeed, where would many of us be?

Dickendall

Author's note: I can't possibly devote a paragraph to all the Labrador breeders who have been influential over the years in America, but there is one more—the Dickendall Kennel of Kendall Herr, always helped and supported by her husband Dick. I first met Kendall in the '70s when she began showing Ch. Dickendall's Flip Flop C.D.X., WC, so I have known her well for a long time. She has devoted her life to breeding Labradors and a few Border Terriers, and I feel that she has had a tremendous influence on the breed. Some of her best known Labradors have been Ch. Linershwood Sticky Wicket from Jo and Derek Coulson in England, Ch. Allegheny Eclipse from Claire Senfield in Virginia, a sharing of Am./Can. Ch. Powhatan Black Badger C.D.X. with Michael Woods of Newfoundland,

and Ch. Broyhill Hennings Casino with Dorothy and Jack Galvin of Ohio. Ch. Dickendall Snazzy was one of Kendall's favorite bitches, dam of Am./ Can.Ch. Dickendall Waterdog Jazz by Am./Can. Ch., OTCh. Ballyduff Storm. In the mid 1980s, Kendall and her friend, June Kagawa (kennel name Davaron) went to England and brought back Eng. Ch. Receiver of Cranspire, who is a beautiful dog, and has had a huge impact on Labradors everywhere. I've asked Kendall to put down some of her thoughts:

Dog breeding is something most of us fall into by mistake, and continue out of the love of dogs and the joy of raising puppies. It somehow gets out of control. There's a quest to breed the perfect dog in conformation, temperament and health. The ideal, perfect dog is never achieved, but this makes us try even harder. During this futile attempt, through years of upgrading, we do achieve a well above average dog, one most pet owners are proud to own with an easy-to-live-with temperament. Most are happy, healthy and functional.

Unfortunately this is not a perfect world and we are dealing with unpredictable nature. Things turn up that we have never imagined and certainly didn't plan. We all go through our fair share of HD [hip dysplasia], OCD [osteochondritis dissecans], entropion and epilepsy. However, I went through a disaster that shook the Labrador world.

My partner and I leased a six year old dog from England. He was a top show dog there. A top producer, he had sired quality offspring in Europe, Australia and the United States. He was with me for a year and a half. He was a joy to live with and he produced many lovely puppies. They were

Ch. Dickendall Ruffy, SH owned and bred by Kendall Herr, Dickendall.

natural gun dogs and improved conformation quality consistently. Then the worst happened. It was discovered that he was a carrier of PRA, a blinding eye disease.

When you aren't personally involved with a problem you tend not to think or learn much about it. I was thrown into the middle of a major problem I knew nothing about.

Having a kennel full of children and grandchildren by this dog, I was forced to learn very fast. I read everything I could and talked to people all over the world about PRA. My first gut reaction was to scrap everything. Then my reaction evolved to a wait and think about it, to digest all I could about this problem. There were too many contradictory things that didn't make sense about what was thought to be fact about PRA.

Since this dog was so famous it caused mass hysteria in the Labrador world. His progeny were damned. They were put down or given away and rumors flew. The consensus was to get rid of all his descendants—only then would the Labrador breed be saved from PRA. Later it was finally realized that the answer to this problem is not so simplistic.

The positive side of this situation is that it brought PRA in Labradors out of the closet. People began to talk. PRA has been in Labs since day one. It has been covered up, denied, misdiagnosed and, due to the late onset nature of the disease, simply never found out. We have heard rumors for years of different dogs producing and having PRA, but nothing concrete ever came of it. They were just rumors, and like all dog rumors, they had to be discounted because of lack of proof.

This incident, for some reason, caused people to talk and to admit to having problems. We now have several volumes of confirmed carriers of PRA published. It is now known that most all lines of Labradors have PRA represented in them. You would think this information would make PRA easy to eliminate. However, years after the PRA hysteria, there somehow doesn't seem to be nearly the number of affected showing up that we ought to be seeing if this truly is caused by a simple recessive gene. Too many combinations factor into this problem. Because of the mode of inheritance, this thing is impossible to figure out.

The son or daughter of a carrier can be fine, not being affected and not carrying the gene or genes for PRA, or they can be affected or be a carrier. There is no way to tell the carriers from the non-carriers. If you have a carrier of eye disease five or ten generations back in your pedigree, the disease can still be carried through successive generations unnoticed by anyone. Pushing it back in a pedigree gives a false sense of security. You are not safer the farther back it is. The truth is, at this time, there is no way for breeders to have a clear knowledge regarding all the factors surrounding eye disease. Everyone looks for a scientific or easy answer to tell them what is right or wrong and what to do. Unfortunately breeding isn't as scientific as we think it should be. What should happen doesn't usually happen. We just have to take a chance, most breeding is all a gamble.

A real downside of this is people. While trying to save the breed from PRA, some have been breeding, not to produce good dogs, but to avoid the problem. Many have found that, by bending over backwards to get away from it, they end up right in the middle of it again in a line that was

Ch. Dickendall Arnold owned by Kendall Herr, Dickendall, and June Kagawa, Davaron; bred by Liz Muthard and Ted Rosenberg.

previously thought to be 'clean' or end up with worse genetic problems.

You have to breed to produce a quality, balanced dog in all aspects including health, conformation and temperament. When you breed entirely to avoid problems, you usually end up with mediocrity and possibly other problems. Don't become overwrought by a problem that occurs in only a very small percentage of the total picture. Always breed the best to the best and consider all factors. Common sense tells us not to breed to known individuals that are affected or carriers. We can only breed from what we know for a fact, not what you think might be there. Don't try to cull entire lines from your breeding plans or you'll find there's nothing left to use. We never really know 100% what we are doing when breeding, what pedigrees really contain or what different combinations might produce. All anyone can do is try to keep everything in perspective when planning a breeding, then keep the good and discard the bad. That is what breeding has always been about. Breeding is very personal—after considering all aspects of a breeding, you must do what you are comfortable with.

Kendall has been through a lot with this situation, and so have others whose dogs have been discovered as carriers also. Right now she has two outstanding black dogs, Ch. Dickendall Ruffy, SH who has been producing some dogs with terrific natural retrieving ability, and his son, Ch. Dickendall Arnold, who has produced many show winners. Current research holds hope for a test for PRA carriers that will put an end to this kind of heartbreak.

* * * * * * *

There are many more kennels of note in this vast country of ours— breeders who have been active for a long time, and some who are relatively new and people who keep only a few dogs, and others who own 20 or more. In an attempt to include as many kennels as possible I've elected to produce a *gallery* of photos of American Labrador Retrievers (from the many pictures sent to me) that features one dog per kennel, along with the kennel name and state.

*Ambleside Maraschino C.D.
at 8 yrs. owned by Wendy
Huttner, Ridgeway—Pennsylvania; bred by Julie Sturman,
Ambleside—Pennsylvania.*

*Ch. Hawksmoors Kea
owned and bred by Kate D.
Perry, Hawksmoor—
Pennsylvania.
(Photo at 10 mos.)*

*Can. Ch. U-CD, Woodhaven's Silk-
N-Silver C.D.X., WCX, Can. C.D.,
WC bred and owned by Laura
Michaels, Woodhaven—Michigan.*

*Left to right,
Hennings Mills
Crown Jewel and Ch.
Chafern Court Star of
Fabracken (Imp.)
owned by Jack and
Dot Galvin, Hennings
Mill—Ohio.* Graphite
by Meredith Sessions.

*Am./Can. Ch. Winroc Upper
Crust and Brie C.D., WC
owned and handled by Victor
and Diana Pintel,
Mistypoint—California; bred
by Mr. and Mrs. A.L. Foote,
Winroc, reg.—California.*

*Ch. Follytower Blackberry, JH
(Imp.) owned by Carla Frey,
Saltmeadow—Connecticut; bred
by Mrs. Margot Woolley,
Follytower.*

Ch. Pinetree's Smooth Sailin' C.D., JH owned and bred by Patsy C. Jones Pinetree—Oklahoma.

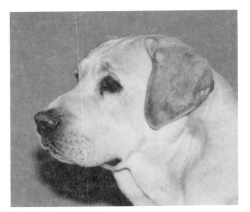

Ch. Bold Aaron C.D., WC owned by Winnie Limbourne, Wingmaster— California.

Ch. Beechcroft's Edgewood Tomarc owned by Mark and Mary Hausman, Edgewood— Pennslyvania; bred by Mary Wiest, Beechcroft—New Hampshire.

Ch. Marshland Blitz owned and bred by Dennis and Pam Emken, Marshland— California. Photo by Charles Tatum.

Ch. Balnamores Chikara C.D., JH bred and owned by Marge and Chris Hutchins, Balnamore—Texas

Am./Can. Ch. Ramblin's Amaretto, WC BOB 1986 LRC, Inc. National Specialty owned by Anne K. Jones, Wapato—Oregon; bred by Mr.and Mrs. M. Peckham and Georgia Gooch, Ramblin— Washington.

*Ch. Folklaur Aurora C.D.,
CGC, TDI
(at 8 1/2 yrs.) bred and
owned by Laura Dedering,
Folklaur—New Jersey.*

*Ch. Jollymuff
Orange Blossom
owned and bred by
Diane B. Jones,
Jollymuff—New
Jersey.* Photo
by Bernard W.
Kernan.

*Ch. Cacao's Mini Willey
(chocolate) owned and
bred by Edna Pillow,
Cacao—New Hampshire.*
Photo by Gilbert.

Ch. Somersett Troublesome Minx C.D., WC co-owned by Merlyn Foote, Somersett—Washington and Mary Jane Sarbaugh, Wyntercreek—Washington.

Ch. O'Henry's BW of Liberation (2 1/2 yrs.) owned by Susan Owens and Brenda Durham; bred by Susan Owens, O'Henry, Texas. Photo by John Ashbey.

Ch. Graemoor Tim co-owned by Kendall Herr, Dickendall—Texas and Betty Graham, Graemoor—Virginia; bred by Stephen and Betty Graham, Graemoor—Virginia.

Can. Ch. Plantiers Ruthless Ruthie C.D., WCI, MH (chocolate) owned by Dick Plantier; bred by Nancy Brandow. Photo by Chuck and Sandy Tatum.

Ch. Inselheim Just Jokin', a two-time specialty winner, owned and bred by Barbara Reisig-Beer, Inselheim—Michigan.

Ch. Shamrock Acres Benjamin owned by Dr. and Mrs. Richard Whitehill; bred by Sally McCarthy, Shamrock Acres—Wisconsin. Photo by Rich Bergman.

Ch. Jayncourt Ajoco Justice (Imp.) owned by Anthony Heubel and Janet Farmilette, Mijans—New Jersey; bred by Jane and Peter Palmer, Jayncourt.

Am./Can. Ch. Cedarwood Aspenlane C.D., WC owned and bred by Diann and Gary Sullivan, Cedarwood— Washington. Photo by Carl Linmaier Photo.

Ch. Highlands Bronze Chieftain (chocolate) owned by George and Lillian Knobloch, Highland—New Jersey.

Ch. Gairloch's Lambeth Walk (1980-1993) foundation stock for Carol Quaif's Carenna Labradors—Georgia.; bred by Margaret Crothers, Gairloch—Pennsylvania. Photo by Graham.

Ch. Shookstown Solo Smasher owned by Stephen and Betty Graham, Graemoor— Virginia; bred by George Bragaw, Shookstown— Maryland.

Ch. Am./Can. Ch. Ebonylane's Midnight Bandit owned by Robert and Barbara Holl, Hollidaze— Indiana; bred by Mike and Pat Lanctot, Ebonylane—Canada.

Ch. Killingworth Thunderson, owned and bred by Lorraine Taylor, Killingworth— Connecticut, with his friend Killingworth Homer.

Can. Ch. Sunnydaze English Leather C.D., JH (chocolate) owned and bred by Linda Squires, Sunnydaze— Washington.

Ch. MHR Romany Jester C.D., MH owned by Alan Kottwitz and Sandy Stanley, Romany—Idaho. "Jess" became the first retriever to earn a conformation title, NAHRA Master Hunting Retriever title, and an AKC Master Hunter title.

Left, Ch. Killingworth Bonnie of Dimeno C.D., CGC owned by Julie Sturman, Ambleside— Pennsylvania; bred by Sue Ostermueller, Dimeno, reg.—Connecticut.

Below, Ch. Cedarwood Squire O'Fawnhaven C.D., JH (chocolate) owned by Barbara and Don Ironside, Fawnhaven—Washington; bred by Diann and Gary Sullivan, Cedarwood— Washington.

Below left to right, Ch. Hennings Mills Master Blend (chocolate) owned by Charlotte Veneziano, Venetian—New York; Am./Can. Ch. Flying Cloud's Tai Pan (black) owned by Theresa and Rufus Winsor— Vermont; and Ch. Willcare's Masterpiece (chocolate) owned and bred by Susan Willumsen, Willcare—New Hampshire. Photo by Sandy Tatum.

Ch. Winroc Goforit of Sundalane, JH, a second generation specialty winner, owned by Mr. and Mrs. A.L. Foote, Winroc, reg.— Pennsylvania; bred by Mrs. A.L. Foote and Della Stephens, Sundalane— California.

Left, Am./Can. Ch. Chelon's Firestorm, WC 1990 BOB LRC, Inc. National Specialty owned and bred by Cheryl and Lon Ostenson, Chelon— Washington.
Photo by Fox and Cook.

Below, The Labradors of Broadway owned and bred by Gene and Maryanne Czerwinski— New Jersey.

Ch. Ballyduff Lark (Imp.) owned by Mary Wiest, Beechcroft, reg.— New Hampshire; bred by Mrs. Bridget Docking, Ballyduff—England.

Right, Ch. Bench Mark Shoals Dune C.D., JH, TT owned by Gretchen Meyer, Seasalt— Pennsylvania; bred by Susan Newell, Bench Mark—Illinois.

Below left to right, Ch. Forecast Beloit, Ch. Forecast Hofstra, and Ch. Forecast Wheaton owned and bred by Betty Curtis, Forecast—Connecticut.

Ch. Blacmor's Carbonear owned and bred by Peter and Audrey Wolcott, Blacmor— Connecticut.

Left, Ch. Stonecreek's Poison Ivy bred and owned by Mrs. R.L. Flowers, Stonecreek—California; co-owners Darrell and Beverly Kelly.

Front to rear left, Flaxenfields Lusty Leila, Brentville Marietta of Lawnwood (Imp.) Mallardhurn Elonor (Imp.), Shalimar Flaming Star; center row front to rear, Flaxenfields Fancy, Mallardhurn Clive (Imp.), Flaxenfields Uncle Harry; black dog, Mansergh Mantuan (Imp.) . . . all owned by Richard and Lola Heckard, Flaxenfields (1974)—Hawaii.

Ch. Briary Blythe owned by Sue E. May, Maytyme—Missouri; bred by Cy and Marjorie Brainard, Briary—Washington.

Ch. Trelawny's Swashbuckler bred and owned by Joan Clarke, Trelawney—Pennsylvania.
Photo by Ashbey.

Below left to right, Ch. Tagalong's Buttercup, Ch. Tagalong's Topper of June Lake, Siridan's Vagabond Millicient, Tagalong's Cleopatra, Ch. Jet's Golden Girl, Tagalong's Marc Antony, Tagalong's Clickety-Click, Ch. Tagalong's Camptorhynchus owned and trained by Andy and Betty Anderson, Tagalong—California.

Ch. Winroc Picaro, WC co-owned by Merlyn Foote, Somersett—Washington, and Barbara Nowak, Broyhill—California; bred by Mr. and Mrs. A.L. Foote, Winroc, reg.—Pennsylvania.

Rocky Acres Rett owned by E. Ann Metzler, Rocky Acres—Pennsylvania; bred by E. Ann Metzler, Rocky Acres, and Ginger Watkins. Photo by Chuck and Sandy Tatum.

Ch. Finchingfield Chauncy Clarke co-owned by Margaret J. Sutor, Yesterday—Pennsylvania and Marilyn O. Reynolds, Finchingfield—Virginia. Photo by Gilbert.

Ch. Belvedere Adam (1989) owned and bred by Grace Mary Lawson, Belvedere—Hawaii. Photo by Mike Johnson.

A head-study of Am./Can. Ch. Rainell's Dynasty owned and bred by Lorraine and Lorrie Getter, Rainell—New Jersey.

Left to right, Ch. Jagersbo Walking Stick and Ch. Jagersbo Splash Down owned and bred by Eric Bergishagen, Jagersbo—Michigan. Photo by Bernard W. Kernan.

*Barbaree's Daisy Duke C.D. owned by Nancy Beach;
bred by Linda Oldham, Barbaree—New York.*

*Ch. J Sun Farms
Summer Breeze bred
and owned by Terry
De Pietro, J Sun
Farms—New Jersey
and Thomas J. Feneis,
Cedarhill—New
Jersey.* Photo by
R. Barber.

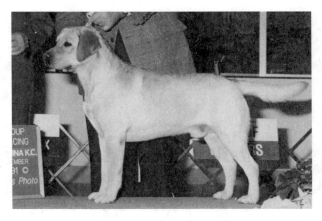

*Ch. Sugar Hollow's
James Bond owned
and bred by Don and
Martha Neblett,
Sugar Hollow—
North Carolina.*
Photo by B. Baines.

Ch. Stonecrest Swift Current owned and bred by George and Louise White, Stonecrest—Rhode Island. Photo by Claire White-Peterson.

Am./Can. Ch. Monarch's Black Arrogance C.D., WC (at 10 yrs.) owned by John and Barbara Shaw, Blackthorn—Washington; bred by Frank and Loreen Wilson, Monarch—Oregon.

Kellygreens Kahlua (chocolate) owned and bred by Sally Kelly, Kellygreen—Pennsylvania. Photo by Robin.

Am./Bah./Bda./Can./
Dom./SoAm./Vez. Ch.
Sunnybrook Acres Ace
O'Spade Can./Dom.
C.D., Bda./PR./Vez.
C.D.X., Bda. TD, Bah.
U.D., Am. U.D.T.X., WC
(at 10 mos.) owned by
Mr. & Mrs. John
Ippensen, Sunnybrook
Acres—Missouri; bred
by Raymond Kleissle,
Sunray—Texas.
Photo by Petrulis.

Specialty winner
Ch. Balrion Over To
You (Imp.) owned by
Ray and Linda
Schiele, Linray—
Missouri; bred by
John and Glenda
Crook, Balrion—
England.

Am./Can. Ch. Rocheby Joseph's
Coat C.D., JH, CGC
(Imp.-chocolate) owned by Nina
Mann, Harbortop—Washington;
bred by David and Marion
Hopkinson, Rocheby—England .
Photo by Brant Photographers, Inc.

Ch. Kupros Live Spark (imp.) owned by Clare Senfield, Allegheny—Virginia; bred by Mr. and Mrs. Peter Hart, Kupros— England.

A 1984 litter of Gairloch puppies bred by Margaret and Jim Crothers, Gairloch— Pennsylvania.

Ch. Mijans Hot Stuff owned by Janet Farmilette, Mijans—New Jersey, and Fran Opperisano, Springharbor— Pennsylvania.

Ch. Grovetons Landmark owned and bred by Eileen Ketcham, Groveton—New York.
Photo by Ashbey.

Counterclockwise top left, Am./Can. Ch. Chocorua's Seabreeze (yellow-10 yrs.), Am./Can. Ch. Chocorua's Silent Dignity (yellow-7 yrs.), Chocorua's As Pretty Does (black-3 yrs.) and Lindall Chase (Imp., black-2 Yrs.) owned by Marion Lyons, Chocorua—New Hampshire.

Eng./Am. Ch. Lindall Mastercraft (Imp.) owned by Mel Pfeiffle, Hampshire—New Hampshire: bred by Linda and Allen Porter, Lindall—England.
Photo by Leslie.

Ch. Northwoods Sandman owned and bred by Karen and Janet Schultze, Northwoods— New York.
Photo by Ashbey.

Ch. Chebacco J Robert owned and bred by Mary Swan, Chebacco— Massachusetts.

Specialty winner Ch. Finchingfield Impetuous owned and bred by Marilyn Reynolds, Finchingfield—Virginia.
Photo by Charles Tatum.

Ch. Saddlehill Hemingway C.D., JH (at 4 yrs.) co-owned by Susan Eberhardt and Ben and Beverly Kulp; bred by Susan Eberhardt, Saddlehill— California.

Ch. Valleywood Nighthawk owned and bred by Chris Kofron, Valleywood—Ohio. Photo by M.B. Roseberry.

Ch. Lobuff's Seafaring Banner (3 yrs.) owned and bred by Jerry Weiss and Lisa Agresta, Lobuff— New York.

Ch. Shadowvales Just So owned by Prescott Chubet, Tweedcroft—Virginia; bred by Mike and Huguette Beattie, Shadowvale—Canada.
Photo by Gilbert.

Ch. Finchingfield Navigator owned by Jeff and Joan Ingelli, Inglenook— Wisconsin; bred by Marilyn Reynolds, Finchingfield— Virginia.
Photo by Martin Booth.

Ch. Tabatha's Windfall Abbey, JH owned by Annie and Ron Cogo, Windfall—Michigan; bred by Carol Heidl, Tabatha—Ohio.

Specialty winner
Am./Can. Ch. Davoeg
Silky Beau owned and
bred by John Doherty,
Davoeg—Washington.
Photo by Chuck Tatum.

Ch. Arosca's Born in
Sweden (Imp.) owned by
Andrea Robertson; bred by
Gunilla Andersson,
Arosca—Sweden.
Photo by Bill Meyer.

Specialty winner Ch.
Dickendall Buckstone
Apple, JH owned and
bred by Faith
Hyndman, Buckstone—
Pennsylvania and
Kendall Herr,
Dickendall—Texas;
co-bred by Rosalind
Moore, Moorwood—
New York.
Photo by Ashbey.

All-breed BIS winner Ch. Snowden Hill's Blackmail owned and bred by Gladys Rogers, Snowden Hill—New York.
Photo by Ashbey

Three generations-left to right bottom, Campbellcroft Bristol Cream U.D., JH; Ch. Marstad's Tread Lightly C.D.; left to right top, Ch. Marstad's Loose Change, JH; Ch. Campbellcroft Snapshot Bo owned and trained by Terri Herigstad, Marstad, reg.—California.

Left to right, Agber's Daniel Aloysius owned and bred by Agnes Cartier, Agber—New Jersey (handled by Joy Quallenberg); judge, Jerry Weiss, Lobuff—New York; and Spenrock's Brown Bess (chocolate) owned and bred by Janet Churchill, Spenrock—Maryland.
Photo by Hilly.

Ch. Tabatha's Inspiration, WC owned and bred by Carol Heidl, Tabatha—Ohio.

Ch. Anderscroft Mijans Bravo (1983) co-owned by Jane Anderson, Anderscroft, reg.— Connecticut and Joan Heubel; bred by A. and J. Heubel and Helen Warwick, Lockerbie— New York.
Photo by Gilbert.

Ch. Ayr's Sweet and Sassy owned by Joan Urban, Misty Glen— Pennsylvania; bred by Nancy Martin, Ayr— Pennsylvania.

Ch. Lobuff's Bare Necessities owned by Beverly Shavlik and Sally Sasser, Teracroft—North Carolina; Lisa Weiss Agresta, Lobuff—New York; and Emily Biegel, Toll House—New York; bred by Guide Dog Foundation for the Blind.
Photo by Ashbey.

Int. Ch. Sandylands Rip Van Winkle (Imp.) owned by Gordon and Debbie Sousa, Breezy—New Jersey; bred by Gwen Broadley, Sandylands—England.

BOB 1987 LRC, Inc. National Specialty Am./Can. Ch. Campbellcroft's Angus C.D., WC owned and bred by Don and Virginia Campbell, Campbellcroft, reg.—California

SECTION V
Labradors in Other Countries

■ **Chapter 1**

Australia

■ **Chapter 2**

Belgium

■ **Chapter 3**

Canada

■ **Chapter 4**

Finland

■ **Chapter 5**

France

■ **Chapter 6**

Netherlands

■ **Chapter 7**

New Zealand

■ **Chapter 8**

Norway

■ **Chapter 9**

Soth Africa

■ **Chapter 10**

Sweden

Labradors in Other Countries

I have often said that the good disposition of our dogs must rub off on the owners. I wrote to a number of people in other lands—some I knew only slightly, and some I'd never met. However, all have generously taken the time to write something about Labrador Retrievers in their country. The following chapters and photographs are from their correspondence. I am indebted to each of the authors for their contribution.

Chapter 1

The Labrador Retriever in Australia

Author's note: Mrs. Norah M. "Gilly" Gilbert of the Jaywick Kennel in Queensland has written something of the history of Labradors in "Oz," and Mrs. Dorothy Sutch, Duffton Labradors, brought the information and some of her early photographs to me when she came to the States to judge. Mrs. Gilbert and Mrs. Sutch both came to Australia from England more than 40 years ago. Mrs. Gilbert's first stud dog was a son of Ch. Sandylands Tan, imported by Mrs. Sutch. Mrs. Gilbert has brought out 20 Labradors from England and, of course, Mrs. Sutch and others have also imported. Mrs. Gilbert has been a judge in Show, Obedience and Field Trials, but has given up the two latter licenses for physical reasons just this past year. Mrs. Gilbert's daughter, Mrs. S.M. Conduit is now a partner in Jaywick Kennels.

Queensland

It was a daunting task to recall and mention Labradors of the past in Australia, and I am bound to omit many and upset some people. However, in my opinion, the ones I have included I believe made the most impact on present day Labradors in our country.

In Victoria, after the early imports of Liddly dogs and some from other breeding, Eng. Sh. Ch. Wendover Kinley Coleen and her son, Wendover Jonah, arrived. Coleen was in whelp to Eng. Ch. Ruler of Blaircourt, and owing to the ship's breakdown, whelped on board and landed when the pups were nearly three months old! (This was always a hazard with ship transport, and I suffered a similar case in Queensland later.) However, these two dogs and their offspring made a lasting imprint on the breeding of black Labradors.

Eng./Aust. Ch. Poolstead Probable, a yellow, came out soon after, and was used extensively. I sent a champion bitch in whelp by him to New Zealand where she became the foundation of a dynasty there. Aust. Ch. Mythras of Lawnwood, and Aust. Ch. Lawnwood's Peppercorn were imported by Mrs. J. Drinkwater's Tesdin Kennel in Victoria and were also used quite a lot. However, the most widespread influence, I believe, was Aust. Ch. Sandylands Tan. He was imported by Mrs. Dorothy Sutch from Mrs. Broadley, and his effect was very wide in England as well as Australia. His grandson, Aust. Ch. Diant Jaysgreen Jasper, was imported later and he also had a great impact. In Southern Australia, Aust. Ch. Pinchbeck Nokeener Harvest Home was the one most used, and later Aust. Ch. Sandylands Greta figured in many pedigrees, especially mated to Jasper.

In New South Wales, the late Mrs. H. Sapio of Queensland was in partnership with H. Scott in Sydney, so many of her imports were shown

Aust. Ch. Sandylands Tan and his grandson, Ch. Diant Jaysgreen Jasper were both influential imports for the breed in Australia.

Aust. Ch. Duffton Drambuie (Aust. Ch. Diant Jaysgreen Jasper x Aust. Ch. Sandylands Greta) at four years of age.

*Aust./N.Z. Ch. Diant
Piper of Jaywick
(import U.K.), owner—
Mrs. N.M. Gilbert.*

there and in Queensland. Aust. Ch. Diant Leading Light and Aust. Ch. Rookwood Woodpecker were campaigned and used in both areas. Leading Light came to Queensland and was behind many top trial dogs. He also sired the all-purpose dog, Aust. Dual Ch. Tenarden Easy Rider who was an obedience and tracking dog as well.

In Queensland my first bitch, Aust. Ch. Clacton Gay Lady of Sandylands (Liddly and Poppleton breeding), became the dam of six champions and was the foundation of the Jaywick Kennels. Aust. Ch. Ballyduff Cetus came to Mr. and Mrs. Pope in 1969 and Aust. Ch. Cornlands Chive of Jaywick was imported by me. These two yellow dogs sired excellent litters and, because I always made it a habit to only purchase U.K. stock from kennels which worked and showed their Labs, many of ours proved themselves in field and obedience as well as show. But from all my imports I suppose the best and most influential in the breed were Aust. Ch. Rookwood Blackamoor and Aust. Ch. Rookwood Treacle Tart, CM.

When early interest in the chocolates began, I bought Tibshelf Coffee of Jaywick, and bred the first chocolate litter in Queensland, many of which are behind today's good ones of that colour.

There were a number of other imports, but surely the most successful has been Aust./N. Z. Ch. Diant Piper of Jaywick, top show dog in Queensland for five years and, at over ten years, my faithful companion still. He is the only Lab in Queensland to be an Aust. and N.Z. Champion Challenge Certificate winner at the Brisbane and Sydney Royal; Best In Show (All Breeds) in both countries and the Lab Club Show.

In Australia we have Non-Slip Retrieving Trials—only one dog is worked at a time over a set course of three runs, all different. Points are given for steadiness, taking a line, marking, facing cover, using nose, tenderness in retrieving, etc. Directions can be given by handlers by signal, voice or whistle, and runs are a combination of water and land.

I used to run my own dogs in Retrieving Trials. In fact, many years ago, at one Novice Trial, first, second and third places were champion father, champion mother and daughter as all my Labradors came from working and show lines.

I have always maintained that our Labrador **is** the most versatile in the world. Another facet to add to the Labrador's accomplishments here is 'cadaver' dog (finding people in the bush); also drug finders, trackers, gun dogs, guide dogs and other service dogs. Incidentally, our Labrador Standard is the same as the U.K.

New South Wales

Mrs. Pat Dunstan of Strangways Labradors in New South Wales wrote, "Not enough emphasis can be placed on the breed's versatility. They do like a job to do and are so easy to teach."

Mrs. Dunstan has bred many show champions, as well as the versatile Aust. Dual Ch. Strangways Top Hat owned by Mr. J. Ellen and Mrs. Dunstan. He is a black dog by Aust. Ch. Arraloob Show the Way out of Strangways Miss Moppet.

The coveted title of Dual Champion is well represented in Australia in all three coat colors. The chocolate dog, Aust. Dual Ch. Avokah Hot Choclyt CM, C.D. (Aust. Ch. Baringa Woomera C.D. x Bridgefield Gentian), was B.I.S. LRC of Queensland 1982, 1983; BOB Brisbane Royal 1985. He was bred and owned by Merrilyn Walsh.

To complete the color representation, there is Australia's first triple champion—the yellow dog Kadnook the Prophet. He is a Show Champion, a Field Trial Champion and a Retrieving Trial Champion bred by Jill McMasters and Wayne Poholke. He was sired by Strangways Statesman x Kadnook the Silhouette, and was purchased as a youngster by Charlie Ball, an excellent gun dog trainer. Although strictly "show bred," he proved he could win in the field.

Author's note: There are two types of trials: Australian Retrieving Trials and Field Trials. Australian Retrieving Trials are open to all gun dogs and include three stakes: Novice, Restricted and All-Age. Depending on the stake, dogs are required to do land and water retrieves, doubles, triples, blinds, etc. Cold game is used and released from a catapult or thrown by hand.

Field Trials have the same stakes, but are run on live game and under actual hunting conditions. They are open to all gun dogs, but are broken down into three types: (1) Spaniels and Retrievers (find, flush, retrieve); (2) Pointers and Setters (find, flush and seek dead); (3) Utility - German Short-hairs, Weimaraners, Brittanies, Viszlas, etc. (find, flush, seek dead and retrieve).

Entries for these trials can vary from as few as eight or nine dogs to as many as 45. Springers, Cockers, Goldens, Curlies and Flatcoats all compete in the section for retrievers, but Labradors are by far the most prominent."

Australia is a huge country that is divided into states, and there is a Labrador Retriever club in each state and numerous breeders. It is impos-

Aust. Dual Ch. Strangways Top Hat, owners—Mr. J. Ellen & Mrs. P. Dunstan.

Aust. Triple Ch. Kadnook The Prophet, owned and trained by Mr. Charles Ball.

Chocolate dog,
Aust. Dual Ch. Avokah Hot Choclyt, CM.

sible to include everyone, however I would like to mention several breeders with notable contributions.

In Victoria, the partnership of Frank Keys and Keith Prior imported two special dogs to their Waintree Kennel: Aust. Ch. Rookwood Blonde Boy and Aust. Ch. Balrion Knight Errant. Both dogs were winners and produced winners, such as Aust. Ch. Waintree Talking Boy and Aust. Ch. Waintree Capangown.

Also producing good dogs in Victoria are Mrs. J. Drinkwater's Tesdin Kennel and Mrs. H. Nichol's Tarbert Labradors.

In New South Wales, Mrs. Anna Spanswick has been breeding Labradors for more than 30 years. She imported Poolstead Pioneer, later an Australian champion and a very influential dog. Aust. Ch. Ballyduff Carol came to the kennel to produce many good Labradors, and in the late seventies two yellows came out from Mrs. Hepwoth: Aust. Ch. Poolstead Public Speaker, a dog, and Aust. Ch. Poolstead Popular Choice, a bitch. Several other imports have come later, all having good influences on the breed.

The Driftway Kennel of Guy Spagnolo has had many winners. His bitches, such as Driftway Dusky Dreamer and Aust. Ch. Driftway Dynasty, have been especially good producers. Not long ago, Aust./N.Z. Ch. Balnova Maelstrom joined the kennel, his lines combining well with the Driftways.

Also in New South Wales is the Gunnislake Kennel of Mr. and Mrs. Hugh Gent. Some of their famous dogs have been Aust. Ch. Gunnislake Stormer and his grandson, Aust. Ch. Gunnislake Shamrock, along with Aust. Ch. Gunnislake Charade and Aust. Ch. Gunnislake Pepper.

Chapter 2

The Labrador Retriever In Belgium

Author's note: This short history of the Labrador in Belgium has been written by Mrs. Carine Berthe-Bougard, and translated by Mrs. Laura MacArthur.

Before going into the details of the Labrador in Belgium, it is important to point out that the Belgium concept of breeding Labradors differs from that of English breeders. Some critics have accused our British friends of separating the 'showlines' from the 'working lines,' creating almost two different breeds. However, we in Belgium have tried to keep the basic type and physical qualities of the breed according to the Standard, and maintain maximum working ability as intended by pioneer breeders in Great Britain at the turn of the century. Thus, our small country is proud of its dual champions!

They are:

- **Belgian Dual Ch. Paducah Ivory Black** (Ch. Kupros Lucifer x Unchained Melody of Tintagel Winds). This bitch belongs to Jef Verrees and was bred by Mrs. Mac Arthur. Her record:

Show:	Work:
5 x 1 EXC	9 x 1 EXC
1 x VDH	7 x CACT
2 x CAC	3 x CACIT
2 x RCAC	2 x RCACIT
1 x RCACIB	2 x RCACT

- **Belgian Dual Ch. Vivacity of Tintagel Winds** (Int. Ch. Sandylands Rip Van Winkle x Ch. Rhapsody of Tintagel Winds) is owned by Philippe Lammens and was bred by Mrs. Leith-Ross. Her record:

Show:	Work:
9 x 1 EXC	3 x CACT
5 x CAC	4 x 1 EXC
5 x CACIB	
6 x RCAC	
5 x RCACIB	

- **Belgian Dual Ch. Iota Bois de Lauzelle** belongs to her breeder, Mr. Francis Stache. Her record:

Show:	Work:
1 x CACIB	6 x CACT
2 x CAC	7 x RCACT
4 x RCAC	3 x RCACIT
10 x EXC	1 x 1 EXC

[Note: These three dual champions are all bitches.]

Belgian Dual Ch. Paducah Ivory Black owned by Jef Verrees and bred by Mrs. MacArthur.

Belgian Dual Ch. Iota Bois de Lauzelle is owned and trained by her breeder, Mr. Francis Stache.

Belgian Dual Ch. Vivacity of Tintagel Winds owned by Philippe Lammens and bred by Mrs. Leith-Ross.

B.F.D.VDH. I.B. '89 World Ch. Kupros MacDuff at Zany's (Eng. Ch. Kupros Master Mariner x Kupros Kirsh) owned by Mr. J.M.K. Verrees and bred in England by Mr. and Mrs. Peter Hart.

This is the proof that we can produce both looks and working ability! But how did we manage this? The real beginnings of Labradors in Belgium began in the 70s with a few dogs mostly imported from Great Britain. The best known were Ch. B.I.B. Harefield Silver Titbit and Ch. B.F.I.B. Mansergh Spade Guinea (Mrs. de Halloy), Ch. B.I.B. Harefield Belle (Mrs. Billon) and Ch. B.I.B. Taiaut du Mat Noir (Mrs. de Heusch).

Then, in the early 80s, Mrs. Felicity Leith-Ross's lines (of Tintagel Winds) were imported from France and became the foundation of many of our present kennels such as: Paducah, Sweettrees, of Misty Dreams, of Lucifer's Delight, du Bois de Lauzelle, of Sweetheartfellows, and Dual's Hope. The different combinations based on the Leith-Ross lines (whose foundation couple was Ch. Kupros Lucifer and Ch. Ballyduff Sunflower) have produced many champions whose names you will find at the end of this article.

At the same time, other dogs were also influential, such as Ch. B.I.B. Crawcrook Castaway (W. Van den Broeck) and the American and Swedish lines imported by Mrs. Gidefors (of Fisherman's Mascot).

At the end of the 80s, our Labrador world changed and became influenced by the following:

–B.F.D.VDH.I.B. World Ch. Kupros MacDuff at Zany's (Mr. Verrees)
–B.F.Lux.D.VDH.Fin.I.B.Euro. & World Ch. Blondella Bonny Lad (Mr. Verrees)
–Eng./Am. Ch. Receiver of Cranspire (Mr. Gad)
–The Beechcroft lines (imported by Mrs. Smith and Mrs. Gidefors)
–The Ballyduff lines (imported by Mr. Breyne)

It is possible that the 90s will be influenced by a dog whose progeny is already in Belgium and France—Eng. Sh. Ch. Rocheby Royal Oak recently imported and belonging to M. Gad in France.

With this article, you will find photographs of some of the champions living in Belgium and all descending from the bloodlines mentioned.

Author's note: Mme. MacArthur has been good enough to send the following explanation of the titles shown on the Belgian dogs. "I would like to add," she said, "that to become a Belgian National or International Conformation Champion as dog must have a placement in a field trial.

Conversely, a Belgian Field Trial Champion must obtain a minimum of a 'very good' in a show. These are prerequisites for all the retriever breeds and require a great deal of effort and money on the part of the owner."

EXC	Excellent
VDH	West German title
CAC	Certificat d'aptitude au championnat. This is a show qualification the equivalent of the English CC.
RCAC	Reserve
CACIB	Certificat d'aptitude au championnat international de beaute'. This is like the CAC, but some shows have a large enough entry to give an international qualification. With two CACIBs one year apart, you become an International Champion.
RCACIB	Reserve. If a dog is already a National or International Champion, his win then goes to the dog in second place.
CACT	Certificate d'aptitude au championnat de travail. This title concerns only field trials.
RCACT	Reserve
CACIT	Same as the above, but more on the international level—the trials usually being more difficult.

These are all titles associated with show results, not work:

Ch. B.I.B.	Champion Belge et international de beaute'
Ch. B.F.I.B.	Ch. Belge, Francais et Int. de beaute'
B.F.D.VDH. I.B.	Belgian, French, East German, West German and Int. de beaute'
B.F.Lux.D.VDH. Fin. I.B.	Belgian, French, Luxembourg, East and West German, Finnish and Int. de beaute'

Belgium Ch. B.I.B. Sweettrees Dark Sensation owned by Mrs. Laura MacArthur and Mr. Francis Stache.

Belgium Ch. B.I.B. Must du Bois de Lauzelle (Ch. Blondella Bright Shade's x Sweettrees Jill) is owned by Mrs. Carine Berthe-Bougard of Sweetheartfellows Labradors.

Chapter 3

The Labrador Retriever in Canada

When I think about the people in Canada and their Labradors, they do not seem like residents of another country. Many of them have traveled to the United States for shows along the border and even farther to specialty shows, and many Americans have made the trek North. Because the judging system for Canadian shows is similar to the system used in the U.S. the transition is easy, however only ten points are required for a Canadian championship. This effortless transition holds true for field trials, too, but all trials in Canada are run on cold game. Field trial stakes have somewhat different titles, however the basic point system for a championship is similar to the U.S. One additional note: In Canada the WC and WCX are recognized as official titles for retrievers by the Canadian Kennel Club.

Whether it be at field trials, obedience trials or shows, there have been many good friendships established between the Canadians and Americans. The names of the late Frank and Vina Jones of Annwyn Labradors come to mind immediately because they came often to visit. Frank was a popular judge in America, and he and his wife attended many specialty shows. The Annwyn Kennel imported Lisnamallard Tarantella (later Am./Can. Ch.) and Irish Dual Ch. Castlemore Coronet (later Can. Ch.), and bred a number of good Labradors. Some of the other early breeders in Canada were Bill and Ruth Grimsbey (Nascopie), and Bill Blyth whose Blyth Kennels produced among others, four dual champions: Can. Dual Ch. Blyth's Ace of Spades, Can. Dual Ch. Blyth's Queen of Spades, Can. Dual Ch. Blyth's Pat, and Can. Dual Ch. Blyth's Knave of Spades. Hugh Crozier imported Can. Dual Ch. Castlemore Shamus and Can. Ch. Crozier's Castlemore Sean C.D., and had many other good dual purpose dogs. His death last year was a great loss to the breed. Sandy Briggs, was also the breeder and owner of many winning Labradors, both in Canada and America. Two of her champions were Am./Can. Ch./Can. OTCh., F.T. winner Wimberway's Wateaki, Am. C.D., WC and his sister, Am./Can. Ch. Wimberway's Wanda, Can. C.D., C.D.X., WC.— a truly versatile duo. Two other kennels that should not be forgotten are Monroe Coleman's Carnmoney and E. Chevrier's Avandale; both provided successful breeding stock for many lines in Canada and the U.S.

Audley

The Canadian province farthest to the east is Newfoundland, the cradle of the breed we know as Labradors. There are two well-known Lab kennels in Newfoundland: Audley of Lady Barlow, and Waterdog of Dr. Michael

Can./Am. OTCh.
Waterdog's Raine Storm
(Can. Ch./OTCh.
Ballyduff Storm U.D.
(U.S.A.), WC x
Waterdog's Seawizard
Sadonia C.D.) owned and
handled by Dr. Michael
Woods, Newfoundland,
Canada.
Photo by Ashbey.

Can./Am. Ch.
Ebonylane's Aslan is
the top producing sire
of all time in Canada
with over 100 cham-
pion offspring. He was
owned by Dr. Ken
Bentley, Quebec, and
bred and leased by Pat
and Mike Lanctot.

Can./Am. Ch. Chablais
Myrtille owned by Jean
Louis Blais and
Madeleine Charest
shown winning Best
Puppy at the LRC of
Central Connecticut
Specialty, 1990. Photo
by Ashbey.

Lady Barlow and Sandringham Chive greeting the Princess Royal (Princess Anne) at Government House, St. Johns, Newfoundland, 1991.

Woods. Lady Barlow has done the "Gundogs" column for the magazine, *The Labrador Quarterly,* for a number of years, and has been a wonderful source of information to me for my *Legends in Labradors* book and for this one, too. Sadly, she has just lost her old yellow fellow, Sandringham Chive, from the kennel in Norfolk, England of H.M. Queen Elizabeth II. The present Earl of Malmesbury, decendant of the orginal developer of the Labrador Retriever in England, and his wife are friends of Lady Barlow, and have visited her several times.

Waterdog

Dr. Michael Woods' Waterdog Kennel has had some lovely dogs over the years. His import, Can./Am. Ch. Powhatan Black Badger C.D.X. from Major and Mrs. Aikenhead in England, has had an exceptional influence on the breed in Canada and the U.S. In addition, the lovely yellow dog, Can. Ch./OTCh. Ballyduff Storm, WC and the specialty winners, Am./Can. Ch. Waterdog's Raine Storm and Am./Can. Ch. Waterdog's Raine Dancer, all have proved to be effective breeding stock. George White, a good friend of the Woods, showed Badger and some of the other "Waterdogs" in the States. Michael is a conformation and obedience judge in both countries.

Ebonylane

Pat and Mike Lanctot, of Ebonylane fame, moved from Quebec to Nova

Can./Am. Ch. Shadowvale's Jill at Ranbourne owned by Martin and Valerie Walters.

Eng. Sh. Ch./Can./ Bda./Am./Mex./Int. Ch. Bradking Black Charm C. D., WC owned by Huguette and Mike Beattie, Shadowvale Kennels. Photo by Dick and Donna Alverson.

Can. Ch. Castlemore Bramble imported from Ireland by Dale Haines, Selamat Kennels, Ontario.

Scotia in 1989. They have both semi-retired from breeding to allow more time for travel and judging. The Lanctots owned the Best in Show winners: Can./Am. Ch. Shamrock Acres Ebonylane Ace C.D.X., WC and Can./Am. Ch. Hollyhock Sam. However, their pride and joy has been Can./Am. Ch. Ebonylane's Aslan, Canada's top producing sire of all time with over 100 champions. Some of their other notable Labradors included: Can./Am. Ch. Ebonylane's Midnight Bandit; Can./Am. Ch. Ebonylane's Buccaneer Gold; and Can./Am. Ch. Ebonylane's Yellow Poplar.

Huntsdown

Moving westerly, the Huntsdown Kennel of Mrs. Anne Mugglestone is in Hampton, New Brunswick. Some of her good dogs have been Can./Am. Ch. Huntsdown Valleywood Spice; Can./Am. Ch. Huntsdown Jubilation and Can. Ch. Huntsdown Buddha Beechcroft, Best of Breed at the Labrador Retriever Club of Canada and The Labrador Owners Booster Club.

Chablais

In Quebec, the Chablais Kennel of Jean Louis Blais and Madeleine Charest has come forth rapidly with some big winners. Perhaps the most well-known is Can./Am. Ch. Chablais Myrtille who won Best in Sweep-stakes at four specialties: Labrador Owners' Club (Can.) 1990, LRC of Canada 1990, LRC of Central Connecticut 1990, and LRC of the Potomac 1991; Winners Bitch and Best of Winners, Mid-Jersey LRC 1990 and LRC of the Potomac 1991; BOB in two Specialties, LOC (Canada) 1991 and LRC of Greater Boston 1991; Judge's Award of Merit at LRC, Inc. National Specialty (U.S.) 1991 and 1992, and many Bests of Breed and Group placements in all-breed shows in the U.S. and Canada. Another youngster is the chocolate female, Shakespeare Mislyn de Chablais (Eng. Sh. Ch./Am./Can. Ch. Lindall Mastercraft X Shadowvale Mistral Blackvelvet) Reserve Winners at the LRC of Central Connecticut 1992, Open Chocolate winner LRC of Mid-Jersey and Ox Ridge K.C. 1992.

Savanes

Also in Quebec is Can./Am. Ch. Superbe Brise des Savanes, bred and owned by Maurice Legare. She was Winners Bitch and Best of Winners at three specialties: LOC 1991, LRC, Inc. National Specialty (U.S.) 1991, LRC of Central Connecticut 1992 as well as Best of Breed at LRC of Mid-Jersey LRC in 1992.

Ranbourne

The Ranbourne Kennel of Martin and Valerie Walters is also in Quebec, and they are the owners of the lovely Can./Am. Ch. Shadowvale's Jill at Ranbourne, bred by Michael and Huguette Beattie as well as Can. Ch. Ranbourne This Bud's for You.

Shadowvale

Moving on to Ontario, the Shadowvale Kennel of Huguette and her late husband, Michael Beattie have had some wonderful Labs. The Labrador community was both shocked and saddened by Michael's sudden death in 1993. The Beatties had two beautiful black bitches, both from England. Eng. Sh. Ch./Can./Bda./Am./Mex./Int. Ch. Bradking Black Charm C. D., WC from Arthur and Peggy Kelly's Bradking Kennel and Can./Am./P.R. Ch. Heatherbourne Forget Me Not from Mrs. Heather Wiles. A nice yellow male also came from the Bradking Kennel, Can./Am./Bda./Ch. Bradking Rangeways Mr. Chips and a black dog, Can./Am. Ch. Bradking Mike, both of whom have been very successful producers.

Selamat

Dale Haines, Selmat Kennel, in the Province of Ontario imported two important chocolates from Mrs. Carvill in Ireland, Can. Ch. Castlemore Bramble and Can. Ch. Castlemore Pride, WC. "Bramble" was BIS at the LOC of Canada Specialty in 1980. These fine littermates sired by Eng. Ch. Sandylands Mark out of Castlemore Chlohelga proved to be good producers for this kennel.

Oaklea

Another Welshman to emigrate to Canada with his English wife, Eileen, is Ken Grant of Oaklea Labradors. The Grants have been primarily known for their yellows, and have done a lot of winning with Can./Am. Ch. Finchingfield Ivan of Oaklea—BOB at both Miami Valley LRC and LRC of the Potomac. Ivan's lovely daughter, Can./Am. Ch. Selamat's Oaklea Yellow Rose has done well, too—BOB Labrador Owners' Club (Canada) and BOS at the Mid-Jersey LRC and the Winnebago LRC. Both Ken and Eileen have judged the Sweepstakes classes at various specialty shows. By the way, the name "Oaklea" is on their race horses too.

Can./Am. Ch. Finchingfield Ivan of Oaklea (Am. Ch. Briary Brendan of Rainell x Am. Ch. Briary Bustle)—BOB at LRC of the Potomac, 1990; owned by Ken and, Eileen Grant, Oaklea. Photo by Ashbey.

Can./Am. Ch. Rickway's Sun Raider (Lachienvale Big Mac x Accipiter Cattle Annie), bred by Lorne Love and owned by Ron Ursel. Photo by Mikron Photos, Ltd.

This yellow winning brace from the Stonedale Kennel is made up of Can. Ch. Stonedale's Bavarian Cream and daughter, Can. Ch. Stonedale's Tessa. Photo by Purebred Photos.

Can. Ch. Amaranth All of Me finished his Canadian title at seven months of age and won multiple awards at Canadian specialty shows.

Rickway

Lorene and Joyce Love established their breeding stock on imported lines from the Ferntree Kennel in Australia. After the shock of tragic death of their first import, Ferntree Front Runner, they were able to acquire a half-brother to "Runner," and a second dog from Olga Martyn's Lachienvale Kennel who became the sire of the Love's first show dog of note, Can. Ch. Rickway's Sun Raider. A third import, a black bitch, Lachienvale Lydia when bred to Int. World/Fr./Am. Ch. Sandylands Rip Van Winkle produced the delightful show dog, Can. /Am. Ch. Rickways Tuscaroura ("Breezy") owned by Sherry Ursel. "Breezy's" daughter (sired by Am./Can. Ch. Rainell's Dynasty), Am./Can. Ch. Breezy's Whirlwind, JH, is owned by Jackie MacFarland and Gordon Sousa. In 1992, she was BOB at the U.S. National Specialty under English judge, Janice Pritchard. "Spooky" was the first winner of this prestigious event to hold a Hunting Retriever title. The Loves are also proud of another "Lydia" daughter, Can. Ch. Rickways Independence C.D.X. who ammassed enough points in the obedience ring to become Canada's Top Obedience Labrador Retriever for 1992 and #3 Sporting Dog.

Redsky

Grace McDonald's Redsky kennel name is permanently registered with the Canadian Kennel Club, and located in Manitoba. To qualify for a permanent registration by Canadian Kennel Club rules a kennel must have produced five champions under that prefix. Grace McDonald started her kennel in 1965, and has produced multiple generations of obedience trial champions starting with OTCh. Redsky's Dandy Little Honey. Can. Ch./ OTCh. Redsky's Divine Designate, WCX has recently retired to allow her daughter, "T.F.," to compete.

Stonedale

Paul and Diane Crouch were initially interested in chocolates, but they have branched out recently, importing several dogs from England such as Can. Ch. Charway Ballydipper who was BOS under English judge Ken Hunter at the Canadian Labrador Owners Club. They now have all three colors.

Amaranth

Another winner at the Canadian Labrador Owners' Club, Can. Ch. Amaranth All of Me, bred, owned and handled by Joan Calder won his Canadian championship by age seven months, was a Best Puppy in Show winner, and the L.O.C. top puppy for 1990. Joan has bred three obedience trial champions, and another, Can. Ch. Amaranth Preachers Kid C.D.X., WC, with two legs on a U.D. As soon as she obtains her last leg (which she probably has by now) she will become Joan's first show and obedience champion.

Springfield

Alberta Province seems to be a real stronghold for Labs. Shirley Costigan's Springfield Kennel has had some really good show champions. Can./Am. Ch. Springfield's Uhuru was a multiple all-breed Best in Show winner and has won several specialty stud dog classes. Can. Ch. Springfield's Meadow Muffin was 1987 B.I.S. winner at the LRC of Canada Specialty.

Ranchman

The Ranchman Kennel of Marion R. Reid located in Medicine Hat has had some lovely dogs, having imported quite a few from England which have left their stamp on stock in Canada.

Beautawn

Bill Gugins has been breeding Labs under the name Beautawn since 1980, and said, "I believe that I have contributed to the breed as all my dogs work as well as look like Labradors. I am a very avid hunter, and any dogs that I keep in my breeding program must have hunting desire and ability."

Windanna

The Windanna Kennels of Charlie and Judy Hunt have been in operation since the mid-'70s, and during this time have produced over 50 home-bred champions, 32 Companion Dogs, ten Companion Dogs Excellent and two OTChs. On the field side, 12 WC's, one WCI and one WCX plus seven NAHRA Started dogs. "We try to encourage our puppy people in all phases of the Labrador as we believe Labs are truly all-around dogs." They have both been charter members and extremely active in the Labrador Retriever Club of Canada and have held offices in the Alberta Kennel Club and the Westwind Sporting Dog Club. Both judge conformation, and they are both North American Hunting Retriever (NAHRA) judges.

The yellow bitch, B.I.S.S. Can. Ch. Beautawn's Instant Replay C.D.X., WC (Can. Ch. Shadowvale's Just Reward x Beautawn's Brandy on the Rock C.D.X., WC) or "Tinker" as she is known was bred and owned by Bill Gugins.
Photo by Mikron Photos.

Can. Ch. Windanna Opus Won (Am./Can. Ch. Braemar Oakmead Magnum Force x Windanna's Pallas Athena C.D.) bred and owned by Charles and Judy Hunt. Photo by Mikron Photos.

Did you know that there are *two triple champion Labradors* in Canada? They belong to Kerry and Lori Curran in Langdon, Alberta, and Lori has written to tell us about them:

Whistlnwings

We at Whistlnwings are proud to be the home of Canada's only Triple Champion Labradors. Our first one, Can. Ch./Can. FTCh./Can. OTCh. Kenosee Jim Dandy, WCX (Dandy), was given to me as a seven week old pup by her breeder, Jim Harkness. She was a field trial dog by pedigree, although both her parents (Can. FTCh./Am. FTCh. Pelican Lake Andy and Kenosee Jo) were nice looking Labs. Her grandsire was all time High Point Open Dog in Canada, '75, '81 CNFC/Can. FTCh./Can. AFTCh./Am. FC/Am. AFC Pelican Lake Petey Two. Our second Triple Champion is a home-bred daughter of 'Dandy' by Am./Can. Ch. Monarch's Black Arrogance C.D., WC, Can. Ch./Can. FTCh./Can. OTCh. Whistlnwings Kitty MaGee, WCX. We have done all of Dandy and Kitty's training and handling at shows and trials ourselves and both girls earned all their championships before their fifth birthdays, with limited showing and trialing.

Kerry and I are basically field trialers who love Labradors and are dedicated to keeping it a dual purpose breed where the great majority look and work like we think Labs should. We have been 'in Labs' for many years, although we breed sparingly and did not breed our first litter until 1985. Kerry has been field trialing for 30 years and is a popular field trial judge who also had the honor of judging the 1982 Canadian National Retriever Championship. I have been field trialing for 22 years and have also done some showing and obedience trialing and some professional training off and on over the years.

We feel that trying to produce show and field trial Labs in one package is a great challenge . . . but well worth the effort to help preserve our wonderful breed. We have crossed field trial and show lines as one way of trying to accomplish this. Each litter is planned as a step toward our ultimate goal of producing a line or lines of Labs that are sound in mind and body and will have a high percentage of the qualities that, 'with proper training,' will go toward making a dual or triple champion.

To date we have produced nine litters with seven progeny qualified all-age field trial dogs, two of which are field trial champions and another two with points toward their field trial championships. Two offspring are obedience trial champions, two show champions and three others pointed, one is a Senior Hunter with two legs towards his Master Hunter title, and one has her Junior Hunter title. One of the highlights of our breeding was in 1991 when Ch. Whistlnwings Autumn Thunder, WC went Best of Opposite Sex at the Canadian National Specialty. On the same weekend, her litter sister, Can. Triple Ch. Whistlnwings Kitty MaGee, WCX earned her first Open Field Trial win.

We feel strongly that breeders should train and work their dogs because it is very easy to lose those 'unseen qualities' such as intelligence, heart and desire to retrieve and to please in spite of hardship. These qualities are just as important to a Lab as that Lab expression and 'otter' tail, etc.

Left—Can. Triple Ch. Kenosee Jim Dandy, WCX (Can. FTCh./Am. FTCh. Pelican Lake Andy and Kenosee Jo). Right—Can. Triple Ch. Whistlnwings Kitty MaGee, WCX (Am./Can. Ch. Monarch's Black Arrogance C.D., WC x Can. Triple Ch. Kenosee Jim Dandy, WCX).

Finn./Nor. FTCh. & Finn. Sh. Ch. Ethusan Yliveto Finnish Labrador of the Year 1988, 1991, 1992, and 1993.

Finland, Somero International Championship Show, June 1993; judge—Eeva Rautala; BOB, Ch. Caveris Mirage (yellow dog-left) by Ch. Receiver of Cranspire x Caveris Elin; BOS Tweedledum Sweet 'N Rosy (black bitch-right) by Guideline's Copyright x Jayncourt Jingle Jangle.

Chapter 4

The Labrador Retriever In Finland

Author's note: Eeva Rautala of the Finnish Labrador Kennel,Wetten, agreed to write a history of the Labrador Retriever in Finland.

The Finnish Kennel Club, founded in May 1889, is the oldest in Scandinavia. However, the history of retriever breeding is relatively short. It started in the 1950s when a well-bred black bitch, Whatstandwell Sonya, was imported from Great Britain in 1954 by Alderbay Kennels. She became the first Show Champion Labrador in Finland and had three litters. Other imports followed, mainly from Great Britain, but also from Scandinavia and the United States.

One of the objects of the [Finnish] Labrador Club is to keep the Labrador a dual-purpose breed. To emphasize this, the club has since 1982 awarded a trophy and the title 'Labrador of the Year' (Vuoden Labradori) to the best dual-purpose Labrador with awards from both field trials and shows that year. The dog gets points for the highest two field trial and show awards.

Wetten, Horseman's, Ethusan

In the 1960s the breed was dominated by a British-bred stud dog, Int./ Finn./Nor. Ch. Diant Dobrudden Breydon, who was the son of the famous Eng. Ch. Sandylands Tweed of Blaircourt. He was owned by the I Vassen Kennel of the Kankkunen's, who also bred Flat-coats. The Finnish Retriever Club was founded in 1963 and held its first Championship Show in 1970, the Best in Show [BIS] winner being the yellow Labrador dog, Yolk I Vassen. Mrs. Andrea Standertskjold, the present chairman of the Finnish Labrador Club (founded in 1980), had a nice black bitch, Finn. Ch. Tekla I Vassen, born 1968. This bitch was the foundation of her Kennel Horseman's, now breeding Labradors of the working type and pointers. Her second foundation bitch was Roseacre Senta, who was imported from Britain 1979 mated to Eng. Ch. Timspring Sirius. From this litter one was field trial champion, FTCh. Castor Star. A bitch from the same litter, Finn. Ch. Chara Star, won the first Labrador Club Breed Championship Field Trial and became the foundation of Eeva Rautala's Wetten Kennels. Horseman's Kennel also imported a black dog puppy from Norway in 1980, later to become Finn. Ch. and Nordic FTCh. Kevin Keegan av Sverresborg (by Int./ Nord. Ch. Minväns Junior ex Nor. Ch. Ballyduff Kerry), a most famous field trial winner with his five consecutive victories at the Lab Club Breed

Championship Trials (1983-87). He was awarded the title 'Labrador of the Year' in 1983, for the best dual-purpose Labrador. This title was later conquered five times by his son, Finn. Ch. and Finn./Nor. FTCh. Ethusan Yliveto, bred and owned by the leading field trial kennel, Ethusan, of Mr. and Mrs. Matikainen.

Ballyduff Maroon
Int./Nord. Ch. Minväns Junior
Minväns Esmeralda
Scan. FTCh./Finn. Ch. Kevin Keegan av Sverresborg
Eng. Ch. Timspring Sirius
Nor. Ch. Ballyduff Kerry
Spark of Ballyduff
Finn./Nor. FTCh. & Finn. Sh. Ch. Ethusan Yliveto
Powhatan Percy
Eng. Ch. Powhatan Solo
Powhatan Tonic
Finn. Ch. Kamrats Barbara
Lugwardine Judge
Badgerland Jess of Powhatan
Timspring Muslin

Susanset, Rosanan, Follies, Mailiksen

It has to be remembered that for the first decades the Labrador population was rather small in Finland. It started to grow in the 1980s to become the fourth most popular breed in the country with around 2,000 registrations each year in the 1990s. In a country of five million people, that makes the Labrador almost as popular in Finland as in Great Britain or the U.S. In the 1970s the Labrador breeders often used Swedish-owned stud dogs for their bitches. These were often British imports of mainly Sandylands and Ballyduff breeding. One of the top winning kennels in the '70s was

Finn. Ch. Follies Cutty Sark was BIS at the Finnish Labrador Retriever Club Specialty 1992; Best Dog and BOS at the Lab Club Show in 1993; Best Dog and BOS at the Lab Club Specialty 1993.

Mrs. Aspegren's Susanset, with quite a few champions and some excellent chocolates. FT and OBCh. Susanset Illuusia, who was the foundation of Mrs. Rauni Aslamo's Kennel Rosanan, was of her breeding. Mrs. Aslamo also owned the lovely yellow Swedish bitch, Finn. Ch./OBCh. Proud of Sinfonia, who had many big wins at shows and was the breed's Top Winner in 1979-80-81. Another highly successful show dog of this kennel was the British import Finn. Ch. Poolstead Pipit, the Top Winning Labrador of 1983. Illuusia's son, Int./Finn. Ch. Rosanan Dandelion did very well at shows and appears in some winning pedigrees of today, and her granddaughter (by Int./Nord. Ch. Licithas Blizzard), Finn. Ch. Rosanan Taste of Honey, is behind many champions of the Mailiksen kennels. From Mrs. Aspegren's Susanset Kennels came the Best in Show (BIS) winner of the Labrador Club Show 1982, Finn. Ch. Susanset Inez, belonging to the Follies Kennels of Mrs. Helena Kaitila. The present stock of Follies is based mainly on the British import bitches Heatherbourne Partypiece and Finn. Ch. Balrion Witching Hour, her great-grandson being the top male, Finn. Ch. Follies Cutty Sark, who was BIS at the Lab Club Show in 1992 and best male at the Club Show 1993. Several Champions have been bred by this kennel.

Tweedledum, Mallorn's, Aprilmist, Hirsipirtin

Witching Hour's litter brother, Int./Finn./Swed. Ch. Balrion Knights Quest (by Eng. Sh. Ch. Bradking Cassidy ex Eng. Sh. Ch. Balrion Wicked Lady) was also imported as a puppy with his sister in 1982. He became one of the top winning Labradors in this country and sired many Champions. He was BIS at the Lab Club Show three times, in 1984-85-86, and the top winner in the breed in 1984. He also competed at field trials with success and was awarded the dual-purpose title, Labrador of the Year 1984-85. His offspring include the lovely yellow bitch, Finn. Ch. Aprilmist Apricot Flower, his granddaughter bred by the up-and-coming Aprilmist Kennels of Mrs. Mirja Aro-Ikonen. This bitch was the breed Top Winner in 1987.

Another successful breeder in the 1970s was Miss Heikkila, who started with a Swedish-bred bitch, Finn. Ch./Finn. & Swed. FTCh. and OBCh. Duchess, the first field trial champion retriever in Finland and a very good brood bitch with many champion offspring. One of her sons was Finn. Ch. Max, the first Labrador of Mrs. Kirsi Luomanen, and behind some of her present day winning stock, like the BIS winner at the Club Show 1992, Tweedledum Puddle Jumper and Am. Ch. Tweedledum Pop My Cork, litter mates out of Jayncourt Jingle Jangle. Mrs. Luomanen's Kennel Tweedledum has bred and owned many successful show dogs—the original foundation bitch being the Swedish-bred Nattens Drottning in 1978. In 1976 the same kennel imported Mr. and Mrs. Salin's Finn. Ch./OBCh. Nattens Sportsman (by Ballyduff Maroon), who was a highly-successful stud dog in the early 1980s and the breed's Top Winner 1978 and winner of BIS at the first Lab Club Show in 1981. The Tweedledum

Kennels has been involved in many imports through the years—like the British-bred males Kupros Kassidy and Roseacre Madigan. Kassidy (by Sh. Ch. Newinn Kestrel ex Ballyduff Morella) was used extensively at stud and produced many show winners for different breeders. Madigan's offspring also did well at the shows. In addition, he threw chocolate and his chocolate daughters from Miss Anu Saurama's up-and-coming Mallorn's Kennels, M. Aprilfool and Applesauce, are behind the winning chocolate stock of Mallorn's, Loresho and Bubbling Kennels. Madigan's litter sister, the beautiful yellow Finn./Nor. Ch. Roseacre Madcap (by Eng. Sh. Ch. Ardmargha Mad Hatter ex Roseacre Shell), was imported by another established breeder, Mrs. Birgitta Johansson, Mellows Kennels. This kennel has imported British and Swedish dogs, and bred many champions over the years and as well as breeding stock for others. Madcap was very successful at shows and was also a very good bitch. Her daughters are Mellows Pop Primadonna, whose son, Finn. Ch. Mellows Xanthos, has done very well in the show rings, and Mellows Pop Primavera, who produced the All-Time Top Winning Labrador, Int. Finn./VDH Ch./ World Winner '91 Caveris Ellen, bred and owned by Mrs. Carita Hallgren's Kennel Caveris.

Ellen's sire, Hirsipirtin Q-makoira, is bred and owned by Ritva Tervo's Hirsipirtin Kennels and he has been a very prominent sire of numerous show winners in the past seven years. He is by the Norwegian stud dog, well-known all over Scandinavia by his winning stock, Int. Nord. Ch. Licithas Blizzard out of Finn. Ch. Hirsipirtin Emma, an excellent brood bitch with many winning offspring. Hirsipirtin Kennels started with Mellows Katanja in the late 1970s, and another foundation bitch being Finn. Ch. Follytower Hedda from Great Britain. Hedda's son, Finn. Ch. Hirsipirtin Gummiseta, has done very well at shows and produced many show winners. Hirsipirtin Kennels has imported several dogs over the years successfully breeding winning show dogs, as well as breeding stock for other kennels.

Caveris, Pastime's, Palabras, M'ladys,

Mrs. Carita Hallgren, Caveris Kennel, started breeding in 1985 with Finn. Ch. Mellows Honeysuckle and has been very successful in the show rings ever since. The beautiful bitch Caveris Ellen has been extremely successful in Finland, as well as other countries. Not only has she been the Top Winning Labrador for four years in 1988,89-90-91, but also the Top Winning Gun Dog in 1988-89 and winner of BIS at the Lab Club Show in 1988 and again as a veteran in 1993. She was also BIS in Holland over 500 dogs at the Dutch Lab Club Championship Show in 1990, the biggest Continental Lab Show. She has no offspring, but her litter sisters Caveris Elin and Eulalia have produced several top winning dogs including Int.

Int. Finn./VDH Ch./
World Winner '91
Caveris Ellen owned
by Mrs. Carita
Hallgren.

Champions Caveris Mirage and Mimosa by Eng./Am. Ch. Receiver of Cranspire. The imports made by this kennel include Int./Finn. Ch. Charway Huckleberry, and Finn. Ch. Charway Sea Badger (by Eng. Ch. Kupros Master Mariner ex Charway Sally Brown), BIS winner of the Lab Club Show 1989 and a widely used stud dog. Another big winner owned by the Caveris Kennel is the Top Winning Labrador of 1986, Int./Finn. Ch. Pastime's Stepping Stone. This lovely yellow bitch was bred by the Pastime's Kennel of Mrs. Virpi Hallberg. Her sire is the Swedish import Finn. Ch. Fagelangens Hawker Hunter (by Int. Ch. Sandylands Night Flight ex Mallards Caddis Worm), who has sired the most puppies in this country. His offspring have been very successful in the shows over the years, many of them becoming champions. The foundation bitch of Pastime's was the litter sister of his dam, Finn. Ch. Mallards Caddis Cased, a beautiful black bitch and Top Winning Labrador in 1982. This excellent bitch produced some top winning offspring in the 1980s. Her daughter, Finn. Ch. Pastime's Toothsome produced with Hawker Hunter the foundation bitch of Miss Marika Nahkuri's new Kennel M'ladys, whose breeding produced the Top Winning Labrador of 1992, Finn. Ch. M'Ladys Snow-Ball. He is by Finn. Ch. Palabras Spacecraft bred by another up-and-coming kennel, Miss Hannele Jokisilta's Palabras. Another young breeder combining Hawker Hunter and Pastime's lines with her foundation bitch, a daughter of the famous Int. Nord. Ch. Licithas Blizzard, is Miss Tiina Rantanen of the Strongline's Kennels, who has already produced several champions and highly successful dogs.

The breeding and training of guide dogs for the blind have been an active program since the 1950s. A majority of these dogs are Labradors. Labradors have also been used for drug detection for about 20 years.

The Finnish Labrador breeders are rather conscientious about health problems in the breed. Hips have been x-rayed from the start of the

*Int./Finn. Ch.
Strongline's Incandes-
cent (Finn. Sh. Ch.
Pastime's Swinging
Gate x Finn. Sh./Ch.
Track. Ch. Applehill's
Mayday) owned by
Tiina Rantanen and
Mia Tapanainen.*

breeding in this country and eye examinations started in the 1970s. Nowadays The Kennel Club only registers puppies from parents with clear eyes and nearly free hips. The breed club also requires free hips. Elbows are x-rayed on a voluntary basis. The health situation has been rather good. However, one problem has been that some of the widely used stud dogs have later been discovered to be PRA-carriers, which has made breeding plans more difficult for many breeders. However, the general quality of the breed has improved all the time and the best show dogs can compete internationally. A phenomenon that appeared about mid-1980s was the division of the breed to so called show lines and working lines. This is a great pity and has made the breeding of dual-purpose dogs more difficult, as in so many other countries.

During the first decades the Labrador breeding in this country was rather dependent on imported or foreign stud dogs and breeding material, and many of the top winning dogs were imported. Nowadays the Finnish-bred Labradors can hold their own in many ways and imports have declined. Instead, quite a few exports have been made, for instance to Sweden, Denmark, Holland, Belgium, Germany, Hungary, Portugal and to the U.S. and Canada. Opening of the borders in 1988 to all (except so-called quarantine countries) opened the possibilities for wider international cooperation for Finnish breeders and exhibitors.

Outstanding Labradors in Finland

Labrador of the Year (includes both show and field trial wins)
1988 Ethusan Yliveto
1989 Susanset Zorro
1990 Susanset Zorro
1991 Ethusan Yliveto
1992 Ethusan Yliveto
1993 Ethusan Yliveto

Year's Top Field Trial Dog
> 1989 Drakehead Wade
> 1990 Ethusan Yliveto
> 1991 Susanset Zorro
> 1992 Tupla-Pummin Ulpukka
> 1993 Ethusan Yliveto

Year's Top Show Dog
> 1989 Caveris Ellen
> 1990 Caveris Ellen
> 1991 Caveris Ellen
> 1992 Caveris Ellen
> 1993 M'Lady's Snow-Ball

Author's note: My young Finnish friend, Tiina Rantanen of Stronglines Kennel, asked Mr. Veli Erkki Haataja to give an account of field trials in the different Scandinavian countries. It is of special interest to note what the Labrador must do in these very cold climates—thank you, Mr. Haataja, I'd like very much to see a Finnish Field Trial.

Field Trials in Scandinavia

HISTORY

The history of field trials in Scandinavia is not long. The first trials were held twelve years ago, and the first championship trial was only ten years ago. Scandinavian countries held very tight ties developing field trials. Finland, Sweden and Norway had almost the same rules and there was much competition between these countries, but unfortunately there has been some rabies in Finland, and Sweden and Norway closed their borders to Finnish dogs.

HUNTING WITH RETRIEVERS

To understand our working tests and field trials man must first know a little about hunting practices in Finland. There are no driven shoots for small game. (Only elk hunting occurs as partly driven.)

The most popular hunting is wild fowling with approximately 300,000 men and women participating when season starts on 20 August. About one million birds are shot during the season and officials count more than 20% of the birds are lost because difficult terrain, mud, water and high bulrushes prevent hunters from reaching the game. This is the situation where retrievers are most used in Finland. The dog hunts by itself, but in contact with the handler, to find wounded or dead game either shot by the handler or somebody else. Retrievers are also used for flushing the birds, but this ability is not tested in trials. Some dogs spend most of the season in water.

The season lasts to the end of November and at that time some waters have already started to freeze—dogs may have to work in ice. This is why we put a lot of emphasis on dogs' coats. We have some field trial Labradors imported from the United Kingdom, and their coats seem to be too thin for our circumstances.

WORKING TEST

The Working Test is a simple basic test where retrievers' hunting abilities are certified. Only retrievers that have passed a working test obtain the title of champion. Most of retriever breeders do not understand the importance of the working test. Their only goal is a 'beautiful' retriever and they do not care about hunting ability. Well, this is a subject about which one can talk over and over again never reaching any result.

The following abilities are tested in working test:
- how dogs react to other dogs and people
- self-confidence and initiative
- reaction to gun's sound
- how dog used his scent
- eagerness on hunting
- how the game is picked up and how it is carried and delivered
- eagerness to swim
- contact between dog and handler

HOW THE WORKING TEST IS ARRANGED

Game used is previously killed and cold. Birds that are used are crows, seagulls, magpies, pheasant. Rabbit is used for tracking.

In the beginning six dogs approach the judge who follows noting how the dogs react to each other. They should respond in a friendly way and they should not be aggressive or afraid.

Then each dog is judged individually. The first test is water work where a bird is thrown into the water, preferably into bulrushes, about 60 feet away. The dog should retrieve on command.

Next is the most important part that we call free hunt. In an area approximately 150 x 150 feet in size five birds are placed so that the dog cannot see them, then one bird is thrown and a shotgun is fired simultaneously. The judge then gives permission to send the dog. The dog should search the area independently without the handler's help or directions. If dog leaves the area or does not do the work properly then the handler must become involved. The dog should retrieve four to six birds in good time and cover the whole area.

If the dog has done everything well so far, only one task is left—tracking. A dead rabbit is dragged approximately 300 feet in cover and left at the end of trail. The dog is sent to retrieve the rabbit.

Dogs that have passed the working test can enter field trials.

The hunting season in Finland lasts to the end of November. At that time some waters have already started to freeze—dogs may have to work in ice and snow. This is why the Finnish put a lot of emphasis on dogs' coats.

FIELD TRIALS

Field Trials are held with cold game. In Finland we do not have driven shoots and it is not possible to arrange the same circumstances in wild fowling for every dog. The arrangements in field trials are as close to normal hunting situations as possible so there is free hunting, directions, markings, etc.

There are three stakes: Novice, Open, and Winner. Judgment is on quality not competition, i.e., one or more dogs can reach first prize in the same stake or it can happen that no one gets the prize.

After passing a working test, a dog starts field trials in the Novice Stake. Having won first prize in Novice, a dog can advance to the Open Stake where it must gain two first prizes before it can enter the Winner Stake. To become a field trial champion a dog must get three first prizes in the Winner Stake; pass a field trial with live game; *and have at least a second prize in an Open Class in a show.*

A field trial has the same elements in every stake: marking, direction, free hunt and theory on land or in water, or both. In the Novice Stake the distances are short, marks are singles and directions simple, such as "get in." The Open stake is more demanding and it requires a lot of training to get the dog into the Winner Stake. In the Winner Stake, the free hunt can be more than 300 x 300 feet, partly in water and partly on land and the amount of game three to five birds. It takes between 20 to 40 minutes to empty this kind of area. Distances in directions vary between 200 to 500 feet depending on terrain. Directions occur mostly in water. Marks are doubles or triples and the dog must remember falls exactly.

FIELD TRIALS IN SWEDEN, NORWAY AND DENMARK

Sweden and Norway do not have working tests, and their field trials are about the same as in Finland with only small differences. Denmark has a working test that is more like obedience and they also have a so called A-trial that means a real hunting situation, something not used elsewhere in Scandinavia. Cold game trials are similar to ours.

I wish all readers could come to Finland to see our field trials and to see that our Finnish retrievers are the best shooting companion's man can have.

Chapter 5

Labrador Retrievers in France

Author's note: Mrs. Felicity Leith-Ross agreed to give me a picture of the Labrador situation in France. She was fortunate to acquire Ballyduff Sunflower from Bridget Docking who told her right away that she had no business with Labradors if she wasn't prepared to work them. Over the years she's shown and trialed some very influential dogs in France: Int. Ch. Kupros Lucifer, Int./World Ch. Sandylands Rip Van Winkle (who later went to Gordon and Debbie Sousa in the U.S.), Int./World Ch. Peche Des Vergers De La Tour, Ch. Wetherlam Blackberry, Sh. Ch./FTCh. Cherry Brandy of Tintagel Winds and her young dog, Carromer Charlie Chalk. Felicity declares, "I still firmly believe that it's possible to show on Saturday and run in a trial on Sunday, and what's going to be fun this winter is that Charlie believes it too." She has written the following:

The subject of Labradors in France is, apparently, one to avoid! All my efforts have boiled down to statistics, and the conviction that no one wants me to go into the subject. The present president [i.e., of the Retriever Club] assures me that all the club archives prior to 1980 have been lost. (How *can* one lose 70 years' of papers and photos?) After six hours in a damp, mouse-infected warehouse, and a further six at the S.C.C. (French Kennel Club), I can make a brief outline on Labradors in France, but nothing very fascinating to beguile a passionate public.

At the S.C.C. I found show catalogues dating back to 1887. At this time all retrievers were lumped together and only the odd detail on size or coat occasionally gives a clue as to the variety. It was also clear that the popular Curly was losing ground to the elegant Flat, and that the Labrador was primarily considered as an uncouth, cumbersome, semi-mongrel cousin. The Retriever Club de France was formed in 1911 and had, I am told, about 40 members, all wealthy land owners who got together during the shooting season; it was very much a closed circle.

It is easy to understand how, and roughly when, the first Labradors must have appeared in France. At the end of the 19th century the quarantine laws had not come into force, and English dogs appeared frequently on the show bench in Paris at that time. All the retrievers were considered a shooting man's dog. These owners weren't interested in showing so much as showing off their dogs when invited on a shoot. Certainly the first retriever breeds to arrive were the Curlies and Flats, followed by the

Left, a group of Labradors owned by Baron Rothchild about 1955). Photo by Henri Dimont, France.

Fr. Ch. Ballyduff Sunflower and her 10 week old daughter, foundation bitch of Tintagel Winds, owned by Felicity Leith-Ross.

Labradors, and later the Goldens. Many of the French aristocrats had family ties in England (revolution oblige!), and later non-aristocrats with money, land and time (such as the Rothschild family with its ramifications all over Europe) began to take an interest in the retriever breeds.

The first Labrador was registered in France in 1882 or there-abouts, but lost data prevents us from identifying the dog. Population increases were very slow. From 1934 to 1960, only 1,028 Labradors were registered; from 1961 to 1980, 10,000; and from 1981 to 1990, registrations tripled to 33,000.

To Americans these figures won't mean very much, but they do serve to show the abrupt increase in popularity of the Labrador in recent years. The biggest problem is the inability of the Retriever Club to cope with this explosion. Up to the mid-eighties there was no official hip dysplasia control and, until very recently, no eye control. These problems have galloped proportionately faster than registrations. Of 150,000 pedigree dogs all breeds registered in France in 1992, 120,000 were bred from pet stock in pet homes. A majority of Labrador breeders are either pet owners or those who have made the equation that the demand outweighs the supply, and that Lab bitches are usually prolific whelpers. Some notable imports have proved to be carriers of our major breed problems, and proven carriers were, and still are, used at stud. The future looks difficult, and if we want to save what's best in the breed, there's much culling to be done.

As in England and the United States, the tendency in France is toward two distinct breed types—work and show. One or two kennels are fighting to keep the Labrador as a complete dog. I've been lucky enough to have owned the two dogs who have done the most for the breed in the last fifteen years, both of them producing show champions, field trial champions and even dual champions. The first was Kupros Lucifer (Squire of Ballyduff x Kupros My Lady), the second was Wetherlam Blackberry (Wetherlam Storm of Lawnwood x Wetherlam Siskin). Most of the leading kennels either started with progeny of these dogs or used them at stud. Apart from Tintagel Winds, the main show and field kennels are: Anne-Marie and Michel Le Roueil with La Passe De L'Eider Kennels; Muriel and Bruno Perrin with La Plaine De Lavau Kennels; and Martine Roux with Les Hauts De Tara Kennels.

Livers have been pioneered mainly by Michel Germain with St. Urbain and Les Hauts De Pouey, and David Sedze's kennel has been well-known as a working kennel for several years.

Concerning the breed Standard for Labradors—the French breed Standard was revised in 1988 after the 1986 Kennel Club (U.K.) revision. It is interesting to note that the French Standard is an exact word-for-word translation, except for one word, which in my opinion, was wrongly translated and is now the cause of temperament problems in France. *Undue shyness* is defined as *shyness without reason* and not, as translated, *excessive shyness*.

In France a puppy is delivered a 'birth certificate' and not a pedigree. When he or she is over 15 months, the owner takes the dog and the papers for confirmation to a judge. This is done either during a show or at special confirmation meetings. No Labrador is definitely registered until he's been through 'confirmation' successfully. Refusals are based on faults (bite, number of teeth, lack of undercoat, etc.) and no dog can be bred from officially until he or she has successfully gone through confirmation. Relatively few Labradors were shown before 1975, and when the breed increased in popularity, judges qualified in other gun dog breeds found themselves responsible for confirmation for all the retrievers without having much or any knowledge of the breeds. Hence, the problem with the system, and the one word in the Standard that has been given a faulty interpretation. Because of this we're getting more and more Labradors passing confirmation with their tails between their legs and a jump backwards from the judge. When I point out that shyness is a dreadful fault in a Labrador, I get the answer that only 'excessive shyness' is. Who says where excessive begins? I'm astonished to realize how one little word, erroneously translated, can modify a breed's temperament.

It's been a wonderful life and a wonderful adventure. I got into it all by accident, stayed in by pleasure and by passion, and hope that Labradors have been happy to have me in their world.

Eng. Sh. Ch. Rocheby Royal Oak, bred by Mr. & Mrs. Hopkinson, was top sire in England in 1992 and is now owned by Mr. Marc Gad, France. Photo © John Hartley, England.

Chapter 6

Labrador Retrievers in the Netherlands

Author's note: Pieta C.D.M. van Dee-Vogelaar, Fogel Hlara Kennel has sent the following information on Labradors in her country:

After the Second World War the Labrador Retriever almost disappeared in the Netherlands. Just a few were imported and used for hunting.

Between 1954 and 1957 only a small number of Labradors were registered at the Dutch Kennel Club. However, the sixties saw an increase in Labradors imported from the United Kingdom, and breeding programs were started by the Sabo Kennel and the Sunny Loch Kennel. Canis Frisiae Kennel now has a leading role in breeding in the Netherlands, with the six most recent champions from their stock.

The 'big boom' started in the second half of the seventies. The number of Labradors in the Netherlands increased enormously. In 1993 there were more than 15,000 Labs in our country. The annual number of puppies registered is now over 3,000. The Dutch Labrador Club was founded In 1964. The first Club show (1965) had an entry of 51. At the 30th anniversary show of the Dutch Labrador Retriever Club in 1994, the entry is anticipated to be about 750.

. The Labrador is very popular as a pet, however only a few breeders are trying to improve the breed and reach a quality that can be compared with the English Standard. The Netherlands has imports from the most famous English kennels (Sandylands, Wetherlam, Ballyduff, Blondella, Lawnwood, Charway), and a few of them have become champions. Like many other continental countries, most serious Dutch breeders started their breeding program with imports from the U.K. The Dutch Labrador Retriever Club is trying very hard to keep breeding activities under control. The Club uses a set of rules to which breeders should work. All breeding stock should have: (a) at least two show qualifications (a minimum of 'very good'); (b) good hips—at least HD-B; (c) eyes free from PRA and cataracts; and (d) not more than one litter every year. As a result the Dutch Labrador is, in general, of good health and according to the Standard. Nevertheless, there are still too many 'pets' instead of good, typical examples of the breed. In addition, we are now working out a set of rules for the handling of the OCD problem.

In the Netherlands we have only ten C.A.C./C.A.C.I.B. shows every year. The Winner Show in Amsterdam is the most important—with an

The chocolate dog, Dutch Ch. Brown Booby Winston van Toolenburg (Puh's Brown Autumn x Toplight Cracker's Comet)

entry of more than 4,000 dogs of all breeds. For the Gun Dog Group there is the 'Gun Dog Show' at Hertogenbosch.

The Dutch Retriever Club (for all retrievers) organizes two field trials every year (limited entry of only twelve dogs). It is very difficult to become a member of this Club. As one can imagine, it is hard to train a 'fully trained' Labrador with little opportunity to take part in field trials. The Dutch Labrador Club organizes a number of working tests, primarily with dummies.

To become a Dutch Champion it is not obligatory to get a field trial qualification. Four C.A.C.s (under at least three different judges), one of which must be after 27 months of age, are necessary for a final championship. Winning the Winner Show or the Labrador Retriever Club show provides two points.

The Winner title at the Winner Show is a special qualification that can be added to a dog's name —Winner '93.

The Netherlands has always been a very 'open' country. That means, e.g., that at Dutch shows many entries from abroad can be seen. Labradors from Belgium, France, Germany and some Scandinavian countries are frequently seen at shows in the Netherlands. The Dutch all-breed shows that have English judges are especially popular with breeders from other countries. For the Dutch retriever owner it is also rather easy to go to other countries to show their dogs.

Some of the Dutch dogs that have been of substantial influence to the Dutch Labrador population are: Ch. Ladylands Black Arrow (Ch. Sandylands Strinesdale O'Malley x Ch. Black Signet of Powhattan), Ch. Cranspire Skytrain (Cambremer Petrocelli x Poolstead Purpose of Cranspire), Wetherlam Nutcracker (Ch. Lindall Mastercraft x Wetherlam Sheba), and Ch. Balnova Sultan (Boothgates Headliner x Wetherlam Willow Warbler of Balnova).

During recent years the chocolates have become more popular. Wetherlam Nutcracker, who sired four Dutch champions (of which three are chocolate), especially stimulated this interest. Finally, some of the dogs that recently became a Dutch champion:

- **Fogel Hlara Napata** *(Wetherlam Nutcracker x Trinket of Tintagel Winds, Winner '89)*
- **Toplicht Tintagel's Tagel Moon** *(The Dog of Tintagel Winds x Ch. Rodarbal Rainbow)*
- **Brown Booby Winston van Toolenburg** *(Puh's Brown Autumn x Toplight Cracker's Comet)*
- **Balnova Sultan** *(Boothgates Headliner x Wetherlam Willow Warbler of Balnova)*
- **Charway Bally Marine** *(Ch. Charway Ballywillwill x Clarence Charway Sea Aster)*
- **Charway Bally Murdoch** *(Ch. Charway Ballywillwill x Clarence Charway Sea Aster)*
- **Fairywoods Lulu** *(Ch. Balnova Sultan x Ch. Fairywoods Acer)*

Dutch Ch./Ger. Ch./VDH Ch. Balnova Sultan (Boothgates Headliner x Wetherlam Willow Warbler of Balnova).

The chocolate bitch, Bacchus Balou From Galderlane (Dutch Ch. Balnova Sultan x Fairywoods Arrabelle) earned the title Junior World Ch. '91.

Dual Champion Goldaire Justa Honey owned by D.W. & C.J. Adams is one of only six Labradors with this status in New Zealand.

Lance Dickey, Lanmardic Kennels, with FTC Poolmanton Black Gem Q.C. at a New Zealand field trial.

Chapter 7

Labrador Retrievers in New Zealand

Author's note: In 1991, I had the great pleasure of visiting both the North and South islands of New Zealand where I met some wonderful people. A few of them have written a bit about their special Labrador interests for this chapter. Dave and Cynthia Adams were kind hosts to my friend, "Puss" Faiella and to me in their lovely Christchurch home. Dave's main concern and pleasure are field trials and training. We went along to see how the "Kiwis" do it. Here's what he has to say about New Zealand field trial Labradors.

In New Zealand we are fortunate to still have many acres of unspoiled natural habitat for upland game such as pheasant, quail, and chukar. And wetlands for waterfowl like mallard ducks. shovelers, Paradise ducks, Canada goose and Black Swan. The Canada goose season in Canterbury, N.Z. lasts for seven months. The geese congregate around Lake Ellesmere in large numbers and feed on the farmers' grain products in the early mornings and evenings. There is no limit to the number you are allowed to shoot, therefore bags of 50-60 birds are not uncommon. Big, strong, well-trained Labrador Retrievers are very much a part of this hunting scene. Most of these working Labradors carry English bloodlines close up in their pedigrees, therefore the difference in type between working and show has been reduced considerably. Field trialing has also helped narrow this gap as many hunters buy a puppy and then look to the Field Trial Club for advice and help to train their young dog. Many puppies from show backgrounds become very good workers and look like Labradors should.

Field trials started in New Zealand in the Canterbury area in the early 1930's. The first New Zealand Championship was held in 1938 at Mr. Yarr's property on the Selwyn River. There are now thirty-one field trial clubs throughout New Zealand. Each club has monthly club days open to all different breeds of gun dogs. The classes run are Open, Limit, Novice and Puppy. Clubs are authorized to run four annual championships for all breeds: retrievers, spaniels, pointers and setters. Championships are held in rough, rushy, marsh areas with plenty of heavy cover. The water part of trialing is usually over canals, creeks or swift flowing braided rivers.

Trials can consist of two to five sections depending on the size of the club and the grounds available. Each section has a different judge and will contain two or three marks or finds, four to fifteen retrieves in all. At least two of these retrieves must be across water. A dog must retrieve all game to hand to gain an aggregate of points to be in with a chance to win. The winner must have a score of 75% of the points available to be issued a Challenge Point. Six Challenge Points must be gained to become a Field

Trial Champion. In the event of a draw, a runoff is held to establish an outright winner.

All retrieves marked on a blind find are at a minimum distance of 65 meters, and a maximum distance of 100 meters. The areas selected for retrieving trials must be heavy enough to bring out the Labrador's marking abilities, and strength and courage, but still clear enough for the judge to see the dog and judge the event. Ladders and scaffolding are frequently used to elevate the judge and steward to a vantage point.

Judging is on a negative system with points deducted for faults from a standing total of approximately 50 points per retrieve. Areas of apptitude such as control, speed and style are judged over the whole event. The time for the retrieve is set by the judge, depending on the distance to swim and the heaviness of cover, but usually 6-8 minutes is allowed for a three bird retrieve.

Mechanical catapults are used to throw the birds—pigeons, pukekos or ducks. These game birds are shot by club members or hunters and kept frozen until required for a trial. Rabbits are also used for the blind bird finds, but are not popular with trial participants as many Labradors are trained **not** to pick up cold rabbits because of the 1080 poisoning done in Canterbury for vermin, and I presume the same bait is laid all over New Zealand.

The All Breeds Championship is open to all breeds of gun dogs and is probably unique to New Zealand trialing. It is geared to find the ultimate hunting dog, and Labradors excel in this trial, taking out most championships and, at times, filling all five placings. The trial is comprised of two sections, the first being a two bird heel retrieve from across water and out of thick cover approximately 80-100 meters. The dog is judged on his ability to mark the fall of the bird; finding it; and finally, his line back to the handler. The second section is a range, find and flush. Usually two kinds of planted dead game must be found and returned to hand, plus two homing pigeons to be flushed from electronically controlled traps.

After ranging, finding and retrieving the two dead birds, the dog is once more cast off to quarter the ground, keeping within gunshot range of the handler. When the dog winds the homing pigeon and is going into flush, the judge releases the pigeon from the controlled trap, the handler fires a blank shot while the bird is within gun range and the dog is expected to freeze, and is judged on his steadiness to shot and game and the quality of his flush. This event takes approximately twenty minutes from start to finish. Labradors perform well in this type of trial, but must be trained and kept in fit hunting condition to last the distance.

There are a number of noteworthy breeders in the South Island: Goldare, D. and S. Bryne; Ladogo, Mrs. D. Cooke; Lissara, N. and S. Davis; and Mascot, Mrs. S. Jackson, to name but a few.

Author's note: I'd like to add that when I judged The Canterbury Labrador Retriever Club show , there were field trial classes in which the dogs were taken to an area of trees and cover and were actually judged on retrieving dead game with blank shot, et al. There was avid participation, and I was pleased that the winning bitch in the show placed second in the well-attended field class. Profiles of some New Zealand kennels follow:

Southerly Labradors

I established Southerly 25 years ago—with Joan Antrobus joining me eight years ago. Although our kennels are geographically separate, we 'share' dogs and collaborate on breeding programs. My first 'proper' Labrador pup was Ch. Simonville Scuba Q.C. (Qualifying Certificate in the field awarded by the N.Z. Gundog Trial Assn.) She was a lovely bitch and I am so thankful that the standard that was set by her is one that I used as basis for future generations. She was truly dual purpose, something that comes through quite strongly in her descendants. Over the years the most competitively successful dogs we have bred have undoubtedly been: Grand Field Trial Champion Southerly Clouds (owners—I. and J. Hendren) and Grand Show Champion Southerly Shadow (owners—S. and G. Meredith); plus Dual Purpose Labs of the Year—Southerly Scuba Q.C. and Southerly Madam X (owners—D.L. & M. Dickey).

We have also bred guide dogs, T.V. performers, rough shooting dogs,

Grand Champion Southerly Shadow, owned by S. & G. Meredith. "Tommy" is the litter brother of Southerly Scuba Q.C. and the top winning Labrador of all time in New Zealand with 89 C.C., four B.I.S. All Breeds, a B.I.S. Labrador Championship Show 1990, B.I.S. Pal Blue Ribbon Show 1993, Labrador of the Year '88, '89, '90, '91 and '92. He was also Stud Dog of The Year in '90, '91 and '92.

hospital visitors, dogs used in classroom animal care lessons and, most important of all—companions. A busy dog is usually a happy one, and we give preference to new puppy owners who want to DO something with their Lab. Our puppies are well-handled as babies—they all come inside, and all have plenty of opportunity to explore new territory outside. When they go to their homes, they are well-equipped to start their new life upholding the Labrador tradition of being the best, and most versatile dog in the world.

The Labrador Club fosters the general purpose Labrador by holding regular training days for shooters, as well as shows and lectures for breeders and new puppy owners. They also have country walk days where babies are put into carry packs and lunches into knapsacks and thirty plus waving tails disappear into the bush.

We think of Labs as being bird dogs, but many New Zealand hunters use Labs for both goat and deer hunting. They are not used for bringing game down, but are finders. Although Labs don't feature in the obedience ring in large numbers, they do participate, and we had an obedience champion made up last year, Strangways Stardust, bred from show stock.

The Kiwi bird is the New Zealand national emblem. It is flightless and nocturnal, and is hardly ever seen. In a scientific project by the Department of Conservation, Labradors were trained by Mr. Rogan Colbourne to use their noses and sniff out Kiwis for study. Although they have to pass a test before they start working in the bush and forests, the dogs wear muzzles in case they get a little too enthusiastic. One dog may find 20 Kiwi burrows in a week when it would take 20 people a year to locate as many. The Labradors—known for their agility, intelligence and gentle nature—have helped the department find hundreds of Kiwis.

Labradors are not the number one rescue dogs overseas, but they are in New Zealand. Our very watery environment—lakes, rivers and an extensive coastline—mean that the chance of a natural disaster involving one or the other of these is very high. Of course, there is no dog better suited than our Labs for rescue in this environment. Recently the New Zealand Search Dogs Association was formed, and a branch, Alpine Rescue Dogs,

N.Z. Ch. Mardas Corn Barley (imp. U.K.) is a rough shooting dog and field trial winner, as well as a veteran of T.V. commercials. He also serves as a canine hospital visitor and accompanies a veterinarian during classroom talks on animal health care, owner—Mrs. Pat Woollaston, Southerly Kennels.

Southerly Scuba Q.C., a show group award winner and a field trial winner, was awarded the New Zealand Labrador Club Dual Purpose Dog of the Year award in 1988.

is composed of unpaid volunteers who willingly undertake demonstrations to promote the skills of the dogs. The dogs are trained in three environments: alpine and avalanche search; bush search; and disaster work.

—Mrs. Pat Woollaston, Southerly Kennels, Howick, near Auckland, New Zealand

Lanmardic Kennels

Lance and Maree Dickey use the Lanmardic Kennel prefix. Lance is a keen hunter who enjoys working his dogs in rough shooting conditions. He is also a Probationary Field Trial Judge. Maree is a qualified Championship Field Trial Judge for all breeds, and the Spaniel and Retriever groups in New Zealand, and a Star Championship Judge. They both share the showing of their Labs with their daughter Andrea. They owned the New Zealand Labrador Club Field Trial Dog of the Year 1979 and 1980, FC Poolmanton Black Gem Q.C., and four New Zealand Labrador Club Dual Purpose Dogs of the Year: N.Z. Ch. Beldon Drumfire Q.C., an All Breed Best in Show winner and winner of two Field Trial Challenge Points; Southerly Scuba Q.C., a show group award winner and FT winner; Southerly Madam X, New Zealand Labrador Club Field Trial Dog of the Year 1991; and her daughter, Lanmardic Dunedoo, a show awards winner.

Missenden Kennel

The Missenden Kennel of Mrs. Sally Oscar is also on the North Island of New Zealand. This kennel has been well known for many years, and Mrs. Oscar wrote the following:

My first Labrador litter was from all New Zealand lines and born in 1970. I then became more involved and imported my first stud dog from Australia. Over the years I have imported four dogs—two from England, and three bitches, all going back to the English lines that interested me.

*Eng./Aust./N.Z.
Champion Ballyduff
Marshal was im-
ported in 1977 by
Sally Oscar, New
Zealand, and Robert
Pargetter, Australia.*
Photo by Terry
Wilcock.

English, Australian, New Zealand Champion Ballyduff Marshal was imported to New Zealand in 1977 in partnership with Robert Pargetter of Tanton Kennels in Melbourne, Australia. Marshal turned three while in quarantine. He became a valued stud dog in both countries, but unfortunately died prematurely in 1982. We can still see the effect he has had on our Labradors today, several generations later, especially the lovely Ballyduff head.

Poolstead has also played a large part in my kennel, and I have stuck mainly to these two strains. Both, of course, go back to the great Eng. Ch. Sandylands Mark. I used Aust. Ch. Poolstead Probable twice, and then imported my own N.Z. Ch. Poolstead Puzzler, also by Ch. Poolstead Problem. Puzzler has given me some lovely puppies and is still with me, now twelve years old.

Croftsway Labradors

Mrs. Julie Bedford-Amoore's purchase of a yellow bitch puppy as a pet/gun dog in 1975 led to a lifetime hobby. N.Z. Ch. Willowstream Angel Gold Q.C. proved a fantastic buy for her young, novice exhibitor, gaining

*Driftway Dare To
Dance (Aust. Ch.
Driftway Dancing
Brave x Shakaranda
Half Penny), 14
months, and Balnova
Brando (Eng. Ch.
Keysun Krispin of
Blondella x Kupros
Miss Bramble of
Balnova), 5 1/2 years,
are recent imports by
the Croftsway Kennel.*

Grand Field Trial Champion Sandford Tudor Prince, owned and bred by Angela and David Murray.

her show title and working certificate. The highlight of her show career was BOB at the Nationals in 1979. Alas, she was not a good producer, so Aust./ N.Z. Ch. Gemcourt Powder Puff (in whelp to Oakhouse Classical Note of the U.K.) was imported, and so the Croftsway Kennel started. The emphasis has always been on breeding good, sound, typical Labradors that excel in temperament and working ability.

Highlights for the kennel have undoubtedly been the successes at the Labrador Club Championship Shows: Best in Show 1986, 1989 and 1993, all under English breeder-judges. In addition, several Croftsway Labradors have qualified as guide dogs. There have been additional imports, the latest of these being Driftway Dare to Dance (Aust.) and Balnova Brando (U.K.). Brando is the sire of the kennel's current star, N.Z. Ch. Gamelord Kiwi Magic. Julie is also the publisher of *The Labrador Spectrum*, a pedigree directory in New Zealand.

Sandford Kennel

The Sandford Kennel prefix belongs to Angela and David Murray. "In 1985 with a combination of good New Zealand lines, Te Reinga and Satin, we bred Grand Field Trial Champion Sandford Tudor Prince. His success in trialing is due to an excellent temperament with willingness to work and please. At eight years he has accumulated 35 challenges. To date his progeny have also inherited his temperament so the future looks bright for this kennel."

High Peak

Mrs. Susan Poulter has had Labradors since 1962. When she and her husband Dennis emigrated to New Zealand in 1976, they took along Madford Yellow Mustard from Mr. Eley. She promised to see that Mustard lived up to her breed description. So with the help of The Labrador Club and The North Auckland Gundog Club, Mustard was trained and earned her

Q.C. The judge, Mr. Alan Burt, gave her a mark of 96 points, the highest he had ever awarded. Mustard was mated with Ch. Strangways Buff in Australia and produced two male puppies. One of them, High Peak Jolly Swagman, became an N.Z. Champion and he has produced both guide dogs and rescue dogs. The other male from Mustard and Buff, High Peak Fair Dinkum, became a drug detection dog. "Dinkum" and his handler, Mr. Garry Puddy, were featured in a New Zealand television news program. This is surely an example of versatility.

When Mustard was mated with High Peak Throstlenest, a bitch from this union became N.Z. FTCh. High Peak Jessica Q.C.

Chapter 8

Labrador Retrievers in Norway

Author's note: Mrs. Eva Mjelde of Surprising Kennel has provided the following short history of Labradors in Norway.

Labradors did not arrive in Norway until after World War II. Norwegian military officers who were stationed in England during the war brought some Labradors with them when they returned home to Norway after 1945. A yellow dog called Barnawarne Brand (Guld Sandy x Covarne Judy) was probably the first. Later there was a yellow bitch, Knaith Caerlaverock Beetle (Poppleton Golden Russet x Knaith Brilliantine) imported in whelp from Mrs. Wormald's famous Knaith Kennels. A bitch from this litter was mated to another import, Thyrood Lieutenant (Bobby Macamber x Glance's Successor) and a dog from this mating became the breed's first Norwegian Champion in 1958.

At that time the American Ambassador to Norway brought a Labrador dog with him that was used at stud. He was called Normannstone Dwight (Am. Ch. Mumbery Plenty x Bowstones Sanda). Up to the late 60s little else was imported, and nearly all stock in Norway was descended from these few dogs. Growing rapidly popular, the breed became heavily inbred.

Vestvollen

The leading breeder at that time was Vestvollen Kennel. Their foundation bitch, Ch. Lissi, was a result of a father (Thyrood Lieutenant) to daughter mating. Her progeny started off several breeders in Scandinavia. Luckily in 1965 Vestvollens Kennel was able to import Sandylands Rough Tweed (Ch. Sandylands Tweed of Blaircourt x Sandylands Annabel) who became a Norwegian Champion. The stock in Norway was greatly improved by this beautiful black dog.

In the 70s the Labrador increased in popularity in a way not good for the breed, as there was not enough first class breeding stock. In 1970, 330 new Labs were registered—in 1975, there were 1,200 new registrations. Fortunately, the other retriever breeds became popular as well at the same time, and the registration figures for Labradors sank to a more normal level. Breeding material imported from both England and the other Scandinavian countries gradually took over.

Int./Nord. Ch. Licithas Blizzard (Nord. Ch. Baronor Phoenix x Norw. Ch. Licithas Poppet) owned by Anne and Harald Liland of Norway.

Norw. Ch. Surprising's Thelma (Int./Nord. Ch. Licithias Blizzard x Norw. Ch. Surprising's Norah), Norway's Top Dog 1990, owned by Eva and Ole Mjelde, Surprising Kennel, Norway.

Surprising, Licitha, Hrovan, Narjanas

In 1965, Sandylands Georgina, foundation bitch for the Surprising Kennel became the first imported bitch after the post war imports. The Surprising Kennel is still very active today, having recently bred their fiftieth champion, everyone directly descended from Sandylands Georgina.

The Licitha Kennel was founded in 1971. Their foundation bitch was Licitha (Int./Scan. Ch. Cookridge Ram x Samba) who became the breed's first Triple Champion. The majority of breeders today have started out with Licitha stock, one way or another.

Also, from this time, the Hrovan Kennel must be mentioned. Their foundation bitch was the chocolate, Int./Swed./Norw. Ch. Puhs Quidora (Puhs Freddy x Int. Ch. Puhs Chocolate Lady) from the famous Puhs Kennel in Sweden. The Hrovan stock founded the Narjanas Kennel in 1979—it is one of the top kennels today.

Cha, Pangro, Vihahund

Like in all other countries, breeders in Norway have been coming and going. However, most of them have been rather dedicated and always worked well together. The last 10 years or so, the most winning kennels have been: Cha, Pangro, Vihahund, Narjanas and Surprising. In 1990, a Labrador bitch, Norw. Ch. Surprising's Thelma, was Norway's Top Dog All Breeds, an all time record for the breed in Norway.

Norwegian Labradors have been good quality dogs with working abilities as well as being sound. The breed has never been split between field trial and show, and dogs competing in field trials are either show dogs or dogs with show stock backgrounds. In Norway the Standard is always the country of origin, so the English Labrador Standard is the one we use here.

Labradors in Norway are used as guide dogs for the blind; sniffer dogs for the police; avalanche rescue dogs; tracking dogs; and, of course, as family dogs, as well as gun dogs.

FC/Obed. Ch./Show Ch. Brigade Highway Man is one of the few triple champion Labrador Retrievers in the world.

Peter and Jane Horley's Ch. Winston of the Hussars (Sandylands Trade Wind x Charmaine of Cannobie Lee).

Chapter 9

Labrador Retrievers in South Africa

Author's note: Mr. Rod Copestake has taken the time to do a write-up about South Africa. He and his wife, Carmen, and their Breckondale Labradors are known the world over, and I certainly appreciate their help.

As a breed the Labrador Retriever has been known in South Africa for many years, the first registration having been recorded by the Kennel Union of Southern Africa in 1926. The Labrador Retriever Kennel Club of South Africa had its beginnings in 1957 when a small group of enthusiasts gathered in Johannesburg to form a club to promote the best interests of the breed in the country.

This club remains the only body in South Africa devoted purely to the interests of the Labrador, and its championship show attracts by far the largest entry of the breed each year, hence its insistence on appointing only breed specialists to judge the event. It is rightly regarded as the premier event for Labradors on the show calendar. Casting one's eyes down the list of Best-in-Show winners produces a veritable 'who's who' of the history of the breed in the country.

The first Championship Show was held in 1967, so 1992 produced the Club's twenty-fifth anniversary show. The event was suitably celebrated by a record entry that saw over a hundred dogs present on the day of the show.

Since its formation the Club has maintained very close links with the United Kingdom. It has pursued a deliberate policy of inviting British judges to officiate at both its' field trials and the annual championship show. Sadly in recent times, only Mrs. Sandra Halstead (Drakeshead) has been in a position to undertake both responsibilities which she did in 1987. During the 1970s however, South Africa was host to Mrs. Ann Wynyard (1972); Mrs. Audrey Radclyffe (1974) and the late Geoff Robinson (Mallardhurn) in 1977, all of whom attended to both the trials and the shows.

It was during the 1980s that entries at the Championship Show really started to climb and the popularity of the breed as a show dog, working dog and companion began to become apparent. Over the past ten years the Labrador has consistently occupied a position in the top four breeds of Kennel Union registrations.

Of great assistance in promoting the interests of the breed were the British judges who visited us during this period. In 1979 the Championship Show was judged by the late Bridget Docking and she was followed by Mrs. Margot Woolley (1981); Mrs. Gwen Broadley (1984); Mrs. Heather Wiles (1985); Mrs. Sandra Halstead (1987); Mrs. Pat Dunstan (Australia 1988); Mrs. Glenda Crook (1989); Mr. John Steven (1991); Mr. Jim Nolan (1992) and Mr. Bob Plumpton of Australia in 1993. Each and every one of them has proved to be a wonderful ambassador and added greatly to the South African's appreciation of the Labrador with their own knowledge and insight of the breed.

The Gundog Club of South Africa is located in Johannesburg and breed specialists are also regularly invited by gun dog clubs located in the Cape and Natal. In addition, there are approximately thirty all breed clubs offering Challenge Certificates. The majority of these are located in the large commercial areas of Johannesburg and the Witwatersrand, the Cape and Natal.

Five points are required to 'make up' a champion and each Challenge Certificate is worth either one point or two points depending on the number of dogs entered and beaten. The system works effectively, and approximately five or six new champions are created each year, a number that is not considered to be excessive for the breed. Champions are permitted to continue competing for Challenge Certificates, although a Champion Class does exist, the winner of which would compete against the Challenge Certificate winners for Best of Breed.

Singling out individual dogs for special mention in a brief review of this nature is a particularly hazardous pastime but, in reality, the review would not be complete without mentioning a few very special dogs who have done so much to popularize the breed in South Africa. They must include Rose Marie Cabion's Ch. Sleepy Hollow Follytower Old Oak (Ch. Ballyduff Hollybranch of Keithray x Follytower Silsdale Old Chelsea) who was a huge winner in the Cape and a very prepotent sire. Peter and Jane Horley's Ch. Winston of the Hussars (Sandylands Trade Wind x Charmaine of Cannobie Lee) who was campaigned with much the same degree of success and notoriety, during the same period in the Transvaal.

More recently there was Rod and Carmen Copestake's Ch. Balrion Lord of the Manor of Breckondale (Ch. Squire of Ballyduff x Sh. Ch. Balrion Wicked Lady) who won six successive Challenge Certificates at the Labrador Retriever Club Championship Show (four times going Best in Show) between the years 1981 to 1986 inclusive. He was also an all-breed Best in Show winner and holds 48 Best of Breed wins—a record for dogs in the breed. He subsequently sired 19 champions, three who have, in turn, followed their sire's footsteps by going Best in Show at the Specialty Club.

Joan van Niekerk, under her Jeronga prefix, did a great deal to popularize the chocolate in both Cape Town and Johannesburg. She was

Left, Ch. Balrion Lord of the Manor of Breckondale (Ch. Squire of Ballyduff x Sh. Ch. Balrion Wicked Lady) and right, Ch. Sandylands Master Piece of Breckondale.

very successful with her bitch, Ch. Jeronga's Glowing Flame, who was a superb example of the type. Another successful show bitch was Ch. Emanzini's Green Cascade of Merrowspring. She was Reserve Best in Show at the prestigious Goldfields Championship Show, and she matched her sire, Ch. Balrion Lord of the Manor of Breckondale in Best of Breed wins.

Perhaps the most noteworthy single accomplishment was the win recorded by a yellow Labrador bitch, Ch. Breckondale Caprice (by Ch. Sandylands Carl of Jeronga) who was inaugural winner of the Kennel Unions National Championships (all breeds) in 1980. She was later joined by her daughter, Ch. Breckondale Calf Love (sired by Ch. Sandylands Master Piece of Breckondale) as an all-breed Best in Show winner. This started a dynasty of winning Breckondale bitches which continues to this day. Best-in-Show wins at Specialty shows have since been recorded by

Ch. Emanzini's Green Cascade of Merrowspring owned by Joan van Niekerk, Jeronga.

Ch. Breckondale Silver Skates was BIS L.R. K.C. Championship, October 1993. She is owned by Mr. and Mrs. R.N. Copestake.

their direct descendants, Ch. Breckondale True Love and Ch. Breckondale Silver Skates.

Finally no review would be complete without a mention of Mike and Bernadette Gie's locally bred Brigade Highway Man who is one of the world's few triple champions—in obedience, show and field.

Field trialing is a popular activity and a great amount of effort is spent in training dogs to the gun and in mounting field trial events. These are run under the auspices of the breed clubs, and are recognized by the Kennel Union in awarding the title of field trial champion. Equally the Labrador is much in demand as a working dog by the Guide Dogs Association for the Blind and by the Gold Mines for security and detection work—all proof of our breed's huge versatility and skill.

The Labrador supporters of South Africa owe a very special gratitude to the breeders of the United Kingdom who have done so much over the years to provide help and guidance, and who have sent out so many carefully bred youngsters to assist in the development of the breed in this country.

Chapter 10

Labrador Retrievers in Sweden

Author's note: Mr. Jan-Erik Ek of Thornbreaker Kennel, in Soderkoping, Sweden, has sent a history of the breed in his country.

Until the early '70s, the Labrador Retriever was not a breed generally known to the Swedish, however, in 1971 big things happened. The yellow import, Int./Nordic Sh. Ch./Swed. FT Ch. Powhatan Sentry, bred by Major and Mrs. Aikenhead, imported and owned by Mr. Inge and Mrs. Ing-Marie E-son Thoor (later, Ing Marie Hagelin) of the Kamrats Kennel, hit the spotlight by being crowned 'Golden Dog of the Year'—all breeds. That same year Swed. Obedience Ch. Nattens Oberon won the award 'Obedience Dog of the Year'—again all breeds. Two such major awards did not pass the scene unrecognized, and registrations quickly started to increase. Oberon was bred by Mrs. Sigyn Littorin, one of the most respected all-rounders in Scandinavia and, indeed, a very respected Labrador judge, not only in Sweden, but on the continent and in the U.K. Although she did not breed many litters, several 'Nattens' Labradors achieved major awards at championship shows as well as at championship field trials, and several were made up into champions.

Kamrats, Puhs

The Thoors purchased their first Labrador in 1957, Baskervillers Hund Black Beauty, and then imported several dogs from Mrs. Yvonne Pauling's Cookridge Kennel in Yorkshire. They also made up two homebred triple champions, Swed. Ch./OTCh./FTC Kamrats Frida and Swed. Ch./OTCh./FTC Kamrats Buse. The latter was by Eng. Ch. Sandylands Mark out of Norw. Sh. Ch. Ramah Chocolate Chip who was mated to Mark before she left England. Since the mid-'80s, Inge E-son Thoor has run Kamrats Kennel on his own and has made up the yellow male, Int. Ch. Kamrats Magic Man, and the black bitch, Swed. Ch. Kamrats Tilda. In 1960 Kamrats kennel imported the first chocolate Labrador into Sweden, Swed. Ch. Cookridge Cola, who did not only win her title, but was also a Group winner. A daughter out of Cola, the chocolate Int./Swed./Norw./SB Ch. Kamrats Careena, was purchased by Mrs. Brit-Marie Brulin, who later became known world-wide for her super chocolate Labradors bred under the affix 'Puh,' taken from Mrs. Brulin's first Labrador, Kamrats Puh. Later the black Int./Nordic Ch. Cookridge Raamah arrived at Puh's and Careena

Triple Champion Kamrats Buse (Eng. Ch. Sandylands Mark x Norw. Sh. Ch. Ramah Chocolate Chip) owned and trained by Inge Thoor and Ing Marie Hagelin. Photo by Lars Söderbom.

was mated to him to produce the chocolate bitch Ch. Puhs Chocolate Lady. Raamah was a son of Eng. Ch. Cookridge Tango so there were quality chocolates on both sides of the pedigree. Lady mated to the black, Ch. Nattens Domino, produced the chocolate, Ch. Puhs Chocolate Beauty, and Lady to Ch. Puhs Freddy produced Ch. Puhs Quidora, the first chocolate Labrador to go Best In Show at an all-breed championship in Norway. I'm sure, the best-known chocolate Puh Labrador for U.S. exhibitors is Swed./ Norw./Am. Ch. Puhs Superman, who went Best In Show at the 1981 National Specialty and, who I understand, has had a great impact on today's American chocolate Labradors.

Imp's, Aroscas, Country Songs

Ballyduff Maroon, a dominant black dog by Eng. Ch. Sandylands Mark x Ch. Ballyduff Marina bred by Mrs. Docking, was imported at the beginning of the Seventies and produced many champions. His grandson, Ch. Puhs Imp (out of Puhs Cardemon, a daughter of Ch. Puhs Chocolate Beauty, went to Mrs. Inger Olofsson, Imp's Kennel, and she has line bred to him with great success. One example of this is Imp's Batman who in his turn has produced CC winning offspring. Indeed, several breeders of the '60s and '70s purchased their foundation stock from Mr. & Mrs. E-son

Thoor or Mrs. Brulin, one being Mrs. Gunilla Andersson, Aroscas Labradors. Her first Labrador was Puhs Malva who was mated to Ch. Nattens Yellon to produce Swed. Ch. Aroscas Arosca. Later, she imported from Mrs. Gwen Broadley's Sandylands Kennel—one being the black Swed. Dual Ch. Sandylands Mamba (Eng. Ch. Sandylands Mark x Eng. Ch. Sandylands Dancer) who produced many champions. She also imported Nord. Ch. Sandylands Midnight Maestro and, in the '80s, the half-brothers Sandylands Night Flight (who later went to join Dee Fair Kennel in Denmark) and Sandylands April Madness, both by sons of Eng. Ch. Sandylands Mark out of Eng. Ch. Sandylands Longley Come Rain. She recently exported Aroscas Sophisticated Lady to the U.S. where she quickly gained her title. Mrs. Andersson bred Ch. Aroscas Fight who was a very successful yellow dog in the '70s and who went Best In Show at an all-breed championship show in Norway. She also bred Swed. Ch. Aroscas Country Song who was sold to Mrs. Mona Holmquist, Country Songs Kennel. This bitch was a very consistent winner during her career and proved herself as a brood bitch, too. Mrs. Holmquist imported the black male Wishwood Shuttle (litter brother to Eng. Sh. Ch. Wishwood Shaft) bred by Mrs. Mollie Rayment, and he has been producing winning offspring. Mr. Lars and Mrs. Anita Grans bought Country Songs Happy Lass who was by Sandylands April Madness out of Swed. Ch. Aroscas Country Song. She was mated to Shuttle to produce the yellow bitch Boldwinds Hold Me Tight, a very successful exhibit in the breed as well as in Groups and Best In Show finals.

Alvgardens, Jidjis

Mrs. Majvor Nasman of Alvgardens Kennel, started with the black bitch Sandylands Twanah (Eng. Ch. Sandylands Tweed of Blaircourt x Sandylands Tanita) who was the first in a long line to become a champion. This kennel is as flourishing today as in its youth and there seem to be no end to its successes—the number of champions increasing all the time. Early in the '70s, Mrs. Nasman imported the black male, Eng. Ch. Black Eagle of Mansergh from Mrs. Roslin-Williams. He produced several champions—his son out of Twanah, Swed. Ch. Alvgardens Midnight, a chocolate carrier, was used some at stud. A granddaughter of Black Eagle of Mansergh and Sandylands Twanah, Gunsmoke Eliza, joined the kennel in the late '70s This bitch not only become a champion, but a producer of champions that is rarely seen. Her influence on the breed was not only at Alvgarden, but all over the country. Her granddaughter, the chocolate Ch. Alvgardens Shoe Shone, through her son, Ch. Alvgardens Brizard, has been a big winner with several Groups as well as placing in the BIS finals at all-breed championship shows. She is, I'm sure, the most winning chocolate for many years in this country. The dam of Shoe Shone, Swed. Ch. Alvgardens XPrincess, has also produced several other champions and

Int./Swed./Finn. Ch. Gunsmoke Eliza was a successful producer for Alvgardens with 17 champions.

is by the import Ch. Poolstead Pick Of The Pops (Ch. Fabracken Comedy Star x Ch. Poolstead Pictorial). A yellow bitch, Swed. Ch. Jidjis Buttercake, also joined Alvgarden in the '60s. She was sired by Black Seth of Ide out of Dryhill Wedding Cake. She was a Group winner and placed in BIS finals at all-breed championship shows and was a good brood, too, being the dam of Ch. Alvgardens Black Eve. She was bred by Mrs. Mona Iletorp who was co-owner of the Jidjis affix, but later applied for an affix of her own—Ingmos.

Ingmos, Minvans

During the early '70s, Puhs Black Bird (Int./Swed./Norw. Sh. Ch. Nattens Domino x Int./Swed./Norw. Ch. Puhs Chocolate Lady) bred by Mrs. Brulin arrived at Ingmos and mated to the yellow import Swed. Ch. Pendil of Ballyduff produced Swed. Ch. Ingmos Umberto, a very successful black male. His full brother, Ingmos Yster, also became a champion and a noted stud dog. Mrs. Ulla Persson of Minvans Kennel owned Ingmos Yster. Her foundation was an Av. Oppensten bitch (bred by this country's grand old lady in the breed, the late Mrs. Irma Brusewitz-Olsen—acquired in the '60s and, mated to Swed. Ch. Sandylands Wiseman, produced the black CC winner Minvans Cijoppa. Swed. Ch. Minvans Junior was a very consistent winner in the late '70s.

Mallards, Wimsey's, Cindys

Mr. Arnfinn and Mrs. Brit Hävaker's first Labrador was Ch. Puhs Christopher Robin. The Hävakers acquired his granddaughter, Garpabackens Nana, and she proved to be a marvelous brood, producing several winners when bred to Ballyduff Maroon—one being Swed. Ch. Mallards Big Hole Demon. Later the Hävakers imported the black male Ch. Ballyduff Fergus (Ch. Timspring Sirius x Spark of Ballyduff). They also

Swed. Ch. Attikonak
Khatrine owned by
Mrs. Gunilla Ek.

imported the bitch Curnafame Strike, and when mated to Ch. Licithas Faithful Apporter, she produced the well-known black male, Int./Nordic Ch. Mallards Clay Basker, who in turn produced many winners. One of his daughters, Highstone Julie (out of a Ch. Pendil of Ballyduff daughter) became the foundation for Miss Lena Bjornelin Wimsey's Kennel and Julie has produced several winners, one being the yellow CC winning male, Wimseys Tedeum. Wimseys Autumn Passion, a black bitch line bred to

Int./Nordic Ch.
Mallards Clay Basker
(Ch. Licithas Faithful
Apporter x
Curnafame Strike)
bred and owned by
Mr. & Mrs. Hävaker.

Smart Fellows Order From New York owned and bred by Mrs. Yvonne Westerlund.

Julie, won the Bitch CC and BOB under Mrs. R. V. Hepworth at this year's Club Championship show.

Mrs. Inger Lindgren, Cindys Kennel, imported Baronor Phoenix (Eng. Ch. Sandylands Mark x Baronor Vesta), litter brother to Eng. Ch. Baronor Pegasus. He quickly won his title and stamped his mark on the breed— many kennels of today have this dog in their pedigrees. Phoenix sired the big winner, Norw. Ch. Licithas Blizzard, who in turn is the sire of Eng. Ch. Aditis Becky of Foxrush. Another son of Phoenix, the CC winning black, Cindys Lord, mated to Phoenix's full sister, Swed. Ch. Baronor Linnet Of Cindys, produced Swed. Ch. Cindys Vesta. Later Mrs. Lindgren imported the litter brother of Eng. Ch. Kupros Master Mariner, Kupros Major at Lindall, and he is behind winners in this country as well as in Norway and the U.K.

Willows, Attikonak

Mrs. Lili Lagerquist, Willows Kennel, bought her first Labrador in the early '60s, and bred her first litter in 1968. Her initial champion, Swed. Ch. Willows Illbatting, did well in the show ring and, in the early '80s, she imported the black male Powhatan Black Cedar from the Aikenheads. He sired some good-looking working stock, among them Swed. Triple Ch. Askrikes Dennis (out of Willows Leading Lady) and Swed. Ch. Willows Nefer.

Mrs. Gunilla Ek, Attikonak, purchased her first Labrador in the late '60s. In the mid-'70s she imported the black male Grock of Mansergh (by Ch. Groucho of Mansergh) from Mrs. Roslin Williams and he produced winning stock. Successful exhibits from the Poolstead Kennel followed— the yellow bitches Pigtail, Past Participle, and Premonition. The last one, Poolstead Pop Socks, has just been made up, as were Past Participle and

Premonition. Mrs. Ek also bred Swed. Ch. Attikonak Khatrine and Swed. Ch. Attikonak Margreth O'Kelley, both successful exhibits in their youth as well as in their older days. In addition, she bred the winning black male, Ch. Attikonak Mister Mac Cloud, sired by Ballyduff Maroon.

Winnies, Guidelines

Mrs. Pia Razera Brulin, Winnies Kennel, bought two puppies from Mrs. Brulin in 1973—a black male, Puhs Black Thunder (Swed. Ch. Nattens Domino x Puhs Chocolate Lady), and a yellow bitch, Puhs Artiga Marta (Swed. Ch. Chruston Wapanichki of Trewinnard x Gunsmoke Amulette). Black Thunder and Artiga Marta were mated and produced the yellow bitch Swed. Ch. Winnies Actress. When Actress was mated to Ch. Baronor Phoenix, she produced Swed. Ch. Winnies Kliche, a yellow who did a great deal of winning. Kliche' mated to Swed. Ch. Deras Dovregutten (a grandson of Phoenix) produced the group-winning yellow male, Swed. Ch. Winnies Wide Type. Mrs. Brulin also imported the black male Novacroft Arris (Angolcroft William of Novacroft x Novacroft Coffee Time) bred by Mrs. Dorothy Gardner and he has produced many winners. She also imported the black CC winning male Crawcrook Calihban from Mrs. Linda Redmile.

Mrs. Eva Gustafsson, Guidelines Kennel, have often used the services of Mrs. Razera Brulin's stud dogs with successful results, one being Guidelines Mish Mash a black CC winning bitch that has been Group placed, too. Mrs. Gustafsson imported Cambremer Copy Cat (Eng. Ch. Kupros Master Mariner x Cambremer Montclair) from the Brabbans in whelp to Eng. Sh. Ch. Rocheby Royal Oak to produce this country's record CC winner (to date), Guideline's Copy Right, a black male.

Minnows, Thornbreaker, Smart Fellows

In 1971 Mrs. Charlotte Lindell, Minnows Kennel, imported the yellow bitch, Roydwood Right In Line (Roydwood Royal Tan x Eng. Sh. Ch. Roydwood Right On Time) from Mr. Michael Boothroyd, and in 1980 the yellow bitch Sandylands Poser (Eng. Sh Ch. Poolstead Problem x Eng. Sh. Ch. Sandylands Midnight Magic) from Mrs. Gwen Broadley. Poser came in whelp to Sh. Ch. Sandylands My Rainbeau and the yellow male Minnows Pompe and yellow bitch Minnows Polly, both CC winners, are both her offspring. Another Poser daughter sired by Swed. Ch. Baronor Phoenix, the CC winning yellow, Minnows Nelly, mated to Nor. Ch. Surprising Mathias produced the Group winning yellow bitch, Minnows Tilda. Poser mated to Norw. Ch. Licithas Blizzard produced Minnows Winter Whizz, a CC winning yellow male. Recently, Mrs. Lindell has started to mix her show stock with British field trial lines. An example of this is Minnows Walter Scott who recently won his first CC. He is the son of Minnows Zittra (the result of a half brother/sister mating, M. Winter Whizz x M. Polly) mated to Blackthorn Briar (a Scottish-bred field dog).

Jan-Erik Ek, Thornbreaker's Kennel, bought his first Labrador in 1973 from Mrs. Lindell—Minnows Leonora, a yellow daughter of Ch. Powhatan Sentry out of Roydwood Right In Line. When bred to Puhs Tony (son of Am./Swed. Ch. Puhs Superman) she produced, Mr. Ek's Rodarbal Maxi, a chocolate CC winning male who in his turn sired a chocolate CC winning daughter. In 1987 Mr. Ek imported an Eng. Ch. Fabracken Comedy Star daughter, Glebehouse Black Pearl of Fabracken, from Miss Anne Taylor. She became the dam of the CC winning black male, Thornbreakers Talk Of Town. Later he imported Blondella Bally Who, litter brother to Eng. Sh. Ch. Blondella Ballerina. 'Bally Who' has produced many winners including Norway's 1992 top show Labrador, Norw. Ch. Balrion Him of Praise, bred by the Crooks in the U.K.

Mrs. Yvonne Westerlund, Smart Fellows Kennel, bought her first Labrador in 1972, and in 1982, the yellow bitch Minnows Lucinda (Swed. Ch. Baronor Phoenix x Minnows Polly) bred by Mrs. Lindell. In 1985 she imported the black male Stowlodge Stoddart (Wishwood Quincey x Cornlands Brun) bred by the Bevans, and his full sister, Stowlodge Quintette joined him shortly afterwards. Both these dogs have produced winners and Mrs. Westerlund has built up a strong line of dogs as well as bitches thanks to 'Quintette' who has been an excellent brood. Her yellow daughter, Smart Fellows With Class And Style (by Balnova Super Tramp), her black son, Smart Fellows Order From New York, and her black daughter, Smart Fellows Our Dream Of Mite (by Am./Can. Ch. Tweedcroft Debonair) are all big winners in the ring. Order From New York has a runner-up in the Group to his credit and is the sire of several CC winners. In 1988 Smart Fellow's won Best Breeders' Group In Show all-breeds, a major award, at the big International Show in Stockholm.

When it comes to the amount and consistency of winning, no kennels are close to the achievements made by Alvgarden Kennel and Smart Fellows Kennel at present.

SECTION VI
The Basis of Heredity

Left, Ch. Ayr's Sea Mark, WC, owner-breeder Nancy Martin, Ayr. Right, his sister Ch. Ayr's Sea Mist of Kenbru co-owned by Nancy Martin and Joyce Lindsay. Photo by Christine Watt.

Chapter 1

Basic Genetics

The study of genetics can be complicated and difficult to understand, but in the breeding of any animal, the background is extremely important. The more one knows about the ancestors of an individual dog, the more one can predict the qualities of its offspring. Pedigree study can be instructive as to desired qualities, such as cleared eye conditions, good hip status, and if you are really familiar with the dogs in the background, you will know about temperament, retrieving ability, color, good or bad structural points and such important things as coat, marking skills, style, expression, head, feet and beauty. Certainly the more information you have about ancestral qualities, both good and bad, the better you can plan a breeding program. There is one advantage of advanced age for a breeder: One can usually remember that old Ch. What's His Name back in the fifth generation was a good-looking Labrador but produced a lot of hip dysplasia.

Consistent breeding of show quality dogs should be considered an art. To some breeders it comes naturally. Others have to learn this art. Still others will never achieve success in this vital and important facet of purebred dogs.

To some breeders having an eye for a dog is second nature. Breeders lacking this natural talent can become self-taught provided they have the intelligence and motivation to discern between the good and poor examples set before them.

Consistent breeding of show-quality specimens depends on important factors beyond the natural or acquired talents of the breeder. The breeding stock itself is of prime importance and should be the very best the breeder can obtain. Many breeders still operate under the illusion that second best will produce as well as the choice specimen, pedigrees being equal.

Another important element contributing to the success or failure of any given breeding program is that of chance. Everything else being equal, sex distribution, puppy mortality, timing, transmission of the best factors (or the poorest), etc., all depend to a great extent on chance.

There is no shortcut to breed improvement, no miraculous or secret formula that can put Mother Nature out of business and place the breeder in full control. There are, however, many do's and don't's which can be used to minimize the chances of failure and to encourage the chances of success. These do's and don't's are axioms of our breed, yet there are breeders who ignore and bypass them.

The first step in your breeding program is to decide what is ideal. Until a breeder knows what kind of specimen he wants, he is stopped cold and can neither select the best nor discard the worst. This is where the breeder's capabilities and talents come into play. For this is the basis of selective breeding, and the backbone of any breeding program.

Characteristics such as height and coat color are known as inherited traits. They are traits that offspring inherit or receives from parents. Inherited traits are passed along from generation to generation. As a result of heredity, each generation is linked to older generations and to past generations. For example, a dog may resemble his parents with respect to height, head shape and coat color. His grandsire or great grandsire may have also possessed the same identifying features.

A whole science known as genetics has grown up around the study of heredity. Specifically, the science of genetics is the study of how the reproduction process determines the characteristics of an offspring and how these characteristics are distributed.

According to Anthony Smith, writing in *The Human Pedigree*:

Gregor Mendel, a nineteenth-century monk living in Czechoslovakia, is credited as the founder of genetics. Basically, Mendel's work had proved that traits can be passed from one generation to the next, both with mathematical precision and in separate packets. Before this time, it had been assumed that inheritance was always the result of being colored water of a weaker hue. Mendel foresaw genes, the differing units of inheritance (that are named, incidentally, after the Greek for race). Genes remain distinct entities. They do not blend, like that of colored water. They produce, to continue the analogy, either plain water, or colored water or a mixture between the two. Moreover, assuming no other genes are involved to complicate the story, they continue to create three kinds of product in generation after generation. The packets remained distinct.

The mathematics also has a pleasing simplicity at least in the early stages. The human blue-eye/brown eye situation is a good elementary example. There are genes for brown and genes for blue, everybody receives one of each from each parent. To receive two browns is to be brown-eyed. To receive two blues is to be blue-eyed. To receive one of each is also to be brown-eyed because the brown has the effect of masking the relative transparency of the blue.

This also signifies that brown is dominant over blue and will always cover over the recessive blue color. Blue will only be expressed when it, as a recessive, is inherited from both parents.

The clarity of Mendel's vision certainly helped science. It was assumed that all of inheritance was equally clear cut, with a ratio of 3:1, or his equally famous ratio of 9:3:1 (involving two characteristics) explaining all of our genetic fortunes. So they do, in a sense, but the real situation is much more complex. Only a few aspects of inheritance are controlled by a single pair of genes. Only a few more are controlled by two pairs. A feature like height, for example, or coat color may be organized by 20 or so pair of genes. Each pair is working in a Mendelian manner, but the cumulative effect of all of them working together is a bewilderment.

There are literally thousands and thousands of paired genes within each animal. There are enough of them, and enough possible variations, to ensure that each specimen is unique. Never in history has there been a duplicate of any specimen. Never in all of future history will there be another one just like it again. Each dog is a combination that is entirely individual and yet his genes are common to the population they live in. There is nothing unique about them .

Piggybacking now upon Mendel's work and that of later scientists, let us look at how breeders can use this knowledge and breed better dogs.

Each dog contains a pair of genes in each of its cells for each trait that it inherits. One of the genes is contributed by the sire and the other by the dam. When a black Labrador is bred to a yellow one, all the first generation offspring will be black. Each parent contributed one gene for color to each offspring. Since they were different colors, the offspring were hybrid. One parent, contributed a "factor" for black color while the other parent passed along a "factor" for yellow coat color. Why, then, were all the hybrid offspring black? Because black is dominant over yellow.

The recessive characteristic (yellow) was the hidden or masked one that did not appear in the hybrid offspring. A dog can show a recessive trait such as a yellow coat only when both factors (genes) are recessive in one individual. The dominant trait will appear only when one or both genes are present.

To clarify matters a bit, let's see what happens when an all-black hybrid specimen is crossed with another just like it. Every hybrid can pass on to each of its offspring either black or yellow characteristics. Therefore, yellow and black have a 50/50 chance of being transmitted to the offspring. These hybrids have a black (dominant) gene and a yellow (recessive) gene. Lets symbolize them B-Dominant, b Recessive. It is possible to predict not only the possible combinations of factors, but also the probability for each of the combinations. (See illustrations.)

Chance plays a part in both the biological and physical worlds. Mendel was aware of this and knew something of the laws of probability. He used these in explaining his results. These laws say to be wary of interpreting the occurrence of a single random event. However, Mendel goes on to postulate that if large numbers of occurrences of the same event take place at random, there is a kind of order in the result in spite of the uncertainty of the occurrence of a single event.

By moving from the inheritance of a single trait to the inheritance of two traits simultaneously, life gets a bit more complex. Start by breeding a homozygous (pure) black dog that is tall (also homozygous) to a short yellow specimen that is also homozygous for its traits. Naturally enough, the breeding produces tall black offspring, since those traits are dominant. They look exactly like the black parent. Take these hybrid offspring that are hybrid tall-hybrid black and mate them with like specimens. The resultant types are quite interesting. There will be four different types produced. There will be a small black type and a tall yellow one. These types are new combinations of the two traits.

Continuing in this vein, and for all other traits as well, the distribution ratio turns out to be 9:3:3:1. This means for every nine tall black dogs in a hybrid X hybrid mating there will be three tall dogs with yellow coats, three small dogs with black coats and one short yellow specimen.

A quick glance at the above will show 12 tall dogs to four short ones and 12 blacks to four yellows. Both demonstrate the 3:1 ratio already established for the inheritance of a single trait in which segregation occurs.

Mendel and later researchers uncovered the fact that, for example, tallness is independent of color. This is called the law of independent assortment and is supported by numerous experiments. The probability of two or more related events is calculated by multiplying the individual probabilities. Thus, if the probability of one event occurring is 1/4 and the probability of a simultaneous event is also 1/4, then the probability of the two occurring together is 1/4 X 1/4 or 1/16, that is, one in every 16.

In breeding for color in dogs, we find that the majority of factors that determine coat color appear to be single factors, inherited according to Mendel's laws. However, many of these color factors are influenced by other genes that have the ability to modify the expression of the key gene in numerous ways and thus account for considerable variation in the finished product. As an example, while a dog may possess the key genes that have the ability to create the Black and Tan pattern, independent modifying genes may alter its appearance by restricting or by allowing full expression to the tan pigment in its coat, so that it looks like a black dog or a tan dog.

Though the color of a dog's coat may be determined by a single gene or by a pair of genes, the skeletal structure of a dog is determined by the interaction of a large number of genes. It should be easy to understand why something as highly complex as the structure of a dog's head or body is controlled by the actions of multiple hereditary factors.

Movement is a good example. No one gene labeled gait has the ability to determine whether an individual puppy will move properly or improperly. Rather, there are countless genes, working in concert which determine these facts.

What factors enable an individual dog to move in a way that has been designated as correct for its particular breed? Every breed has a characteristic gait, which is determined by its structure—not the structure of the legs, or the feet, or the hips, or the shoulders, but the structure of all the parts working in concert for this breed. Thus, the Chow Chow moves with short steps and stilted action, the Pekinese and Bulldog roll along, and the German Shepherd Dog covers ground rapidly with far-reaching steps and a smooth action. These differences in gait are the result of differences in structure—the manner in which all the body parts are assembled in an individual.

Any attempt to explain multiple-factor inheritance fully would prove to be a real puzzle, for most dog breeders have no formal training in advanced genetics. However, the following facts may serve to give a better understanding of this complex subject:

1. What is seen and described as a single characteristic (leg, foot, tail, etc.) is often affected and influenced in its development by a large number of different and unrelated genes that are capable of independent assortment.

2. It is extremely difficult to sort out the various genes that influence a particular characteristic and to determine the specific effect each has on that characteristic. In other words, just how important is a given gene in the development of a particular characteristic?

3. Some genes have a direct, complete influence on the development of a characteristic (dominant genes). Some have only a partial effect, being neutralized to some extent by the action of the opposing member of the pair of which it is one (incompletely dominant genes). Some genes are completely masked and have no effect unless such genes comprise both members of a given pair (recessive genes).

4. The combination of multiple-gene effects together with environmental influences is the rule rather than the exception in such characteristics as body length, height, weight, head and muzzle development, tooth characteristics, foot size and shape, muscle and bone development, and such recognized faults as loose shoulders, flat ribs, cowhocks, weak pasterns and splay feet. As

an example, body size depends upon some genes that affect all the tissue and upon others that influence only certain regions, such as the legs, neck, head or tail. In addition, diet, exercise and other environmental influences determine the degree to which genes are able to stimulate and produce growth of the different tissues, organs and body parts.

There are more than 135 breeds eligible for registration with the American Kennel Club. None of the breeds is purebred in the true genetic sense of the word. All of them are subject to variations of form and type which may account for considerable differences in appearance between specimens of the same breed. Unlike certain strains of laboratory mice, which have been standardized by inbreeding and selection, no breed of dog exists which duplicates its own kind without variation.

Major differences between breeds are probably due to independent genes which may be found in one breed and not in another. To understand the manner in which complex parts such as the body, legs, head, and other structural parts are inherited, the following will be necessary:

1. Observations of a large number of animals, resulting in careful and accurate records of the differences in structure which exist within the breed.

2. Accurately recorded breeding tests between the animals of contrasting structural types, and recorded observations of their resulting offspring. This may well require the crossing of breeds at one or more genetic research laboratories, as was done in the controlled experiments done by Dr. C.C. Little at the Jackson Memorial Laboratory of Bar Harbor, Maine. In this way, extreme types can be compared and the inheritance of marked differences in structure can be studied.

3. The making available of these records to scientists who are qualified to analyze them. The task of breeding and raising a large enough number of animals representing different breeds, the recording of observations of their structural types and the types of their offspring, is beyond the finances and ability of any one person or any one institution. However, such data could be collected by breeders at no additional expense and a small amount of additional work. Each breeder's records could be sent to a central laboratory for analysis and any resulting conclusions could, in turn, be made available to breeders.

What kind of questions pertaining to inheritance in dogs can geneticists answer right now? Information pertaining to a great variety of subjects is available, including: color differences found in the coat, eyes, and skin of most breeds of dog; differences in the length, quantity, texture and distribution of hair; various reproductive problems, such as fertility, fecundity, the production of stillborn or non-viable young, monorchidism; various abnormalities of the eye, malformations resulting from arrested development, such as harelip, cleft palate, cleft abdomen, etc.; diseases as hemophilia and night blindness; differences in ear, eye, nose, jaw, foot and tail characteristics; differences in head size and shape; and numerous physiological differences resulting in characteristic patterns of behavior.

Many breeders have practiced line breeding by grandfather to daughter breeding, but have only skirted around the edges of inbreeding which might include full brother to sister matings shying away from carrying it to its full potential. As a means of finding out which animals have the best genes, inbreeding deserves more use than it has received. Not only does it uncover recessives more surely than any other method, but it increases the relationship between the inbred animal and its parents and other relatives so that the animal's pedigree and the merits of the family to which it belongs become more dependable as indicators of its own genes.

Considerable inbreeding is necessary if family selection is to be very effective. The gene is the unit of inheritance, but the animal is the smallest unit that can be chosen or rejected for breeding purposes. To breed exclusively to one or two of the best specimens available would tend to fix their qualities, both good and bad. In fact, that is the essence of what happens under extreme inbreeding. Moreover, the breeder will make at least a few mistakes in estimating which animals have the very best inheritance. Hence, in a practical program, the breeder will hesitate to use even a very good stud too extensively.

The breeder also is far from having final authority to decide how many offspring each of his bitches will produce. Some of his basic stock may die or prove to be sterile or will be prevented by a wide variety of factors from having as many get as the breeder wants. Bitches from which he wants a top stud dog may persist in producing only females for several litters.

The ideal plan for the most rapid improvement of the breed may differ from the plan of the individual breeder chiefly in that he dare not risk quite so much inbreeding deterioration. If the object were to improve the breed with little regard for immediate show prospects, then it would be a different story. This is an important point and deserves more attention.

Inbreeding refers to the mating of two closely related individuals. Most breeders practice inbreeding to a limited extent, even though they may call it close-line breeding. Actually, the breeding of half brother X half sister, as well as niece X uncle or nephew X aunt is a limited form of inbreeding. For purposes of this discussion, however, inbreeding will refer to the mating of full brother X full sister, father X daughter, and son X mother. Most breeders probably consider these three categories as representative of true inbreeding.

It would certainly be interesting to know exactly what percentage of inbreeding takes place in various breeds and what results are obtained. Speaking in generalities, it would probably be safe to say that only 1 or 2 percent of all champions finishing within the past 10 years were the products of inbreeding. On this basis, it would be reasonable to conclude that the practice of close inbreeding on these terms is relatively rare.

In the breeding of domestic animals, such as cattle, chickens, etc., as well as plant breeding, inbreeding is regarded as a most valuable tool to fix a desired type and purify a strain. This raises the question as to why inbreeding has not gained more widespread acceptance among dog breeders. By combining inbreeding with the selection of those individuals most nearly ideal in appearance and temperament, the desired stability of the stock is quickly obtained.

Breeding the offspring of the father X daughter or son X mother mating back to a parent is called backcrossing. To illustrate this, suppose an outstanding male specimen is produced and the breeder wants more of the same type: The male is bred back to his dam, and the breeder retains the best bitch puppies in the resulting litter. By breeding these back to the excellent male (backcrossing), there is a good chance that some of the puppies produced as a result of this backcross will resemble the outstanding sire. In backcrossing to a superior male, one may find some inbreeding degeneration in the offspring, but this is improbable according to Dr. Ojvind Winge in his book, *Inheritance in Dogs*.

The mating of brothers X sisters is far more likely to produce inbreeding degeneration. This is because a brother X sister mating is the most intense form of inbreeding. Studies show that those breeders who have attempted to cross full brothers and sisters, for the purpose of fixing good characteristics in their stock, give very contradictory reports of their results. It has been found that the mating of brother X sister results in somewhat decreased vitality in the offspring.

It may happen that abnormal or stillborn individuals are segregated out in the litter if special genes are carried in the stock. Everything depends upon the hereditary nature of the animals concerned. Inbreeding degeneration is of such a peculiar nature that it may be totally abolished by a single crossing with unrelated or distantly related animals. However, if it had made its appearance, the breeder should know it was present in the hereditary make-up of his stock.

Most of the studies on inbreeding are in agreement. The decline in vigor, including the extinction of certain lines, follows largely the regrouping and fixing (making alike) of recessive genes which are, on the whole, injurious to the breed. However, along with the fixing of such recessives, there is also a fixing of gene pairs that are beneficial and desirable. It is a matter of chance as to what combination gene pairs a family finally comes to possess, except that selection is always at work weeding out combinations that are not well adapted to the conditions of life. There is a common belief that inbreeding causes the production of monstrosities and defects. Seemingly reliable evidence indicates that inbreeding itself has no specific connection with the production of monstrosities. Inbreeding seems merely to have brought to light genetic traits in the original stock.

One of the most interesting and extensive investigations of inbreeding in animals was done by the U.S. Department of Agriculture. Thirty-five healthy females were selected from general breeding stock and mated with a like number of selected males. The matings were numbered and the offspring were kept separate and mated exclusively brother X sister. Only the best two of each generation were selected to carry on the succeeding generations.

Each family became more like itself, and while this was going on, there was a gradual elimination of sub-branches. There was a decline in vigor during the first nine years, covering about 12 generations. This decline applied to weight, fertility and vitality in the young. During the second nine years of inbreeding, there was no further decline in vigor of the inbred animals as a group. This stability was interpreted to mean that after 12 generations, the families had become essentially purebred—that is, no longer different with respect to many genes.

What does all this mean in relation to breeding good dogs? Inbreeding coupled with selection can be utilized to fix traits in breeding stock at a rapid rate. These traits may be good or they may be undesirable, depending entirely upon the individual's hereditary nature. Inbreeding creates nothing new—it merely intensifies what is already present. If the hereditary nature of an individual already contains undesirable traits, these will naturally be manifested when the recessive genes become grouped and fixed. This applies to the desirable traits as well.

The term genotype refers to the complete genetic make-up of an individual, in contrast to the outward appearance of the individual, which is called phenotype. In selecting puppies to retain for breeding stock, breeders must rely on phenotype because they have no way of knowing an unproven individual's genotype. Inbreeding can reduce genotype and phenotype to one common denominator.

Suppose that an outstanding specimen appears as the product of inbreeding. What would this mean in terms of breeding? It would mean that this specimen has a greater chance of passing on his visible traits rather than possible hidden ones. Prepotent dogs and bitches are usually those that are pure for many of their outstanding characteristics. Since such a limited amount of inbreeding has been carried on in most breeds, prepotent specimens have become pure for certain traits more or less by chance, for they have appeared in most breeds as products of outcrossing, as well as by line breeding. Since line breeding, especially close line breeding, is a limited form of inbreeding, the same good and bad points apply to line breeding but in a much more modified degree. The practice of inbreeding appears to be extremely limited in dogs, so one must assume that breeders are willing to trade slower progress for a lower element of risk with respect to degeneration.

Assume that you have selected a bitch to be either line bred or outcrossed and the proper stud dog who complements her has been selected. The breeding has been made, the puppies have begun to grow up. Hopefully, it will be a good breeding and the results will yield several good prospects, all carrying the dam's good traits but showing a great improvement in the areas where she needed help. What if it doesn't turn out this way? What if the breeding results in general disappointment with none of the puppies showing much improvement? You might well ask how this can be possibly happen when all the proper aspects were taken into consideration in planning this breeding.

Remember the concept of dominance? Test breeding is the only true way of determining whether a dog or bitch is especially dominant. Here again, line breeding comes into play, for the closely line-bred dog or bitch has a much better chance of being dominant by virtue of a concentrated bloodline than the dog or bitch that is not line bred. When selecting a stud to complement your bitch, take into consideration the qualities of his parents as well. For example, suppose a stud is sought to improve the bitch in head. Obviously, a dog with a beautiful head is chosen, but it is also important that his parents had beautiful heads. Then the stud can be considered homozygous for this trait. If the dog selected does not have parents with beautiful heads, or only one parent had a beautiful head, he is said to be heterozygous for this characteristic and his chances of reproducing it are diminished. Dominant dogs and bitches are homozygous for more of their traits, while less dominant dogs and bitches are primarily heterozygous in their genetic make-up.

A great majority of dogs and bitches are probably dominant for some of their traits and not especially dominant for others. It is up to the breeder to attempt to match the proper combination of dominant traits, which is why the dog and bitch should complement each other—the best practical way of attempting to come up with the right combinations. There are some dogs and bitches that are completely non-dominant in their genetic make-up when bred to a dominant partner, so good things result provided their partner is of top quality. When a non-dominant bitch is bred to a non-dominant stud, the resulting litter is bound to be a disappointment. When

---

a dominant bitch is bred to a dominant stud, it is possible that the resulting litter will be a failure. This explains why some "dream breedings" result in puppies that do not approach the quality of either parent.

There are some dominant sires that pass on their ability to their sons which, in turn, pass on their producing ability to their sons, etc. Likewise, there are dominant bitches that pass on their producing ability to their daughters, granddaughters, great granddaughters, etc. Thus, some lines are noted for their outstanding producing sires and/or bitches. Such a line is a true producing bloodline. A producing bitch, usually with a heritage of producing bitches behind her, bred to a proven stud dog will usually come through with those sought after champions. To this, only one additional qualification need be added—that the breeder exercise some degree of intelligence.

Much discussion between breeders has centered on the subject of which parent contributes the most, the sire or the dam. As we have seen, each contribute 50 percent of their genetic heritage or an equal amount; but by so doing, their respective factors of dominance and recessiveness are brought into play. Thus, in reality, there is not an equal contribution. If there were, there would be no outstanding producers.

The producing bitch is a very special entity. Those fortunate enough to own or to have owned one will surely attest to this. When a bitch has produced champion offspring, she is singled out for recognition. While the stud dog's production is unlimited, depending upon his popularity, this is not true in the case of the bitch. Many stud dogs, in achieving a producing record, have sired hundreds and hundreds of puppies. The average bitch will produce between 20 and 30 offspring in her lifetime, which drastically limits her chances of producing champions in any great numbers. Taking this limitation into account, it becomes quite obvious that bitches who produce quality in any amount must possess an attribute different from the average. That attribute is dominance.

The producing bitch may or may not contribute the qualities she herself possesses. Her puppies will, however, bear a resemblance to one another and to subsequent puppies she will produce, regardless of the sire. Whether closely line bred or outcrossed, whether bred to a sire of note or to a comparative unknown, the consistency of quality and type will be apparent in the offspring.

Occasionally a bitch will come along with little or no producing heritage, yet she will be a standout in producing ability. We must assume that such a specimen inherited a genetic make-up different from that of her immediate ancestors, or perhaps the potential was always there, but remained untapped until some enterprising breeder parlayed it to advantage. There are known instances in which specific bitches produced only with one particular dog. In such cases, the desired results are achieved through an ideal blending rather than dominance.

The availability of a true producing bitch is necessarily limited. Whereas all are free to breed to the outstanding sires of the breed, few have access to the producing bitches. Their offspring can and should command top prices; demand always exceeds supply. Their bitch puppies are especially valued, for it is primarily through them that continuity is achieved.

The producing bitch imparts something extra special to her offspring. Though all but impossible to define, this something extra is determined genetically. She is also a good mother, conscientious but not fanatical, calm and possessing an even temperament.

In summary, a basic knowledge of genetics will allow the breeding of better specimens and thus improve the breed. It is not possible to be a successful breeder by hit-and-miss breedings. Hoping that Dame Fortune will smile on you is trusting to luck, not scientific principles.Utilizing the contents of this chapter and other parts of this section will enable a conscientious breeder to score and score well in the winner's circle.

Colors in the Labrador Retriever

In this section we will deal with the inheritance of color in the breed. There are three certainties in breeding Labradors for color. The first is that a dominant black will throw only black puppies. The second is that yellow bred to yellow will produce ONLY yellow puppies and the third is a dominant chocolate bred to another like it will produce only chocolates.

Were it this simple breeding for color would be a piece of cake. "A good dog is a good color" is a statement that is often quoted and one with which most breeders would agree. Color has always held a fascination for the breeder. No sooner is a breeding made than the breeder begins to wonder what colors the litter will contain. Unfortunately, many breed on a hit or miss basis and are completely surprised by the results.

As we begin this discussion of color, please keep in mind that very few dogs are completely dominant for their outside (phenotype) appearance. Hybrids (those that have a different inside makeup called genotype) make up the vast majority of the breeding pool. Over the years, breeders have crossed blacks, chocolates and yellows until today most of our dogs carry some type of hidden genotype and are therefore hybrids.

The yellow color seems to contain factors that many of us are not aware of. First off, there are three types of yellow Labrador. For our purposes they will be known as class #7 yellows—which carry no recessive genes, class #8 yellows—which can, when properly bred produce blacks and chocolates and a class #9 yellow which carries chocolate capabilities.

To try to clarify all this a bit let us look at some of their physical makeup which differentiates them, one from the other. The class #7 and class #8 yellows carry darker nose coloring while a class #9 yellow often has a browner or Dudley nose. The class #7 dog will not throw chocolate colors regardless of the genetic makeup of the dog to which it is bred. This class #7 dog is also known in other Sporting breeds and is sometimes called a dilute black. In fact, he can be regarded as a black who lacks the extension factor (the ability to extend black color through the entire coat). The eye rims, lips, paws and skin color is often dark color. This phenomena was noted by Templeton and Stewart in their articles on Coat Color which appeared in the *Retriever International Magazine.* Proof of this is to be found in the seminal work of C.C. Little contained in his book *The Inheritance Of Coat Color In Dogs.* Templeton and Stewart make use of research done on a colony of Labrador Retrievers at the University of Oregon Health Sciences Center. In this study class #5 chocolates were bred to class #7 yellows to produce 100 percent black offspring.

Carrying this hypothesis even further, the class #9 yellow can truly be regarded as a chocolate dog in disguise. Like his class #7 yellow counterpart, he lacks the ability to extend his chocolate color out into his coat. His Dudley nose, lighter lips and eye rims indicate his presence. The class #8 yellow is an interesting fellow himself. He is more flexible as he can produce blacks and chocolates when bred correctly.

The following illustrations are meant to give you, the reader, a clearer picture of what happens when you mix the paint pots of the breed together.

The Labrador Club of Greater Denver and Lee Darrigrand graciously gave permission to use their logo as the breed representation in these illustrations.

HIERARCHY OF DOMINANCE IN THE LABRADOR RETRIEVER

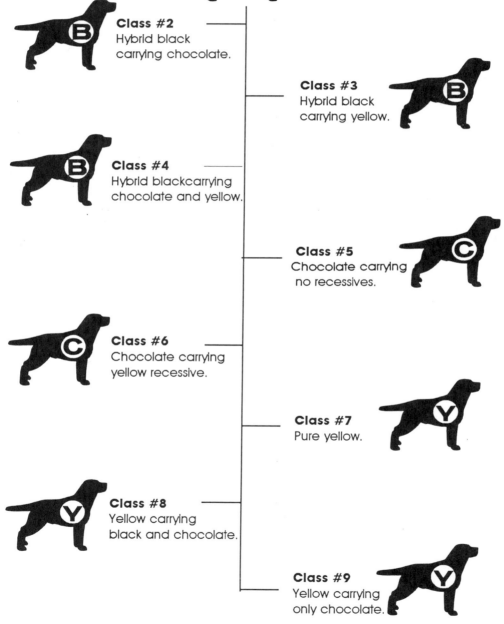

Class #1
Dominant glack
carrying no recessive.

Class #2
Hybrid black
carrying chocolate.

Class #3
Hybrid black
carrying yellow.

Class #4
Hybrid blackcarrying
chocolate and yellow.

Class #5
Chocolate carrying
no recessives.

Class #6
Chocolate carrying
yellow recessive.

Class #7
Pure yellow.

Class #8
Yellow carrying
black and chocolate.

Class #9
Yellow carrying
only chocolate.

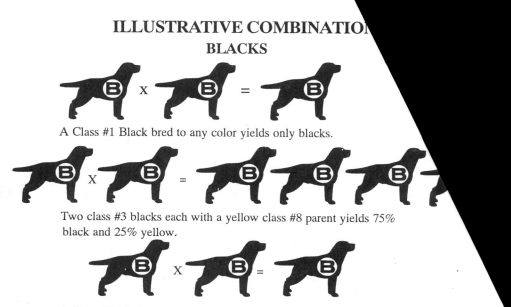

A Class #1 Black bred to any color yields only blacks.

Two class #3 blacks each with a yellow class #8 parent yields 75% black and 25% yellow.

A Class #3 black with one yellow parent bred to a class #2 black with one chocolate parent and not carrying the yellow gene yields 100% black.

A class #3 black with a yellow recessive bred to a class #5 chocolate not carrying the yellow recessive yields 100% blacks.

A class #3 black with a yellow recessive bred to a class #6 chocolate carrying a yellow recessive yields 75% blacks and 25% yellows.

A class #3 black with a yellow recessive bred to a yellow yields 50% black and 50% yellows.

A class #2 black carrying a chocolate recessive bred to a chocolate with a yellow recessive yields 50% blacks and 50% chocolates

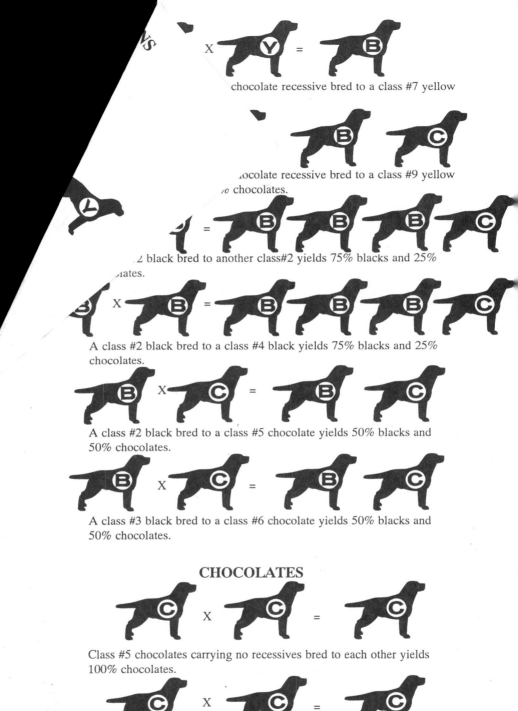

... X ... Y = ... B

chocolate recessive bred to a class #7 yellow

...ocolate recessive bred to a class #9 yellow

...o chocolates.

... = B B B C

...z black bred to another class#2 yields 75% blacks and 25%
...lates.

...B X B = B B B C

A class #2 black bred to a class #4 black yields 75% blacks and 25%
chocolates.

B X C = B C

A class #2 black bred to a class #5 chocolate yields 50% blacks and
50% chocolates.

B X C = B C

A class #3 black bred to a class #6 chocolate yields 50% blacks and
50% chocolates.

CHOCOLATES

C X C = C

Class #5 chocolates carrying no recessives bred to each other yields
100% chocolates.

C X C = C

A class #5 chocolate bred to a class #6 chocolate yields 100% chocolates.

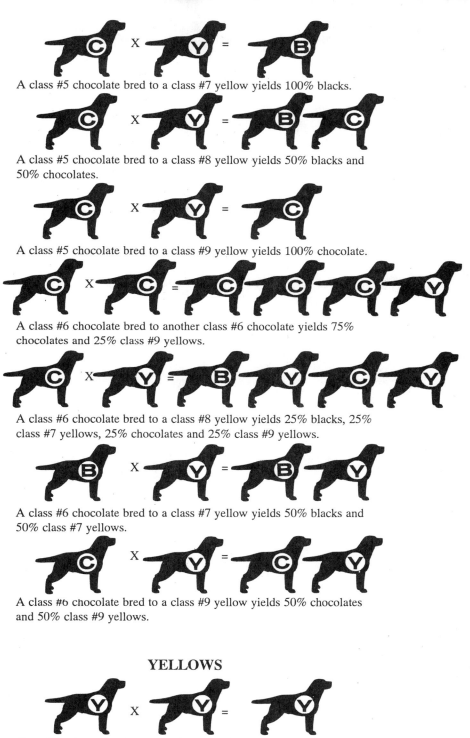

A class #5 chocolate bred to a class #7 yellow yields 100% blacks.

A class #5 chocolate bred to a class #8 yellow yields 50% blacks and 50% chocolates.

A class #5 chocolate bred to a class #9 yellow yields 100% chocolate.

A class #6 chocolate bred to another class #6 chocolate yields 75% chocolates and 25% class #9 yellows.

A class #6 chocolate bred to a class #8 yellow yields 25% blacks, 25% class #7 yellows, 25% chocolates and 25% class #9 yellows.

A class #6 chocolate bred to a class #7 yellow yields 50% blacks and 50% class #7 yellows.

A class #6 chocolate bred to a class #9 yellow yields 50% chocolates and 50% class #9 yellows.

YELLOWS

Class #7 yellows bred together yield 100% class #7 yellows.

A class #7 yellow bred to a class #8 yellow carrying a chocolate recessive yields 100% yellows.

A class #7 yellow bred to a class #9 yellow yields 100% yellows.

A class #8 yellow with a chocolate recessive bred to a similar class #8 yellow yields 3 class #8 yellows and 3 class #9 yellows.

A class #8 yellow with a chocolate recessive bred to a class #9 yellow yields 50% class 8 yellows and 50% class #9 yellows.

Class #9 yellows bred together yield 100% class #9 yellows.

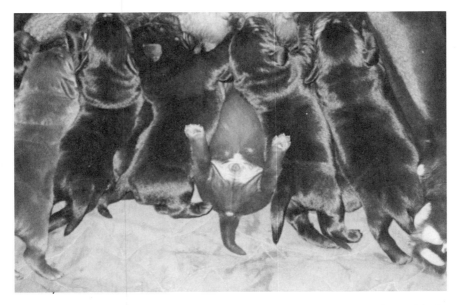

A litter of black and chocolate Labrador Retriever puppies from a dam with the black coat color. Photo by Annie Cogo.

Chapter 2

The Three Colors

We know from the early history that the Labrador was a black dog. From all the manuscripts, records and illustrations, we know this to be true. However, it has been noted that there was the odd brown whelp in the Scottish kennel of the Duke of Buccleuch, and we know for a fact that the first registered yellow was born of black parents at the kennel of Mr. Charles J. Radclyffe. It has been told that many people culled the yellows at birth thinking they were weaker or less desirable. I don't know what happened to the chocolates, but they may have suffered the same fate. Fortunately there have been breeders through the years who have thought very highly of the yellow Labrador, and have concentrated their efforts on developing that particular color. Major Radclyffe's Hyde Ben (or Ben of Hyde) was born in 1899. Many black bitches were bred to Ben, and through them, the yellow offspring or blacks carrying the yellow gene began to move out into various parts of England. Several people recognized their beauty, quality and ability, and therefore continued to pursue excellence in the yellow Labrador. Mr. Radclyffe's daughter-in-law, Mrs. Audrey Radclyffe, has said, "I've been breeding Labradors since 1929, and have always kept yellows because the family did and, of course, because I like them. My dogs have always been genuine dual-purpose dogs."

Lorna, Countess Howe, also had some yellows, but the Knaith Kennel of Major and Mrs. Wormald, the Staindrop Kennel of Mr. Edgar Winter, and the Braeroy Labradors of Mrs. May MacPherson of Scotland are some of the breeders who concentrated on the yellow color. There were conformation champions, but there were also some exceptional field trial dogs. Two well-known yellows were Dual Champion Knaith Banjo and Dual Champion Staindrop Saighdear.

Since World War II, the Labrador Retriever has bloomed, and in all three colors all over the world. However, there are many more black and yellow blossoms than there are chocolate. I will try to explain why. When I got into the breed in 1961, the first Lab I acquired was black, my next two were yellow. There were *very* few chocolate Labradors in my area, and the odd one encountered at dog shows was usually not a good specimen. My veterinarian had suggested that I attend several dog shows to see what a good Lab should be. He said that no one should be breeding without knowing the Standard, and it certainly taught me a lot to actually see the dogs and talk to their owners. The few chocolates that were shown were just not up to snuff. In general, they were tall and lanky with fine bone, and light-yellow eyes, and they were just not appealing. But as time went on, there were several black dogs imported from England that carried the chocolate factor. When I bought a black male, who later became my Ch. Great Scot of Ayr (Ch. Lockerbie Sandylands Tarquin x Ch. Sandylands Spungold), from Mrs. Dorothy Francke, I became the owner of a black dog who produced black, yellow and chocolate puppies. At that time there were a few other people scattered around the country who had an interest in breeding chocolates, and my old fellow sired quite a few litters of chocolates. He produced some nice puppies, and some even became champions. He definitely was one of my all-time favorite dogs—he had a super temperament, and everyone loved him. So, when his black daughter was mated with a popular stud dog of our area, Ch. Dickendall Flip Flop C.D.X., who was also black, we were not terribly surprised to have a litter of all three colors. I kept a chocolate female puppy because she was the best-looking of all, and she became my brown star—Ch. Meadowrock's Fudge of Ayr. She was a character—just so full of life and so much fun! We got her show championship and then did all the enjoyable other things: tracking, field work and obedience. I wish we had the Hunting Retriever Tests then because she was a keen retriever and earned her Working Certificate easily.

I guess you can tell that I thought the world of this wonderful chocolate girl. I have two of her great-grandchildren now, but I know I'll never have another one like her. So the "chockies" are special to me, and I love to see a really good one. They have come a long way, winning Specialties in the U.S. and having some super wins in England, in Europe and the Scandinavian countries.

There were a few early English kennels that concentrated on the chocolate color: the Tibshelfs of Mr. Severn and the Cookridge Labradors of Mr. and Mrs. Pauling. Ch. Sandylands Tweed of Blaircourt was a black that carried the chocolate gene, and when mated with Cookridge Gay Princess, produced the first chocolate to achieve a title in the U.K., or anywhere, Ch. Cookridge Tango. As Mrs. Pauling has said, "Tango proved for the first time that a good chocolate could compete on equal terms with the top Labradors of any colour. I find that when breeding chocolate to chocolate it is better to have a black background and later to breed the chocolate offspring back to black. One must keep the coat and eye colour true."

It is interesting to me that many of the most influential dogs in Labrador history have been black dogs that carry the chocolate gene, some carrying yellow, as well—Eng. Ch. Ruler of Blaircourt, Eng. Ch. Sandylands Tweed of Blaircourt, Am. Ch. Lockerbie Sandylands Tarquin, Eng. Ch. Sandylands Mark, Eng. Ch. Follytower Merrybrook Black Stormer, Eng./Am. Ch. Lindall Mastercraft, Eng. Ch. Fabracken Comedy Star, and now Eng. Ch. Kupros Master Mariner.

A lot has been said here about the yellows and the chocolates that brings us to the quote that we've all heard: "A Labrador is a *black* dog." Many people don't like this combination of words, but I think if one looks at the overall picture of the dogs that work with their owners in the field, the field trial dogs, the dogs that work at many other jobs, the show dogs, the pet dogs and the original dogs from Newfoundland, we can understand the dominance of the black color. There is another saying that is definitely true: "A good dog can be any color."

Most breeders that I know prefer black or yellow Labradors. The primary reason seems to be the desire to keep the pigment of the yellows as dark or black as possible. I think there are three different kinds of pigmentation in the yellow Lab. The first, and most desirable, is the yellow with very black pigment on the nose, eye rims, pads and skin (seen easily on the tummy). The second, and by far most often seen, is the yellow with black coloring that fades on the nose in winter and seems to keep fading a bit with age. The skin color of these Labradors is usually pink rather than black. The third group lacks dark pigmentation and has been called many different names: NBP meaning *no black pigment*; *yellow-livers*; and from Great Britain, *peppermint creams* (which I think is quite distinctive). They are not albinos— that would be no color at all. This latter group is made up of yellow-coated Labradors with brown/pink eye rims, noses and lips—the same pigmentation as a chocolate. Genetically they are *bbee* (two genes for chocolate pigment and two genes for yellow coat color). This why most Lab breeders do not want to mix yellow and chocolate.

Janice Pritchard wrote a very good article about these yellow-livers in her English *Dog World* column in 1990 in which she writes, "Regarding chocs, here are a few basics to bear in mind:

1. To breed chocs, the colour must be carried by both parents.
2. Any two Labs producing a choc pup shows that both of them carry the choc gene.
3. Any Lab with one choc parent is automatically a choc gene carrier.
4. The offspring of a choc gene carrier (be it yellow or black) have a one in two chance of themselves being choc gene carriers.

Pedigrees on the following dogs appear on the next page:

- **American Dual Champion Alpine Cherokee Rocket**
- **American Champion Shamrock Acres Light Brigade**
- **American/Canadian/Bermuda Champion Spenrock's Banner**, also from this litter: American Champion Spenrock Ballot, American Champion Lovat Annie Laurie and American Champion Great Scot of Ayr.

Eng. Ch. Ruler of Blaircourt
Eng. Ch. Sandylands Tweed of Blaircourt
Eng. Ch. Tessa of Blaircourt
Ch. Lockerbie Sandylands Tarquin (Imp.)
Eng./Am./Can. Ch. Sam of Blaircourt
Sandylands Shadow
Diant Pride
Am./Can./Bda. Ch. Spenrock's Banner, WC (By) 1964
Am. Ch. Great Scot of Ayr (Byc)
Am. Ch. Spenrock Ballot (By)
Am. Ch. Lovat Annie Laurie (By)
Eng./Am./Can. Ch. Sam of Blaircourt
Ch. Sandylands Sam
Diant Pride
Ch. Sandylands Spungold (Imp.)
Eng. Ch. Sandylands Tweed of Blaircourt
Pentowen Sandylands Tiptoes
Sandylands Charm

Ch. Kinley Comet of Harham (Imp.)
Ch. Whygin Gold Bullion
Whygin Popsicle
Ch. Shamrock Acres Casey Jones
Ch. Whygin Gold Bullion
Ch. Whygin Gentle Julia of Avec
Whygin Black Gambit
Ch. Shamrock Acres Light Brigade(Y) 1964
Ch. Rupert Dahomey
Ch. Whygin Poppet
Cedarhill Whygin
Ch. Whygin Busy Belinda
Aust. Ch. Michael of Kandahaar
Bengali Sari (Imp.)
Aust. Ch. Bengali Princess

Dual Ch. NFC Shed of Arden
Dual Ch. Grangemead Precocious
Huron Lady
Dual Ch. Cherokee Buck
Eng./Am. Ch. Hiwood Mike (Imp.)
Grangemead Sharon
Grangemead Angel
Dual Ch. Alpine Cherokee Buck (B) 1955
Glenhead Sweep (Imp.)
Dual Ch. Bracken's Sweep
Bracken of Timbertown
Nelgard's Madam Queen
Dual Ch. Little Pierre of Deer Creek
FC Ladies Day at Deer Creek
Tops of Bigstone

"Chessa" and friend. Photo by Jorge Gonzalez, Becerra Productions.

An Armfull of love—Labrador puppies in all three colors, Clare Senfield, Allegheny.

Ch. Shadowvales Statesman C.D.X., TDI Cert. owned by Leslie C. Weiner, Huntcrest— Illinois.

Ch. Sandylands Marshal, JH owned by H. Price Jessop, Blackamoor— Virginia.

Am./Mex./Int. Ch. JanWood's Secret Agent owned by Jan Grannemann, JanRod—California and D.M. and A. Smith.

Left to right:
Ch. Country Place
O'Hennings Mill,
Bradking Beverly and
Hennings Mill's Crown
Jewel, retired founda-
tion bitches of Dorothy
and Jack Galvin,
Hennings Mill—Ohio.

Scrimshaw Placido Flamingo
(10 mos.) owned by Barbara
Barfield, Scrimshaw—New
Hampshire. Yellow Labradors
can vary in color from light
cream to fox-red.

World Winner/Am. Ch.
Misti-Dawn Analore Sojourn (1993)
owned by Nancy Schroeder, Misti-
Dawn—Ohio.

Ch. Chucklebrook Fannie Farmer and her daughter, Ch. Chucklebrook Mouse Feathers owned by Mr. and Mrs. L.G. Pilbin, Chucklebrook— New Hampshire.

Right, Swed./Am. Ch. Puhs Superman, BOB 1982 LRC, Inc. National Specialty, owned by Mel Pfeifle, Hampshire— New Hampshire.

*Ch. Meadowrock's Fudge of
Ayr, WC owned and bred by
Nancy Martin, Ayr; co-breeder
Diane M. Beishline.*

SECTION VII
Becoming a Breeder

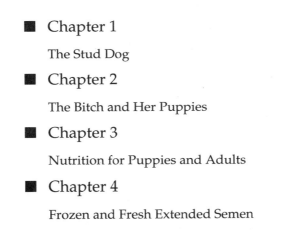

Left, Ch. Lockerbie Brian Boru, WC is a Top Producing Stud Dog with 61 champion offspring. He was owned by Marjorie Brainard, Briary, and bred by Helen Warwick, Lockerbie.

Below, Eng./Am. Ch. Receiver of Cranspire owned by Mr. Marc Gad, France, and bred in England by Ken Hunter. Receiver is a Top Producing Stud dog with 60 champion offspring.

Chapter 1

The Stud Dog

The dog you select to stand at stud should have certain things going for him. First, he should be masculine in appearance and, at least in your appraisal, conform closely to the breed Standard. A major mistake made by breeders is keeping a dog that is overdone in some features in the hope he can overcome a bitch with deficiencies in these areas. It doesn't work that way. It is futile to breed an oversize dog to a small bitch in the hopes of getting average-sized puppies. The hallmark of a good breeder, one who understands basic genetics, is breeding to dogs who conform to the Standard. Extremes should be avoided because they only add complications to a breeding program down the road.

Second, it is important that the stud dog come from a line of Labrador Retrievers that has consistently produced champions on both his sire's and dam's sides. Such a line helps to ensure that he is likely to be dominant for his good traits. A bitch should also come from a good producing line. When a dog is found that has excellent producing lines for three generations on his sire's and dam's sides, there is an excellent chance that he will be a prepotent stud.

The third consideration is appearance. If the male is not constructed right, he is not going to be a great show dog. While the dog doesn't have to be a great show winner to attract the bitches, it helps. There are outstanding examples of non-titled dogs being excellent studs. However, they are somewhat rare.

There is more to breeding than just dropping a bitch in season into the stud dog's pen and hoping for the best.

A subject seldom discussed in the literature about stud dogs is the psyche of the dog. A young stud dog needs to be brought along slowly. If he is a show dog, he most likely has a steady temperament and is outgoing.

Early on, he should be taught to get along with other male dogs, but he should never be allowed to become intimidated. Good stud dogs have to be aggressive for breeding. Dogs who have been intimidated early seldom shape up. However, running, playing and even puppy-fighting with litter mates or other puppies don't have detrimental effects.

Until he is old enough to stand up for himself, the young male should be quartered first with puppies his own age and then introduced to bitches as kennel mates. It's not a good idea to keep him in a pen by himself. Socialization is extremely important. Time for play as a puppy and a companion to keep him from boredom helps his growth and development.

His quarters and food should present no special problems. Serious breeders all feed their dogs a nourishing and balanced diet. Studies in colleges of veterinary medicine and by nutritionists at major dog-food companies have shown that the major brands of dry dog food come as close to meeting the total needs of the dog as any elaborately concocted breeder's formula. Many breeders spice up the basic diet with their own version of goodies, including table scraps, to break up the monotony or to stimulate a finicky eater. However, this is more cosmetic than nutritional and is unnecessary. Dogs are creatures of habit and finicky eaters are man-made. Labrador Retrievers are uniformly good eaters and doers. Do not let your stud dog get fat and out of condition.

The most important aspect of being the owner of a stud dog is to make sure he can produce puppies. Therefore, at around 11 to 12 months of age, it's a good idea to have a check on his sperm count by a vet. This will indicate if he is producing enough viable sperm cells to fertilize eggs. Sometimes it is found that while a stud produces spermatozoa, they are not active. The chances of this dog being able to fertilize an egg are markedly reduced. While this problem is usually found in older dogs, it does happen in young animals. Thus, the sperm count examination is important and should be done yearly.

One should also be concerned with a stud dog's general health. Sexual contact with a variety of bitches may expose the dog to a wide range of minor infections and some major ones. If not promptly identified and treated, some can lead to sterility. Other nonsexual infections and illnesses, such as urinary infections, stones, etc., can also reduce a dog's ability to sire puppies. Since it is not desirable for any of these things to happen, stud dog owners need to be observant.

It's a good idea to have your vet check all incoming bitches. A studdog owner, however, should insist that the visiting bitch come with a veterinarian's certificate that the bitch is negative for canine brucellosis. While checking for obvious signs of infection, the vet can also run a smear to see when the bitch is ready to breed. The dog should also be checked frequently to see if there is any type of discharge from his penis. A dog at regular stud should not have a discharge. Usually he will lick himself frequently to keep the area clean. After breeding, it is also a good idea to rinse off the area with a clean saline solution. Your vet may also advise flushing out the penile area after breeding, using a special solution.

The testicles and penis are the male organs of reproduction. Testicles are housed in a sac called the scrotum. The American Kennel Club will not allow dogs who are bilateral cryptorchids (neither testicle descended), unilateral cryptorchids, or monorchids (dogs that have only one testicle descended) to be shown.

The male's testicles are outside the body because the internal heat of the body curtails the production of sperm. There is a special muscle that keeps them close to the body for warmth in cold weather and relaxes and lets them down to get air cooled in hot weather.

In the male fetus, the gonads, or sex organs, develop in the abdominal cavity and migrate during gestation toward their eventual position. Shortly before birth they hover over an opening in the muscular structure of the pubic area through which they will descend to reach the scrotal sac. This external position is vital to the fertility of the animal, for production of live sperm can only proceed at a temperature several degrees cooler than normal body temperature. The glandular tissue of the testes is nourished and supported by arteries, veins, nerves, connective tissue and ductwork, collectively known as the spermatic cord. The scrotum acts as a thermostat.

As noted above, there are many involuntary muscle fibers that are stimulated to contract with the environmental temperature, pulling the

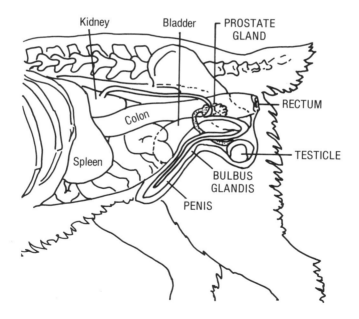

Left side of dog showing genital organs and related parts.

testes closer to the body for warmth. Contraction also occurs as a result of any stimulus that might be interpreted by the dog as a threat of physical harm, such as the sight of a strange dog or being picked up. This contraction does not force the testicles back up into the abdominal cavity of the adult dog because the inguinal rings have tightened and will not allow them to be drawn back up. The tightening of the rings usually occurs at about 10 months of age.

There are a number of reasons why a dog may be a monorchid or cryptorchid. For example, the size of the opening through the muscles may be too small to allow for easy passage of the testes, or the spermatic cord may not be long enough for the testes to remain in the scrotum most of the time; and, as the proportions of the inguinal ring and testes change in the growing puppy, the time comes when the testes may be trapped above the ring as they grow at different rates. Also, there exists a fibrous muscular band that attaches both to the testes and scrotal wall, gradually shortening and actually guiding the testes in their descent. Possibly this structure could be at fault. The important thing about all of this that it helps the prospective stud dog owner learn about the anatomy of the reproductive organs of the dog.

One should be gentle when feeling for a pup's testicles. The scrotal muscles may contract and the still generous inguinal rings may allow the disappearance of the parts sought.

It's a good idea to get the young stud dog started right with a cooperative, experienced bitch—one of your own preferably. By introducing the young and inexperienced stud to an experienced bitch, his first experience should result in an easy and successful breeding. A feisty, difficult bitch could very well frustrate the youngster, and as a result he may not be too enthusiastic about future breedings. Remember, one wants a confident and aggressive stud dog. There may be difficult bitches when he is an experienced stud, so it's best to bring him along slowly and gently for his first matings.

When the bitch is ready to breed (as your stud gains experience he will not pay too much attention to her until she is really ready) both animals should be allowed to exercise and relieve themselves just before being brought together. It's also a good idea not to feed them before mating. Bring the bitch in first. The place should be quiet and away from noise and other dogs. Spend a few minutes petting and reassuring her. Then bring the dog in on a lead. Do not allow him to come lunging in and make a frustrated leap at her. This can cause her to panic and bite him out of fear.

After a few minutes of pirouetting around together, she throwing her vulva in his face and him trying to lick fore and aft, take off the lead. Allow them to court for a few minutes. She should tell you she is ready by being coquettish and continually backing up into the dog.

Now comes the important time for the future success of the young stud: The dog needs to learn that the owner is there to help and should not back away from breeding the bitch just because someone is holding her.

Plan ahead and make sure there will be a large, nonskid rug on the floor. Place the bitch on the rug and face her rump toward the dog. Pat her on the fanny to encourage the dog to come ahead. Generally speaking, he will. As a rule he will lick her again around the vulva. Some dogs will go to the bitch's head and gently lick her eyes and ears. Encourage him, however, to come to the bitch's rear. If he is unsure of himself, lift the bitch's rear and dangle it in front of his nose.

Encouraged and emboldened, the male will mount the bitch from the rear and begin to probe slowly for the opening to the vulva. Once he discovers it, he will begin to move more rapidly. This is a critical time. Some young dogs are so far off the target they never get near the right opening. If this happens, gently reposition the bitch so he can have a better angle. This may occur any number of times. He may get frustrated and back off. Don't get excited as this is normal in a young dog. He may even get so excited and confused that he swings around and tries to breed her from the front.

Get him back on track. Again, gently get him to move to the bitch's rear and encourage him to proceed. At this time there may be a red, bone-like protuberance sticking out from the penis sheath. This, of course, is the penis itself. When, as a dog continues to probe and finds the opening, he will begin to move frenetically. As he moves in this fashion, a section just behind the pointed penis bone begins to swell. It is capable of great enlargement. This enlargement of the bulbous takes place due to its filling with blood, and it becomes some three times larger than the rest of the penis. In this way the dog, once having penetrated, is tied to the bitch; it is entirely due to the male, the bitch having no part in the initial tying.

When a tie has occurred, the semen is pumped in spurts into the vagina. The bitch then helps to keep the penis enlarged as she begins to have a series of peristaltic waves that cause a slight tightening and relaxing of the vagina. Some males will stay tied for up to one hour and others for as little as five minutes. A five-minute successful tie is just as satisfactory as a longer one because the semen has moved up through the uterus and fallopian tubes to the ovarian capsules by the end of five minutes.

Once the dog and bitch are successfully tied, the male may characteristically try to lift his rear leg over the bitch and keep the tie in a back-to-back position. Other dogs merely slide off the back of a bitch and maintain a tie facing in the same direction. It is always a good idea to have two people involved during the breeding, with one person at the bitch's head and the other at the male's.

Occasionally, a fractious bitch may be sent for breeding. She can be frightened about being shipped or spooked by strange surroundings. Certainly one doesn't want the dog to be bitten by a frightened bitch nor to have one's fingers lacerated. The easiest solution to this problem is to tie her jaws loosely with wide gauze. This muzzle should tie behind her ears to make sure it doesn't slide off. Pet her, reassure her, but hold her firmly during the breeding so she doesn't lunge at the dog.

After the tie has been broken, there sometimes will be a rush of fluid from the bitch. Don't worry about it, however, as the sperm is well up the fallopian tubes. Place the bitch gently in a quiet pen, apart from other dogs, and give her fresh water and an opportunity to relieve herself. The dog should be petted and praised. Once the dog is fully relaxed, be sure the penis is back in the sheath. Then, he too should be put in a separate, quiet pen with fresh water. It's not a good idea to put him back with a group of male dogs.

How often can the dog be used at stud? If the dog is in good condition he should be able to be used every day for a week. Some serious breeders who, when faced with many bitches to be bred to a popular stud, have used the dog in the morning and the evening for at least three days. If a dog is used regularly, he can be used from day to day for a long time. However, if a dog is seldom used, one cannot expect him to be able to service bitches day after day for any great length of time.

Nature is most generous with sperm. In one good mating a dog may discharge millions, and a copious amount of sperm is produced in dogs who are used regularly. Frequent matings may be possible for a short time, but for good health and good management they should be limited to about three times a week. An individual bitch should be serviced twice—once every other day—for the best chance of conception.

For some breeders, breeding to a stud of their choice is often difficult, especially in countries that have quarantine restrictions. In the United States, the basic cost of shipping and the chances of making connections with a popular stud can produce a great deal of frustration. The use of frozen sperm opens up many new possibilities. At the time of this writing, there are more than 30 AKC- sanctioned collection stations. There should be many more in the near future.

Collecting sperm from dogs is not like collecting from cattle. One collection from the latter produces enough to inseminate more than 100 cows. The largest amount collected at one time over the many years of research in dogs was 22 vials. Usually two to three vials are used to breed a bitch two to three times.

The estimated time to store enough semen to inseminate 30 bitches differs by age, health, and sperm quantity and quality. Estimate approximately a month for a young dog, approximately three months for a dog of eight or nine years of age or older.

It doesn't take one long to recognize that, in the early stages, those males of outstanding quality will make up the main reservoir of the sperm bank. The collection centers suggest that collection be done at a young age, three to five years.

Limitations in quality and quantity due to old age lengthen the period necessary to store enough sperm for even a few bitches. In addition, the daily routine of a dog's life may limit freezability: The settling down in a new environment, changes in diet, water, or minor health problems. It is also not uncommon to get poor freeze results from a stud dog who has not been used for a month or longer. For the dog, once he settles down, the process of collection is a pleasant experience.

The following information on artificial insemination written by Diann Sullivan is reprinted by permission of *The Labrador Quarterly* (Hoflin Publishing Ltd., 4401 Zephyr St., Wheat Ridge, CO 80033-3299):

> Artificial insemination [AI] has been recognized as possible in dogs for some two hundred years. Semen is collected from the male and introduced into the reproductive tract of the female. When done properly, it is as successful as natural mating. It will not spoil a dog or bitch for future natural breedings and in fact, may desensitize a bitch to accept penetration.
>
> The main reason for AI failure is that it is used all too often as a last resort after trying and failing at natural breedings, when it is too late in a bitch's cycle for her to conceive. The use of artificial insemination as a back-up to a natural mating where a tie was not produced helps assure that as complete a mating occurred as was possible. Bitches who have had a vaginal prolapse and may have scar tissue present after the protruding vaginal wall has been clipped and healed, may reject intercourse due to pain. It is also very useful when the stud dog manager finds he has a spoiled bitch in or one who has had little association with other dogs. Using an AI when natural mating is somehow impossible will provide a satisfactory service versus frustration on everyone's part.
>
> The equipment needed includes one pair of sterile gloves (available through a pharmacy or your doctor), one inseminating rod (through dairy stores or International Canine Genetics), one 12 cc or 20 cc syringe (from stores, pharmacies), one artificial vagina and collection tube (ICG) or the sterile container that housed the syringe, a small piece of rubber tubing to attach the rod to the syringe and a non-spermicidal jelly (K-Y). To sterilize equipment after use, wash thoroughly in warm water and a drop or two of mild liquid dish soap. Rinse well with distilled water and dry completely with a hair dryer to avoid residual minerals that act as a spermicide.

On a safe surface within reach, lay out the package of sterile gloves, not touching the left glove to contamination. Glove your right hand with the right glove. On the sterile paper that the gloves are wrapped in, dispense a little jelly. Attach the collection tube to the smallest end of the artificial vagina (AV). Be sure it is securely in place. Roll down two plus inches on the large end of the AV to make it somewhat shorter. Place the AV and attached tube next to your body. We have the stud dog waiting in a crate within reach until the bitch is securely muzzled and standing ready.

The stud dog handler sits comfortably on a stool facing the bitch's left side. I use my left hand to support her stifle and can hold her tail out of the way with the same hand. Using the right hand, the stud dog helper pats the top of the bitch and encourages the stud dog to "get her!" The thumb and forefinger of the right hand grasps the bottom of the vulva to open it for easy penetration of the dog's erect penis, as he is actively mounting. When he is fully penetrated, the right hand can then hold the bitch's hock to add to the support the left hand is giving to her left stifle.

The stud dog may dismount without a tie occurring. If he is fully erect and dripping seminal fluid, the pre-warmed AV is slipped over his penis and held in place with the left hand. The right thumb and forefinger grasp the penis above the bulbous enlargement and apply steady pressure as the penis is pulled down and back for duration of the collection. If a collection is preferred without allowing penetration, the dog is stimulated into erection as he is actively mounting the bitch. Grasping the penis back behind the developing bulbous will produce thrusting at which time the AV is slipped over the enlarging penis. If collection is being done without an AV, the penis is brought down and back and the syringe container tube is carefully held under and away from the tip of the penis. The pressure from the right hand around the bulbous will cause the ejaculation which is carefully caught in the casing. Watch the collection tube fill. When you see a significant third and clear portion on top of the settled, thickened sperm, withdraw the AV.

Put the stud dog away in a kennel or area with enough room for him to safely retract his penis and in a clean environment. The bitch handler should sit comfortably on his stool and left the bitch's rear up over his knee so her rear is tilted up significantly.

Attach the inseminating rod to the syringe securely. Cut the rods to make them easier to handle. Slip the smooth end of the rod into the collection tube and all the way to the bottom. VERY SLOWLY (so as not to rip off those little sperm tails), draw up the seminal fluid into the syringe. Draw up an extra few cc's of air.

Carefully place the syringe and rod back inside your shirt for warmth, and carefully glove the left hand and apply the pre-dispensed K-Y jelly to the left fingertips.

Palm up, carefully insert the left third (middle) finger in and up to where the cervix can be felt. Gently slip your third finger-tip just through the cervix. Carefully glide the inseminating rod along the palm side of the third finger to where the smooth tip can be felt by the fingertip. SLOWLY, use the syringe to pass the seminal fluid into the bitch. If you notice leakage, gently pass the finger tip and rod tip in a little further and continue to in-seminate. Leaving the third finger in place during insemination acts as the body of the penis to block fluid loss.

Remove your finger after two minutes and continue to mas-sage the vulva every thirty seconds or so, maintaining the tilt of her rear end for at least ten minutes. The massage of the vulva causes her vaginal canal to contract and pull the fluid up.

Crate the bitch for at least one hour after the breeding.

If the dog's sperm count is good and the sperm has good motility, breed three to four days apart to allow for the complete rebuilding of the stud dog's sperm count.

We must each continue to learn new and improved tech-niques to facilitate healthy pregnancies and practice methods that improve conception rates. Utilizing simple artificial insemina-tion as a back-up to unsuccessful natural matings or as a choice in difficult matings increases the number of successful litters. AI allows the stud dog manager a reliable choice to assist his mat-ing strategy for each bitch. AI is extremely useful in achieving a breeding early in the estrus, near when she may be ovulating. Following with either a successful natural mating or another successful AI every three or four days throughout her standing heat, would help insure that active sperm is available to the rip-ening ovum.

It is wonderful to receive the phone calls reporting the ar-rival of a litter that would not exist without the use of artificial insemination. Its reliability is constantly reinforced, and plays a strong role in improving conception rates.

Natural breedings are preferable to artificial insemination. While ex-tenuating circumstances with some bitches may necessitate AI, both the libido in the stud dog and the receptiveness of the bitch are inherited traits. In all his aspects, the Labrador Retriever is a natural dog, including his reproduction abilities. Reputable breeders never want to see the day when artificial means for breeding are the norm rather that the exception.

Chapter 2

The Bitch and Her Puppies

It has been said that a really good bitch is worth her weight in gold. Really good doesn't necessarily mean she will win Westminster. However, she should be a typical representative of the breed from a top-producing bloodline. In the previous chapter on the stud dog, emphasis was placed on a line of champion ancestors. This holds true in bitches as well, although it is somewhat harder to obtain because of the limited number of puppies they produce when compared to the male.

A bitch should be in good health before she is bred. Take her to the veterinarian to have her examined. This includes checking for heartworm and other parasites and making sure she is not carrying a sexually transmitted disease like brucellosis, a cause of sterility and abortions. All this should be done several months before she is due in season.

If there are any problems, they can be remedied. It is also important that the bitch is parasite free. Check for this once again just before she is to be bred as parasites can be debilitating to the puppies.

Her diet should continue along normal lines with plenty of exercise as she should be lean and hard. A fat bitch spells trouble in the whelping box.

Once she has been bred there is nothing special to do for the first few weeks. Again, a good, well-balanced diet, fresh water and normal exercise are extremely important. Most of the good commercial dry foods provide this. Slightly increase her food intake after the third week and feed her twice a day to make digestion easier. After week seven has gone by, feed her at the same level but spread the meals over three feedings. Throughout her pregnancy, she should be getting regular exercise. In the last three weeks, walk her briskly on lead, but don't let her physically overextend herself.

The average whelping time is 63 days after conception. No two bitches are alike and whelping can occur from the 59th day to the 65th day.

There are a number of things that can be done to prepare for the arrival of the puppies. First, prepare a comfortable, quiet place for the bitch to whelp. Either make or buy a whelping box. This box should sit above the floor a minimum of two inches to be out of drafts. It should have enough room for the dam to lie just outside an area where the

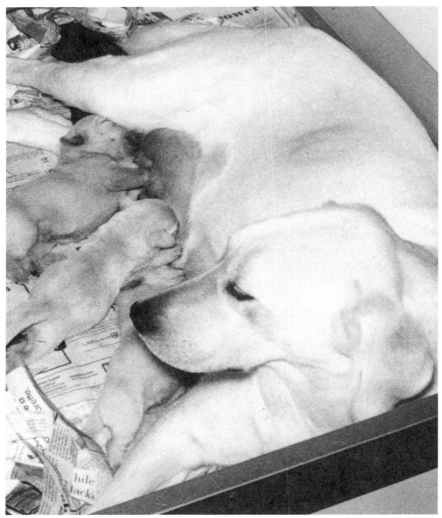

Ch. Shamrock Acres Cotton Candy owned by Mrs. James R. Getz, Aymes, and bred by Mr. and Mrs. James McCarthy, Shamrock Acres, was a Top Producer with 12 champions of record.

Left, Int./Mex./Can./Am. Ch. Franklin's Golden Mandigo C.D. and Am./Can. Ch. Concho's Chivas Regal with five of their litter of seven champions at the 1976 LRC, Inc. national Specialty. Both dogs are on the Top Producers list. Photo by Rich Bergman.

puppies will snuggle but allow her some respite from them when she needs it. It should have a lip to keep the puppies in. It should also have enough room for her to whelp the puppies without feeling crowded and should allow an assisting person room to help. The whelping area should have a generous supply of newspaper to allow the bitch in labor to dig as she tries to nest. The floor itself should be covered with a rough surface like indoor-outdoor carpeting to allow the puppies to gain traction while they are nursing. After a few weeks, cover the area with newspaper because the mother will probably no longer clean up after the puppies, and it can get messy.

There should be an outside heating source either under the flooring or just above to make sure the puppies don't get chilled. Newborn puppies are unable to generate enough body heat to insulate themselves. It's imperative to supply that warmth externally. Listen for crying because this indicates something is wrong and it's often lack of warmth. Puppies will pile on one another to help keep warm. After about 10 days an external heat source is not as important. If the puppies are scattered around the box and not heaped together, the heat is too high.

There are some other supplies that are needed. Since the puppies usually don't come all at once, a place is needed to keep the puppies that have arrived in sight of the mother but out of the way as she whelps the next one. Most people use a small cardboard box with high sides. Get a clean one from your supermarket. At the bottom of this box put a heating pad or a hot water bottle. Cover it with a rough towel. Make sure it doesn't get too warm. After the dam has cleaned each puppy by roughly licking it with her tongue and drying it off, she may wish to nurse it. Let her try, but most of the time mother nature is telling her to prepare for the next whelp. If the bitch starts to dig at the papers on the floor of the box, remove the puppy and place it in the cardboard box.

Sixty-Three Day Whelping Table

Date Bred (JAN)	Puppies Due (MAR)	Date Bred (FEB)	Puppies Due (APR)	Date Bred (MAR)	Puppies Due (MAY)	Date Bred (APR)	Puppies Due (JUN)	Date Bred (MAY)	Puppies Due (JUL)	Date Bred (JUN)	Puppies Due (AUG)	Date Bred (JUL)	Puppies Due (SEP)	Date Bred (AUG)	Puppies Due (OCT)	Date Bred (SEP)	Puppies Due (NOV)	Date Bred (OCT)	Puppies Due (DEC)	Date Bred (NOV)	Puppies Due (JAN)	Date Bred (DEC)	Puppies Due (FEB)
1	5	1	5	1	3	1	3	1	3	1	3	1	2	1	3	1	3	1	3	1	3	1	2
2	6	2	6	2	4	2	4	2	4	2	4	2	3	2	4	2	4	2	4	2	4	2	3
3	7	3	7	3	5	3	5	3	5	3	5	3	4	3	5	3	5	3	5	3	5	3	4
4	8	4	8	4	6	4	6	4	6	4	6	4	5	4	6	4	6	4	6	4	6	4	5
5	9	5	9	5	7	5	7	5	7	5	7	5	6	5	7	5	7	5	7	5	7	5	6
6	10	6	10	6	8	6	8	6	8	6	8	6	7	6	8	6	8	6	8	6	8	6	7
7	11	7	11	7	9	7	9	7	9	7	9	7	8	7	9	7	9	7	9	7	9	7	8
8	12	8	12	8	10	8	10	8	10	8	10	8	9	8	10	8	10	8	10	8	10	8	9
9	13	9	13	9	11	9	11	9	11	9	11	9	10	9	11	9	11	9	11	9	11	9	10
10	14	10	14	10	12	10	12	10	12	10	12	10	11	10	12	10	12	10	12	10	12	10	11
11	15	11	15	11	13	11	13	11	13	11	13	11	12	11	13	11	13	11	13	11	13	11	12
12	16	12	16	12	14	12	14	12	14	12	14	12	13	12	14	12	14	12	14	12	14	12	13
13	17	13	17	13	15	13	15	13	15	13	15	13	14	13	15	13	15	13	15	13	15	13	14
14	18	14	18	14	16	14	16	14	16	14	16	14	15	14	16	14	16	14	16	14	16	14	15
15	19	15	19	15	17	15	17	15	17	15	17	15	16	15	17	15	17	15	17	15	17	15	16
16	20	16	20	16	18	16	18	16	18	16	18	16	17	16	18	16	18	16	18	16	18	16	17
17	21	17	21	17	19	17	19	17	19	17	19	17	18	17	19	17	19	17	19	17	19	17	18
18	22	18	22	18	20	18	20	18	20	18	20	18	19	18	20	18	20	18	20	18	20	18	19
19	23	19	23	19	21	19	21	19	21	19	21	19	20	19	21	19	21	19	21	19	21	19	20
20	24	20	24	20	22	20	22	20	22	20	22	20	21	20	22	20	22	20	22	20	22	20	21
21	25	21	25	21	23	21	23	21	23	21	23	21	22	21	23	21	23	21	23	21	23	21	22
22	26	22	26	22	24	22	24	22	24	22	24	22	23	22	24	22	24	22	24	22	24	22	23
23	27	23	27	23	25	23	25	23	25	23	25	23	24	23	25	23	25	23	25	23	25	23	24
24	28	24	28	24	26	24	26	24	26	24	26	24	25	24	26	24	26	24	26	24	26	24	25
25	29	25	29	25	27	25	27	25	27	25	27	25	26	25	27	25	27	25	27	25	27	25	26
26	30	26	30	26	28	26	28	26	28	26	28	26	27	26	28	26	28	26	28	26	28	26	27
27	31	27	May 1	27	29	27	29	27	29	27	29	27	28	27	29	27	29	27	29	27	29	27	28
28	Apr 1	28	2	28	30	28	30	28	30	28	30	28	29	28	30	28	30	28	30	28	30	28	Mar 1
29	2			29	31	29	Jul 1	29	31	29	31	29	30	29	31	29	Dec 1	29	31	29	31	29	2
30	3			30	Jun 1	30	2	30	Aug 1	30	Sep 1	30	Oct 1	30	Nov 1	30	2	30	Jan 1	30	Feb 1	30	3
31	4			31	2			31	2			31	2	31	2			31	2			31	4

You may wish to leave the box in the corner of the whelping box. However, if the bitch starts to whirl around while whelping, take the box out. Be sure the bitch can see it at all times.

Clean, sharp scissors, alcohol and string should also be present. The scissors, which along with the string should be sitting in the alcohol, are to cut the umbilical cord if necessary. Cut the umbilical cord at least two inches from the puppy. Later, when the puppy is in the cardboard box, tie off the cord with the string. Disposable towels, washcloths, cotton swabs, toenail clippers, garbage pail and pans for warm and cold water are among the other supplies you should have on hand.

There should also be on hand a small syringe with a rubber bulb on it. These can be found in most drug stores and are called *aspirators* and are like the kind you use for basting, only smaller. If you can't find the proper tool, use your basting syringe. The purpose of this device is to clear the puppies' nostrils and lungs of excess fluid. Some puppies are born sputtering because fluid has accumulated in their nostrils or lungs in their trip through the birth canal. Try to suck the fluid from the nostrils first. Listen for a wheezing sound as this means there is still fluid. The puppy will also cough or choke. If all the fluid is still not out and the puppy is still sputtering, take the next step. Wrap the pup in the rough washcloth and grasping it under the chest and hindquarters, raise it above head level and then swing it down between your legs to try to give centrifugal force a chance to expel the fluid. Be firm but gentle—never do this violently. Repeat two or three times. Hold the puppy face down during this maneuver. This should do the trick. The heat in the bottom of the cardboard box should dry out any excess fluid.

As the time of whelping approaches, the bitch will have been giving all sorts of signs. In the last 10 days, her shape begins to change as the puppies drop down. As whelping approaches, she will seem restless and be unable to settle down for any length of time. She acts as though she can't get comfortable. She will also want a great deal of attention. She may or may not show an interest in the whelping box. Some bitches go to it, sniff around and walk away, while others lie in it and occasionally dig it up. Take her temperature on a regular basis as she grows more restless—101.5° F is normal for a dog. Just before whelping she can take a sudden drop to about 98°. Unless the temperature drops, it's pretty sure there will be no immediate action. Some bitches, however, never have a temperature drop, so one can't rely on this indication. Most bitches whelp at night. There are exceptions to the rule—but be prepared. It's a good idea for someone to stay close by the whelping box to keep an eye on the bitch.

The most important sign to look for after her temperature starts to drop is the breaking of the water sac. There will suddenly be a small pool of water around her. This is often referred to as the *water breaking*. This means that real action is close at hand, at least in a matter of hours.

If her temperature goes down, the first thing is to alert the vet that a whelping is imminent and to stand by if any problems arise.

If this is the bitch's first litter, she may be a bit confused and frightened by all this. Reassure her often. Get her to the whelping box and make her comfortable. She may pace, she may dig or she may settle down, but allow things to proceed on their own. Let her go four or five hours if she seems in no distress. However, if she goes into labor and has not delivered a puppy, check with your vet. Labor means digging up papers, heavy panting, and straining followed by short rest periods. She may also issue large groans as she bears down. All this is normal if it is followed by the birth of a puppy.

As she bears down, sometimes standing in a defecating position, sometimes lying on her side, a sac will appear issuing from her vagina and with one big push, she will force it out. Usually, she will reach back and break the sac, cut the umbilical cord with her teeth, and start to lick the puppy to stimulate a cry. If she does not do so immediately or if she seems confused one must step in, cut the cord, and take the puppy out of the sac. One must then clear its lungs and nose and give it back to its dam to stimulate.

Many dams will eat the afterbirth, which is the bluish/black material attached to the sac the puppy came in. Let them eat a couple. It stimulates delivery of the next puppies. If she makes no move to do so, remove it and put it into a garbage pail. *Keep track* of the afterbirths. You need to make sure they are all accounted for. A retained afterbirth can cause great harm to the bitch. In fact, once she has finished whelping, be sure to take her to the vet to check her and make sure no afterbirths have been retained. The vet may give her a shot of pituitrin or similar drug to induce the uterus to contract and force out anything that's been retained.

Puppies may come one right after the other or there can be hours between deliveries. As long as she does not seem in distress, any pattern can be considered normal. If labor persists for a prolonged time and no puppies are forthcoming, call the vet even though she has whelped one or more puppies already. You may have a problem.

The vet will probably advise bringing her to the clinic where she can be examined to determine her problem. In most cases, it is usually only a sluggish uterus and the vet will give her a shot to speed things along and send her home to whelp the rest of the puppies. On occasion, there is a problem and he might opt to do a cesarean section by taking the rest of the puppies surgically. Usually, he will perform this surgery immediately. Some bitches have a problem and cannot even push the puppies down into the birth canal. The vet may take these puppies by "C" section without having her try to go into serious labor. It's a good idea to have another small box with a hot water bottle in it when you go to the vet so any puppies delivered there can be taken care of.

Now, whether the puppies have arrived normally or by C-section they are pursuing normal puppy behavior. Their primary concerns are keeping warm and being fed. A healthy dam will be able to take care of those needs. Be sure to keep a keen eye on both the dam and the puppies; watch for signs of distress. Crying, being unable to settle down, or looking bloated all mean trouble for the puppies. Call the vet. Watch the bitch to see if her discharge turns from a blackish color to bright red. See if she has milk and if the puppies can nurse from her. It is extremely important to stay vigilant for the next three weeks. It's a critical time.

There are times, however, when you may be faced with either losing the dam through complications from whelping or she cannot nurse her puppies due to a variety of reasons. You are now the mother and must deal with these orphaned puppies. These are difficult times for dog breeders. R.K. Mohrman, director of the Pet Nutrition and Care Center at the Ralston Purina Company has advice if you find yourself in this predicament:

> Several critical problems must be addressed in caring for orphan puppies. Among these are chilling, dehydration and hypoglycemia. These problems are interrelated and may exist concurrently. Close observation and prompt attention if any of these problems develop are essential to survival. Of course, proper feeding of the orphan puppies is extremely important. A veterinarian should examine the puppies to determine if special therapy is needed.

> **Chilling**

> Chilling in newborn puppies can lead to significant mortality. A puppy will dissipate far more body heat per pound of body weight than an adult dog. The normal newborn puppy depends on radiant heat from the bitch to help maintain its body temperature. In the absence of the bitch, various methods of providing heat can be used, such as incubators, heating pads, heat lamps or hot water bottles.

Rectal temperatures in a newborn puppy range from 95° to 99° F for the first week, 97° to 100° F for the second and third weeks, and reach the normal temperature of an adult dog (100.5° to 102.5°F) by the fourth week.

When the rectal temperature drops below 94°F, the accompanying metabolic alterations are life-threatening. Therefore, immediate action is necessary to provide the warmth the puppy needs to survive. A healthy newborn can survive chilling if warmed slowly.

During the first four days of its life, the orphan puppy should be maintained in an environmental temperature of 85° to 90°F. The temperature may gradually be decreased to 80°F by the seventh to tenth day and to 72°F by the end of the fourth week. If the litter is large, the temperature need not be as high. As puppies huddle together, their body heat provides additional warmth.

CAUTION: Too rapid warming of a chilled puppy may result in its death.

Dehydration

The lack of regular liquid intake or the exposure of the puppy to a low humidity environment can easily result in dehydration. The inefficiency of the digestion and metabolism of a chilled puppy may also lead to dehydration and other serious changes.

Experienced breeders can detect dehydration by the sense of touch. Two signs of dehydration are the loss of elasticity in the skin and dry and sticky mucous membranes in the mouth. If dehydration is severe or persistent, a veterinarian should be contacted immediately.

An environmental relative humidity of 55 to 65 percent is adequate to prevent drying of the skin in a normal newborn puppy. However, a relative humidity of 85 to 90 percent is more effective in maintaining puppies if they are small and weak.

CAUTION: The environmental temperature should not exceed 90°F when high humidity is provided. A temperature of 95°F coupled with relative humidity of 95 percent can lead to respiratory distress.

Feeding

Total nutrition for the newborn orphans must be supplied by the bitch-milk replacer until the pups are about three weeks of age. At this age, the pups are ready to start nibbling moistened solid food.

Bitch-milk replacers are:
1. Commercial bitch-milk replacers, e.g. Esbilac, Vetalac, Etc.
2. Emergency home-formulated bitch-milk replacer:
   1 cup milk
   1 tablespoon corn oil
   Salt (a pinch)
   1 drop high-quality oral multiple vitamins for dogs
   3 egg yolks (albumin)
   Blend mixture uniformly

Food Temperature

Since the newborn may have trouble generating enough heat to maintain its body temperature, the milk replacer should be warmed to 95-100°F for the best results. As the puppies grow older, the replacer can be fed at room temperature.

Feeding Methods

Spoon-feeding is slow and requires great patience. Each spoonful must be slowly "poured" into the puppy's mouth to prevent liquid from entering the lungs. The pup's head must not be elevated, or the lungs may fill with fluids. Newborn pups usually do not have a "gag" reflex to signal this.

Dropper-feeding accomplishes the same result as spoon-feeding but it is somewhat cleaner and generally speedier.

Baby bottles with premature infant-size nipples can be used for some puppies. Some doll-size bottles with high-quality rubber nipples are even better. Bottle-feeding is preferable to spoon or dropper-feeding but less satisfactory than tube-feeding. Tube-feeding is the easiest, cleanest and most efficient way of hand-feeding.

Amount to Feed

Puppies being fed by spoon, dropper or bottle reject food when they are full. When tube-feeding, care must be taken not to overfeed, since fluid can be drawn into the pup's lungs. When adequate liquid has been injected into the pup the syringe plunger will become more difficult to push as resistance to flow increases. Basically, a one-pound puppy should consume 21 cc per feeding (when fed four times a day).

Some puppies, during their first feedings, cannot handle the determined amount per feeding. More than the scheduled four feedings may be necessary for the appropriate caloric intake.

Monitor the pup's weight and continue to adjust the pup's intake proportionally throughout the use of the milk replacer formula.

CAUTION: Diarrhea is a common digestive disorder in very young puppies. Consult your veterinarian is diarrhea develops, as alterations in the feeding program may be necessary.

It is helpful to understand how the size and sex of a litter are determined. One of the most informative and entertaining articles on the subject was written by Patricia Gail Burnham, a Greyhound breeder from Sacramento, California. Her article, "Breeding, Litter Size and Gender," appeared in an issue of the *American Cocker Review*. The following information is taken from this article. The number of puppies in a litter at whelping time is determined by several different factors. In the order in which they occur, they are:

1. The number of ova (gametes) produced by the dam.
2. The number of ova that are successfully fertilized and implanted in the uterus.
3. The prenatal mortality rate among the embryos while they are developing.

It is not possible end up with more puppies than the number of ova that the bitch produces. As a bitch ages, the number of ova will often decrease. Bitches don't manufacture ova on demand the way a male dog can manufacture sperm. All the ova a bitch will ever have are stored in her ovaries.

In each season, some of them will be shed (ovulated) into her uterus for a chance at fertilization. Elderly bitches quite commonly produce two- or three-puppy litters. Sometimes, just living hard can have the same effect on a bitch as old age.

If a bitch does produce a large number of ova, what happens next? The ova need to be fertilized. If they are not fertilized, or if they are fertilized and not implanted, they will perish. If a bitch ovulates over an extended period of time and she is bred late in her season, the ova that were produced early may have died unfertilized before the sperm could reach them, and the result could be a small litter.

Sometimes there is a noticeable difference in birthweight. It is a good idea not to consider the small ones as runts. They may have been conceived a few days later than their larger litter mates and may grow up to be average-sized adults.

All the puppies in a litter are never conceived simultaneously, since all the ova are not released at once. Because ovulation takes place over an extended period, some of the puppies may be 59 days old while others may be 64 days old at birth. A few days' difference in puppies of this age can create noticeable differences in size.

The mature size of a dog is determined by heredity and nutrition. Its size at birth is determined by the size of its dam, the number of puppies in the litter, and its date of conception. The small puppies could just be more refined than the others and could always be smaller. Only time will tell.

The sire is always responsible for the sex of the offspring. The rule applies equally to people and dogs. While dams are often blamed for not producing males, they have nothing to do with the sex of their offspring. If the bitch determined the sex of the offspring, all the puppies would be bitches because the only chromosomes that a bitch can contribute to her offspring are those that every female has—homozygous (XX) sex chromosomes.

What's the difference between boys and girls? It's the makeup of their sex chromosomes. All of the chromosome pairs are matched to each other with the exception of one pair. Dogs (and people) have one pair of chromosomes that may or may not match. This is the chromosome pair that determines sex. Sex chromosomes may be either X chromosomes (which are named for their shape) or X chromosomes that are missing one leg, which makes them Y chromosomes (again named for their shape).

All females have two homozygous X chromosomes. They are XX genetically. All males are heterozygous (unmatched). They have one X and one Y chromosome to be XY genetically.

In each breeding, all ova contain an X chromosome, which is all a female can donate, while the sperm can contain either an X or a Y chromosome. If the X-carrying ovum is fertilized by an X-carrying sperm, then the result is female (XX.) If the X-carrying ovum is fertilized by a Y-carrying sperm, then the result is a male (XY).

What influences whether an X- or a Y-carrying sperm reaches the ovum to fertilize it? The Y chromosome is smaller and lighter weight than the X chromosome. This enables the Y-chromosome-carrying (male) sperm to swim faster than the heavier X-carrying (female) sperm. This gives the males an edge in the upstream sprint to reach the ovum that is waiting to be fertilized.

As a result, slightly more than 50 percent of the fertilized ova are male. More males are conceived than females. However, things even up, because males have a higher mortality rate than females, both in the womb and later.

What if ova are not ready and waiting when the sperm arrive? If sperm have to wait in the uterus or fallopian tubes for an ovum to arrive, then the odds change. Female sperm live longer than male ones. As the wait increases, the males die off and leave the female sperm waiting when the ovum arrives.

This is the reason that some breeders advise breeding as early as the bitch will stand to maximize the chance for female puppies. The idea is to breed, if she will allow it, before the bitch ovulates. This allows the male sperm time to die off and leaves the female sperm waiting when the ova arrive. Whether this has a basis in fact is not known.

What can influence the number of males and females in a litter other than the time of the breeding? The age of the sire can influence the gender of the puppies. As a stud dog ages, all his sperm slow down. Instead of a sprint, the race to fertilize the ova becomes an endurance race in which the female sperm's greater life span and hardiness can offset the male sperm's early speed advantage. When they are both slowed down, then the male sperm's higher mortality rate gives the female sperm the advantage.

With the information gleaned from this section, you should have the knowledge to breed good Labrador Retrievers and be a successful exhibitor. Now it's up to you to put into practice what you have learned. Good luck!

Chapter 3

Nutrition for Puppies and Adults

Nutrition of dogs can be maintained at a high level by good, commercial diets. It is not necessary for the owner to be an expert in nutrition, but some background in this science is helpful in understanding the problems that may be encountered in the normal care of your dog.

Dog food is generally prepared in one of two ways—dry and canned. Dry food is usually a blend of cooked cereal and meat. The cereal grains need to be cooked or heated to improve digestibility. Fats are added to increase calories; vitamins and minerals are added as needed. Dry foods contain about 10 percent moisture.

A subject frequently discussed among "dog people" is the addition of supplements to commercially prepared dog foods. Supplements are usually unnecessary because major dog food manufacturers incorporate into their products all the protein, vitamins and other nutrients dogs are known to need. The diet may be specific for a particular life stage, such as adult maintenance or growth, or it may be shown as complete and balanced for all stages of life. When it is fed to normal dogs of any breed, no additional supplements in the form of vitamins, minerals, meats or other additives are needed.

Dry meals are usually pellets, sprayed with oil and crumbled. Biscuit and kibbled foods are baked on sheets and then kibbled or broken into small bits. Expanded foods are mixed, cooked and forced through a die to make nuggets that are then expanded with steam, dried and coated with oil. Food to be expanded must be at least 40 percent carbohydrates or the expansion process will not work.

Soft-moist foods, which are considered dry foods, contain about 25 percent moisture. They can be stored in cellophane without refrigeration due to the added preservatives.

Canned foods come in four types:

1. *Ration* types are usually the cheapest and are a mix of cereals, meat products, fats, etc., to make a complete diet containing 50 to 70 percent water.

2. *Animal tissue* may be beef, chicken, or horsemeat. Generally, this type is not balanced although some companies may add supplements. These sometimes are used to improve the palatability of dry foods.

3. *Chunk* style has meat by-products ground and extruded into pel-

lets or chunks. Some of the cheaper ones have vegetable matter mixed in. A gravy or juice is added.

4. *Stews* are meats or chunks mixed with vegetables.

Nutritional Requirements

The exact nutritional requirements of any dog are complicated by the wide variation in size, hair coat, activity, etc. Diets can be suggested based on body weight, but the final determination must be based on how the individual responds to the diet. Gain or loss in weight and change in activity level must be observed and some adjustments made.

There are generally two exceptions to the rule that supplements are not necessary when dogs receive a complete and balanced diet. These instances are: to correct a specific deficiency due to the dog's inability to utilize the normal level of a particular nutrient and to stimulate food intake, particularly during period of hard work or heavy lactation. This includes hard-working dogs, such as bird dogs, sled dogs, and bitches with large litters that require a high level of milk production. The addition of 10 to 20 percent meat or meat by-products to the diet will normally increase food acceptance and as a result will increase food intake. At this level of supplementation, the nutritional balance of the commercial product would not be affected.

Water: Fresh and clean water should be available at all times. The amount of water needed is dependent upon the type of food provided, but generally a dog gets 25 percent of its total water requirements from drinking.

Protein: Ten of the approximately 20 amino acids that make up protein are essential for dogs. Dogs must receive adequate amounts of these 10 proteins for good nutrition. The natural sources containing these ten proteins are milk, eggs, meat and soybeans. Sources such as gelatin, flour and wheat are incomplete.

Also important is the ratio of nitrogen retained to the amount of nitrogen taken into the body. In this respect, eggs, muscle meat and organ meat are all good. Some legumes, such as soybeans, are only fair. Most other vegetative proteins are poor. As dogs get older, this vegetative type of food tends to overwork the kidneys. This is especially important with chronic kidney disease in old dogs. More dog food companies are making products for each stage in a dog's life—from puppyhood to old age, and including lactating bitches.

Another important aspect of protein is digestibility. A good quality dry ration has about 75 percent digestibility, while canned foods are up to 95 percent. Some typical figures for digestibility:

Horsemeat 91%   Meat scraps 75-86%
Fishmeal 99%   Soybean meal 86%
Liver meal 88%   Linseed meal 81%

The dog's utilization of protein is dependent upon both the biological value and the digestibility. The digestibility of protein in the dog is related to the temperature to which the protein is subjected during processing. Some dog foods that seem to have proper ingredients at the time they are mixed can give disappointing results. This may well be due to processing at high temperatures or heating for long periods of time.

It is generally recommended that the dietary crude protein for adult dogs be 18 to 25 percent on a dry basis. For example, if a canned food is 12 percent protein and has a 50 percent moisture content, then it is really 24 percent protein on a *dry basis*. If the protein is of high quality, such as from milk, eggs or meat, the total needed would be less than if it contained substantial amounts of vegetative proteins.

Fats: Fats and oils have an important effect on palatability. A small increase in fat in a diet may greatly increase its acceptability to dogs. Fats supply essential fatty acids, particularly linolenic and arachidonic acids. Other sources are animal fats, corn oil, olive oil and raw linseed oil. A dietary deficiency of the essential fatty acids leads to defective growth, dry hair, scaly skin and susceptibility to skin infections.

The absorption of vitamins A, D, E and K is associated with the absorption of fats. Rancid fat destroys vitamins A and E. Extended use of rancid fats can cause hair loss, rash, loss of appetite, constipation progressing to diarrhea and even death. Commercial dog foods must use an antioxidant to retard rancidity.

The principal danger of excess fat in the diet is that it contains more energy than is needed and leads to storage of fat and obesity.

Carbohydrates: Requirements for carbohydrates in the dog are not known. The dog can utilize as much as 65 to 70 percent in his diet. Because this is the cheapest source of energy, it composes the major part of commercial foods. Carbohydrates are well utilized if properly prepared. Potatoes, oats and corn are poorly utilized unless cooked. High levels of uncooked starch can cause diarrhea. Milk can upset some dogs as some do not have the lactase enzyme needed to digest lactose, the milk sugar. Fresh cow's milk is 50 percent lactose. In some dogs, a ration with as much as 10 percent dried skim milk may cause diarrhea.

Fiber: Fiber is also a part of the carbohydrate portion of the ration. It is only slightly digested. Some fibers absorb water and produce a more voluminous stool. This can help stimulate intestinal action, especially in old or inactive animals. Fiber aids in the prevention of constipation and other intestinal problems. Most foods have 1 to 8 percent fiber. Reducing diets may have as much as 32 percent fiber. Sources of fiber are cellulose, bran, beet pulp and string beans.

Gross Energy: Dogs expend energy in every form of body activity. This energy comes from food or from destruction of body sources. Carbohydrates and fats provide the main source of energy for dogs. Caloric requirements are greater per pound of body weight for small dogs than for large dogs. For example, a 10-week-old puppy weighing 10 pounds would require 650 calories a day. At 12 weeks and weighing 15 pounds, he would need 840 calories a day. Divide the number of calories contained in one pound of feed into the number of calories required by the puppy on a daily basis to determine how much to offer the puppy initially. Using the example: At 10 weeks, he requires 650 calories a day; divide this by 690 (the number of calories in one pound of a popular dry puppy food) and the answer is approximately 1 pound.

There are various theories on how often to feed a dog. The *Gaines Basic Guide to Canine Nutrition* establishes this schedule: Up to five months, feed three times daily; from five months to one year, feed twice daily; from one year on, feed once daily.

Divide the amount of food needed each day into the appropriate number of feedings to determine the amount of food to give the puppy at each feeding. For example, because a 12-week-old puppy requires three feedings, divide the puppy's one pound of food into three servings of one-third pound each.

Russell V. Brown, writing in the February 1987 issue of *The Basenji*, points out:

> While caloric needs vary with age and activity, a rule of thumb is that for dogs of 5 to 65 pounds the need is $X(33-1/4\,X)$ =kcal/day.* In this case "X" is the body weight in pounds. A 20-pound dog would work out as $20(33-20/4) = 20\,(28) = 560$ kcals per day. For dogs over 65 pounds, the formula is $18X$ = kcal/day. The following adjustments are recommended:
>   a. Age adjustments
>   1. add 10% for dogs 1 year of age
>   2. add 30% for dogs 6 months of age
>   3. add 60% for dogs 3 months of age
>   b. Activity variable
>   1. add 25% for moderate activity
>   2. Add 60% for heavy activity
>   c. Pregnancy and lactation
>   1. from conception to whelping—increase 20%
>   2. at whelping—increase 25%
>   3. 2nd week of lactation—increase 50%
>   4. 3rd week of lactation—increase 75%

5. 4th week of lactation—increase 100%
* Kcal is the scientific term for what laymen call calorie.

Some owners find that the portion-control methods, such as the feeding schedule above, are inconvenient. They opt for the self-feeding method, which is also called the free-choice method. Free choice ensures that the puppy's feed consumption correlates with his rate of growth. The idea behind free-choice feeding is that it provides reasonable assurance that the puppy is obtaining all he needs for growth, even though these needs are essentially changing.

Free-choice advocates believe that dogs know quite accurately what their needs are and eat accordingly. Free choice works especially well for the pup who dawdles over his food for hours. A slight variation on the free-choice method is to feed the pup all he can eat in a specified time, usually 20 minutes. The pup would be fed for those time periods a certain number of times a day. This timed method may not be suitable for the slow or picky eater (or the glutton). Studies have indicated that free-choice eaters tend to turn out heavier by some 23 percent and that these weight differences were mostly in body fat.

Other controlled studies have proven that overfeeding can cause skeletal problems. When overfed, puppies may develop hip dysplasia (a disintegration of the ball and socket joint) more often, earlier, and more severely, than littermates who were fed less. Larger breeds are particularly vulnerable to these skeletal defects.

If in doubt on how much to feed, slight underfeeding is preferable to overfeeding. Studies have shown no serious effects from slight underfeeding. On the contrary, when obesity develops through overfeeding, the number of fat cells increases in the puppy. The chance of a dog being obese as an adult has its roots in overfeeding as a puppy.

Regardless of the feeding method used, food should be served lukewarm or at room temperature. If the food is prepared with an ingredient that can spoil quickly, such as meat or milk, be sure to serve fresh food only.

Estimating Caloric Content

In determining how much to feed a dog, use the following:

a. Dry food usually contains about 1360 calories a pound.
b. Canned food can be estimated at 475 calories a pound.

Minerals. Calcium and phosphorus are needed in a ratio of 1.2 parts calcium to 1 part phosphorus. A deficiency causes rickets and other less serious diseases. Young and old dogs need additional calcium. Common sources are bone meal, skim milk and alfalfa leaf meal. Sources of phosphorus are bone meal and meat scraps. Vitamin D is necessary for proper utilization of the calcium and phosphorus.

Magnesium is needed for bones and teeth, and bone meal is a good source. Sodium chloride should be in the diet as 1 percent salt. Sulfur and potassium are needed and are usually in the foods dogs eat. The best sources of iron are liver and eggs. A strict vegetarian diet will cause iron deficiency. Trace minerals are contained in milk, liver and egg yolks for copper, fish for iodine, and most foods contain cobalt, manganese, and zinc.

Vitamins. Vitamin A is important to vision, bone growth and skin health. Deficiency may cause lack of appetite, poor growth, excessive shedding, lowered resistance to disease and infection. Severe deficiency can cause deafness. On the other hand, too much is harmful and can cause birth defects, anorexia, weight and bone problems.

Vitamin D deficiencies are most often found in large breeds. Deficiencies cause rickets in the young and softening of the bones in adults; they also cause irregular development or eruption in teeth. Sources of Vitamin D are sunlight, irradiated yeast, fish liver oils and egg yolks. Too much Vitamin D can cause anorexia, calcification and other problems.

Vitamin E deficiency may involve reproductive and lactation problems. It may be involved in muscular dystrophy. Natural sources are corn oil, wheat germ oil, fish and egg yolks. It seems to be of some value topically in the healing of wounds.

Vitamin K is involved in blood clotting. It is found in egg yolks, liver and alfalfa. Most dogs can synthesize enough in the intestines.

Thiamine deficiency causes anorexia, weight loss, dehydration, paralysis and convulsions. Overheating during the processing of dog food destroys thiamine. It is also commonly destroyed if dry food is stored in a hot location, such as a feed store without adequate cooling facilities. Best natural sources are raw liver, wheat germ and brewer's yeast. High-carbohydrate diets, particularly bread and potatoes, increase the need for thiamin. Fats may decrease the need.

Riboflavin, niacin and pyridoxine are all B vitamins found in liver, wheat germ, leafy vegetables, yeast and mild. Riboflavin deficiency can cause dry scaly skin, muscular weakness, abnormal redness of hindlegs and chest due to capillary congestion, anemia and sudden death. Niacin deficiency can lead to pellagra or black tongue with oral ulcers. Pyridoxine deficiency can also cause anemia.

Chlorine deficiency causes fatty liver. Best sources are liver, yeast and soybean oil.

Biotin deficiency causes posterior paralysis and seborrhea. Raw egg whites contain a substance that ties up biotin. A diet of all raw egg whites should not be fed. Natural sources are liver and yeast.

Vitamin B-12 is important for blood formation. Dogs used in heavy work need a good supply. Dogs produce B-12 in their intestines and when given foods that have enough B-12 they can function adequately. Large doses of antibiotics may stop this synthesis. Best sources are liver, milk, cheese, eggs and meat.

Vitamin C deficiency may cause delayed wound healing and scurvy-type lesions of the mouth and gums, loose teeth, bloody diarrhea and tender joints. Generally, the bacteria in the gut produce sufficient Vitamin C. However, intestinal problems can affect the amount produced.

The 7.5 percent protein in bitches' milk is equivalent to 30 percent dry dog food, but is probably all digestible. Dry dog food protein is only about 80 percent digestible unless it comes from a meat or fish source. A pup must consume twice as much cow's milk to the protein of bitches' milk, but would then get three times as much lactose sugar that it has difficulty digesting. As a result, pups frequently have diarrhea on cow's milk. Nonfat dry milk is even worse, for without the fat the percentage of lactose is even greater.

Weaning Puppies

It's a good idea to feed puppies a diet of 115 calories for each pound of their body weight three to four times a day. Begin to wean them at four to seven weeks of age. Seven to 10 days should see the puppies no longer dependent on their mother. Often, the dam will begin to wean the puppies on her own. During the weaning process, take the dam away during the day for gradually longer periods of time. Feed the puppies three times a day. Puppies often gulp a lot of air when learning to eat solid foods. Slow them down by spreading the food out on a large pan. Chopped meat and small kibble may be better than finely ground meal because it passes through the intestines more slowly, causing fewer digestive problems.

Feeding Older Puppies

The first step in any puppy's feeding program is to weigh him. From birth through six months, the breeder should weigh and record each pup's growth weekly.

The next step is to determine the diet to be fed. This depends, in large measure, on the stage of growth the puppy has reached. Young puppies require twice as much energy per unit of body weight as an adult dog. But feeding the rapidly growing puppy twice as much food of the adult variety is not the answer. The diet must include a protein with high net protein utilization value. This is because the puppy's digestive tract is immature and cannot fully digest and utilize the energy and nutrients that adult foods include. The total need for all nutrients is double for a puppy, and the nutrients must be in an easily digestible form.

When acquiring a puppy from a breeder, be sure to find out the details of his feeding program. The breeder should provide you with the type of food the puppy is used to, the feeding times and the amount of food to be fed. Whether you agree with the program or not, duplicate it for several days until the pup is accustomed to his new surroundings.

After the puppy is settled, don't hesitate to change food or feeding methods if there is a need to do so. Using the information above, use good judgment in selecting the commercial dog food best suited to his size and needs. Make the change in his diet gradually so as not to cause diarrhea. Dry food is the most popular because it is normally most convenient, feed efficient and economical.

Be sure to choose a high-quality dog food. Not only will it be better for the dog's health, but it will also require less food to meet his nutritional needs. Don't be mislead by how much the puppy eats; it's the performance of the food that counts. Lower quality food is also less digestible and will result in the puppy eating more to compensate. The increased food eaten will further reduce the digestibility of the food.

Don't try to save money by feeding maintenance or low-quality foods. The puppy will end up with a pot-bellied appearance, slower growth, poor muscle and bone development and less resistance to disease and parasites.

Regardless of the form of commercial dog food used, Donald R. Collins, DVM, author of *The Collins Guide to Dog Nutrition*, believes every growing puppy should have liver in his diet. Liver is a good source of most of the good things an animal needs. It can be fed chopped, raw, or slightly braised. To avoid diarrhea, feed small amounts at first and gradually increase to no more than 10 percent of his total diet.

Catering to a dog's nutritional needs is one thing; catering to his desires is another. Do not permit a puppy to dictate his food preferences. This reverses the positions of authority and can cause training problems as well. It could also create nutritional deficiencies.

The goal should be that by the time a pup has reached maturity, his digestive system should be capable of handling all the foods he will eat during his adult life. This program should help him reach the average height and weight for the Labrador's standard.

Material for the content for this chapter is drawn from three main sources: 1) "Nutrition and Feeding of Basenjiis," by Russell V. Brown, appearing in the February 1987 issue of *The Basenji*; 2) "Feeding Your Puppy," by Ann Bierman, appearing in the March 1987 issue of *Golden Retriever*

Review; and, 3) "Supplementation—May be Hazardous to Your Pet's Health," by R.K. Mohrman, published in the March/April 1980 issue of the *Great Dane Reporter*.

Chapter 4

Frozen and Extended Semen

American dogs have made their presence known throughout the world. Dog breeders in such far away countries as Australia, Sweden and New Zealand have made remarkable strides in successfully introducing new breeds to their countries. There is, however, a major problem in importation of high-quality breeding stock. Stringent quarantine rules make it extremely difficult and financially prohibitive to import quality stock. There is a solution to this problem. Artificial insemination has been approved by the AKC under certain controlled conditions for use in this country. However, shipping semen over long distances has proven to be a formidable task.

In October and November of 1986, Howard H. Furumoto, DVM, Ph.D. writing in the *ILIO*, Hawaii's Dog magazine, cast a new light on the problem. Dr. Furumoto writes:

> Recent research on canine semen preservation and storage offers Hawaii dog breeder's a promising future. The technology and expertise are available today to overcome the hitherto insurmountable barriers of time, logistics, and statutory requirements when considering the importation of new bloodlines.

> To properly understand and appreciate the significance of these advancements a short review of the evolution of the two methods of semen preservation are in order.

> When approval was granted by the American Kennel Club to legitimize registration of litters conceived by stored semen and artificial insemination, the way was opened for Hawaii's breeders to take advantage of the golden opportunity presented by the new technology. Here at last was an AKC-accredited program which provided the means to circumvent the quarantine requirements and to eliminate the expense, inconvenience, and stress shipping animals to and from destination points. An added attraction for many breeders was the preservation of valuable bloodlines for posterity by the establishment of frozen semen banks.

> The original work on frozen semen was done by Dr. Stephen Seager and co-workers at the University of Oregon under the auspices of the American Kennel Club. The widespread interest he created led to a collaboration with the University of Hawaii. The objective was to determine whether or not we could duplicate the results obtained by Dr. Seager and his co-workers with the addi-

tional variables of air shipping frozen semen and bitches in estrus cycle. Much to our disappointment the four bitches shipped to Hawaii and inseminated with frozen semen shipped from Oregon failed to become impregnated. Subsequently, other investigators have reported similar negative results.

Because of the unreliable results obtained from the insemination of stored semen, canine theriogenologists began searching for more productive methodologies. Two such programs came to my attention. One effort was led by Dr. Frances Smith who had obtained her Ph.D. from the University of Minnesota. Her dissertation was based on the successful development of a semen extender which prolongs the viability of spermatozoa for up to seven days after collection without freezing.

Dr. Smith is widely recognized by dog breeders throughout the continental United States for her work with topline breeding stock of various breeds. In her experience she has been just as successful in obtaining pregnancies with the use of the newly formulated extended semen as with natural breeding.

The second source of information led me to Mr. George Govette of the Cryogenics Laboratories in Chester Spring, Pennsylvania. Mr. Gavotte has earned the reputation of being the foremost frozen semen specialist in the country, having successfully registered 44 litters out of the approximately 50 now recognized by the AKC by this method. In addition he has reported successful frozen semen usage in Japan.

Gleaning germane information from both sources, Dr. Furumoto wrote a second article in which he briefly described the methods employed in semen collection, extension, preservation, storage, and preparation for artificial insemination.

He then projected the long-term benefits and potential hazards of these new technologies as they relate to breed improvement:

Semen Collection. Semen is collected for a number of overlapping reasons—for qualitative and quantitative evaluation, for immediate insemination when natural breeding fails or cannot be used due to physical and psychological inhibitions, for extending the volume of serum, for semen preservation and storage and for legal reasons (quarantine restrictions).

To collect semen it is generally helpful to excite the dog with the scent of a bitch in estrus. Ejaculation is usually performed by digital manipulation and the semen is collected in a graduated sterile collecting tube fitted to a funnel- shaped latex sleeve which is held around the penis.

Three distinct fractions are observed from the ejaculate. The scant first fraction is clear and is secreted by the glands of the urethral mucosa; the opaque second fraction is secreted by the testicles and contains spermatozoa; the third and most voluminous fraction is clear and is secreted by the prostate glands.

Qualitative and quantitative evaluations are made after the semen is collected. The volume and turbidity of the semen are noted. Microscopically, the sperm concentration, motility, ratio of live to dead sperm cells and the shape and size are evaluated. Fresh undiluted semen is used for immediate artificial insemination.

Semen Extenders and Semen Preservation. After semen evaluation, semen of good to excellent quality is selected for preservation by one of two basic methods: chilling or chilling and freezing. In both methods a vehicle or media for dilution and maintenance called semen extenders are used.

Fresh undiluted semen maintains its viability for 24 to 48 hours. Beyond this period the viability of the semen may be prolonged for approximately 4 more days by suspending it in special media known as semen extenders and chilling. The viability of spermatozoa may be continued over an indefinite period of years by freezing the semen after it is suspended in a suitable vehicle (semen extender). By a gradual chilling process spermatozoa are conditioned for freezing at -70 degrees Centigrade. The extended semen suspension is then shaped into pellets by placing single drops into super-cooled stryofoam wells. Enough frozen pellets are placed in each vial to yield about 50 million spermatozoa. Each vial is properly identified and stored at -70 degrees in a liquid nitrogen tank.

An alternative method of preservation is to pipette the extended semen into straws, one end of which is presealed. When the straw is filled the top end is sealed and the semen is conditioned for freezing as with the pelletized semen, frozen and stored.

Preparation for Insemination. The reverse of cooling and freezing is carried out to prepare frozen semen for artificial insemination. A suitable number of pellets or straws are selected to yield 100 to 300 million spermatozoa and gradually thawed to ambient temperature. At this point an evaluation of the thawed semen quality is made. If viability and motility are satisfactory the semen is introduced in the anterior vagina or cervix of the bitch. At least two inseminations usually 24 to 48 hours apart is recommended.

Long-Term Benefits of Extended and Frozen Semen. Extended or frozen semen ... may be shipped in special compact containers over long distances.

Another attraction of extended and frozen semen is the flexibility and convenience of synchronizing semen shipment with the optimal breeding period in the estrous cycle of a prospective bitch. This advantage is particularly applicable when long distance shipment of stud dogs and bitches is involved in conventional breeding programs.

By far the most significant benefit to accrue from extended and frozen semen is the concentration of proven or select gene pools for the improvement of the breed to more rapidly attain that elusive goal known as the ideal breed standard. By extending and freezing semen many more bitches can be inseminated with 'matching' semen which would complement the desirable qualities of the sire and dam.

Disadvantages of Extended and Frozen Semen. The greatest concern regarding frozen and extended semen is the potential for intensifying or replicating undesirable gene traits. Just as much as the potential for breed improvement over a shorter period exists, there is also the danger of perpetuating undesirable inheritable traits, i.e., juvenile cataracts, subvalular aortic stenosis, hip dysplaysia, etc. within an abbreviated time frame. Therefore a great deal of selectivity and objectivity must be exercised in the utilization of preserved semen. Any abnormal offspring must be dealt with objectively and decisively and either euthanized or neutered so that the genetic defect will not become established within a given line or breed.

Another area of concern is the requirement for meticulous attention to details of proper identification and documentation. One only needs to refer to AKC regulations on 'Registration of Litters Produced Through Artificial Insemination Using Frozen Semen' to appreciate the complexity of these stringent requirements.

Conclusion. Notwithstanding the objectionable features of semen preservation and storage, the technical and scientific feasibility of their application to canine reproduction have been amply demonstrated. The acceptance of the program depends to a large extent, on the interest and support of dog breeders and the professional and technical competence of Veterinarians to deliver the 'goods' when the chips are down. Ultimately, the success of the program depends on the development of special interest and expertise in the handling of extended and frozen semen from collection to insemination. Success breeds success. Nowhere is this truism more important than in the pioneering use of these techniques.

SECTION VIII
Outstanding Winners and Top Producers

■ **Chapter 1**

Outstanding Winners

■ **Chapter 2**

Top Producing Sires

■ **Chapter 3**

Top Producing Bitches

Eng./Am. Ch. Sam of Blaircourt, owned by Mrs. Grace Lambert, Harrowby, and bred in England by Grant and Margie Cairns, Blaircourt, was the first Labrador Retriever to place in the Top Ten in the Sporting Group in the U.S. He was also a Top Producer with 29 American champions. Photo by William Brown, October 1960.

Ch. Shamrock Acres Light Brigade, owned by Mrs. James Getz, Aymes, and Mrs. Sally McCarthy, Shamrock Acres, was the first Labrador Retriever to place in the All-Breed Top Ten Winners.. He is the all-time Top Producer with 93 champions. Photo by Evelyn Shafer.

Chapter 1

Outstanding Winners

The list of Top Producing Show Sires and Dams has been supplied by Mrs. Irene Schlintz who has been compiling show records since 1961. All of the statistics used in her Show Reports for individual dogs are taken from the Phillips Rating System. To qualify as a Top Producer under this system, a sire must have had published in the *Pure-bred Dogs, American Kennel Gazette* the names of five champion offspring during a twelve-month period beginning in March of one year through February of the following year. A dam must have had published in the *Gazette* the names of three champion offspring in the same time period.

To quote Mrs. Schlintz, "Mankind is competitive, so he keeps records of his achievements—the length of the fish he caught, how quickly he was able to get from one place to another, golf scores—in fact, he demands some sort of numerical scoring system in order to find out if he is a winner, or what record he must defeat."

Mrs. Schlintz also included the following items of interest:

1. First AKC Registered Labrador Retriever:

> BROCKLEHIRST FLOSS - 1917 (*)
> AKC # 223339   Whelped: 1/2/12   Color: Black.
> (Brocklehirst Bob x Stewardess)
> Breeder: L. Rankine (Scotland)
> Owner: Charles G. Meyer
>   New York City
>   (*) American Kennel Club Source Book.

2. First Labrador Retriever To Place In The Top Ten Of The Sporting Group:

> ENG./AM./CAN. CH. SAM OF BLAIRCOURT
> S-974776   Whelped: 6/11/57 Color: Black.
> (Hawk of Luscander x Olivia of Blaircourt)
> Breeder: Mr. & Mrs. G. Cairns (Scotland).
> Owner: Mrs. Grace Lambert
>   Harrowby Kennels.

HIS SHOW RECORD:

	PHILLIPS		GROUP AWARDS				
DATE	POINTS	B.I.S.	1.	2.	3.	4	Placements
1960	4,448	3	8	10	5	7	#1 Breed, #4 Group.
1961	4,365	2	11	8	7	6	#1 Breed, #4 Group.
1963	4,339	2	10	6	10	3	#1 Breed, #7 Group.
1964	2,224	1	4	3	3	4	#1 Breed.
							#5 All-Breed.

3. First Labrador Retriever To Place In The All-Breed Top Ten Winners:

CH. SHAMROCK ACRES LIGHT BRIGADE
SA-278706   Whelped: 7/6/64   Color: Yellow.
(Ch. Shamrock Acres Casey Jones C.D. x Ch. Whygin Busy Belinda)
Breeder: Mrs. James McCarthy
Owners: Mrs. James Getz & Mrs. Sally McCarthy
Handler: Dick Cooper.

HIS SHOW RECORD:

DATE	PHILLIPS POINTS	B.I.S.	GROUP AWARDS 1.	2.	3.	4.	Placements
1967	1,358.	0	0	3	5	5	#2 Breed
1968	18,865.	12	45	11	2	3	#1 Breed, #1 Group

4. Most B.I.S. Awards Won By a Male Labrador Rstriever:

CH. CHARISMA'S LONE STAR RICK
SD-255947   Whelped: 5/23/81 Color: Yellow.
(Ch. Franklin's Golden Mandigo C.D. x Tanglewood Sassy Celina)
Breeder: Renee Loyless
Owner: J. & R. Loyless

HIS SHOW RECORD:

DATE	PHILLIPS POINTS	B.I.S.	GROUP AWARDS 1.	2.	3.	4.	Placements
1983	1,294	0	2	2	0	2	#7 Breed
1984	2,967	1	4	5	2	3	#4 Breed
1985	7,074	3	12	4	5	9	#1 Breed
1986	10,359	4	20	8	9	3	#1 Breed
1987	9,010	2	17	8	7	8	#1 Breed
1988	4,171	3	5	4	2	2	#1 Breed

5. Most B.I.S Awards Won By a Female Labrador Retriever:

CH. CHOCORUA'S SEABREEZE
SD-642967   Whelped: 12/19/82 Color: Yellow.
(Ch. Shadowvale's Frosty Knight x Ch. McDerry's Midwatch Star Kist C.D.X.)
Breeder: T. & M. Lyons
Owner: Marion Lyons.
Handler: Norman Grenier

HER SHOW RECORD:

DATE	PHILLIPS POINTS	B.I.S.	GROUP AWARDS 1.	2.	3.	4.	Placements
1984	1,300	0	0	1	3	2	#7 Breed
1985	5,139	2	5	4	3	1	#3 Breed
1986	3,522	0	6	3	1	2	#2 Breed
1987	3,180	0	4	4	3	3	#3 Breed

Ch. Charisma's Lone Star Rick holds the record for the most B.I.S. awards won by a male Labrador Retriever, owner—J. & R. Loyless. Photo by Ernst.

Ch. Chocorua's Seabreeze, holds the record for the most B.I.S. awards won by a female Labrador Retriever, owner—Marion Lyons, Chocorua.

Chapter 2

Top Producing Sires

The following lists include sires with more than 30 Champions of record:

CH. SHAMROCK ACRES LIGHT BRIGADE

(Ch. Shamrock Acres Casey Jones, C.D. x Ch. Whygin Busy Belinda)

Whelped:	July 6, 1964
Breeder:	Mrs. James McCarthy
Owners:	Mrs. James R. Getz & Mrs. Sally McCarthy

The sire of 93 AKC Champions:

Ch. Shamrock Acres Cotton Candy
Ch. Shamrock Acres Klondike Rock C.D.
Ch. Ski's White Christmas
Ch. Kelshires Blueprint
Ch. Shamrock Acres Winter Wheat
Ch. Shamrock Acres Sunny Side Up
Ch. Shamrock Acres Country Boy
Ch. Shamrock Acres Early Bird
Ch. Shamrock Acres Pal Joey
Ch. Shamrock Acres Gay Affair
Ch. Hillsboro Wizard Of Oz
Ch. Shamrock Acres Carousel
Ch.Kelshires First Edition
Ch. Shamrock Acres Golden Rod
Ch. Shamrock Acres Epic Journey
Am./Can. Ch.Shamrock Acres Mighty Casey U.D.T.
Ch. Franklin's Corbi Of Limerick
Ch. Shamrock Norton Of Burywood
Ch. Hillsboro Kalidah Of Oz
Ch. Shamrock Acres Gold Standard
Ch. Shamrock Acres Sandbar
Ch. Franklin's Top Of The Morning
Ch. Royal Oaks Rorschach's Libido
Ch. Burywood Hurricane
Ch. Shamrock Acres MacGeorge
Am./Can./Bda., Ch. Grovetons Apollo Moondust
Ch. Grovetons Apollo Countdown
Ch. Franklin's Whirlaway Barbela
Ch. Royal Oaks Shamrock Acre Ad Lib
Ch. Heatherbrook's Could Be Jazzy
Ch. Shamrock Acres Georgy Girl II
Ch. Franklin's Bug A Boo
Ch. Could Be's Katie Can
Ch. Shamrock Acres Tawny Tasha
Ch. Shamrock Acres Yankee Doodle II C.D.
Ch. Shamrock Acres Royal Oak Star
Ch. Starline Special Occasion
Ch. Wingmaster's Tiara Of Cochise
Ch. Shamrock Acres Royal Oak Byob
Ch. Shamrock Acres Schwechater G
Ch. Shamrock Acres Wild Wind
Ch. Sunnybrook Acres Black Gold

Ch. Franklin's Hickory Grove
Ch. Franklin's Chance Play
Ch. Franklin's Winter Wheat
Ch. Roxanne Norton Of Burywood
Ch. Shamrock Acres Northernlight C.D.X.
Ch. Drumlin's Backyard Bridget
Ch. St. George Spring Mill
Ch. Shamrock Acres Bailiwick Ban
Ch. Arroy's Morgana Le Fay
Ch. Nilo Shamrock Acres Snow Cone
Ch. Winacko's Abraham Of Burywood
Ch. Ringneck Rachel Of Borador
Ch. Sherlab's Spectacular Sport
Ch. Shamrock Acres Top Brass
Ch. Shamrock Acres Donnybrook C.D.
Ch. Royal Oaks VIP O'Shamrock Acres
Ch. Jasland Sun Goddess O'Crisara
Ch. Shamrock Acres Golden Accent
Ch. Franklin's Kolps Recovery Pat
Ch. Tabatha Dodena Of Franklin C.D.
Ch. Hi-Tide Special Attraction
Ch. Shamrock Acres Royal Oak TGIF
Ch. Franklin's Tell Tale Maggie
Ch. Shamrock Acres Mellow Yellow
Ch. Shamrock Acres Rhett Butler
Ch. Franklin's Secretariat
Ch. Shamrock Acres City Slicker C.D.
Ch. Franklin's Ruffian
Ch. Shamrock Acres Royal Oak Buck
Ch. Bounty Grant's Barnstormer
Ch. Danicks Diamond Flush
Ch. Sherlab's Especially Special
Ch. Shamrock Acres Royal Oak Rip
Ch. Riverroad's Summerstraw
Ch. Shamrock Acres Sundance Kid
Ch. Ariste's Brown Betty O'Briggs
Ch. Shamrock Acres Chief Invador
Ch. Shamrock Acres Briarpatch
Ch. Aymes Shamrock Acres Brian
Ch. Timberland Vi-Russ Tiffany
Ch. Could Be's Betsy Ross
Ch. Shamrock Acres Peg O My Heart

Ch. Wyndcall Wild Shamrock Honey
Ch. Shamrock Acres Show And Tell
Ch. Franklin's Bailiwick Rally C.D.
Ch. Chamberlain's Minute Man

Ch. Shamrock Acres Smooth Sailing
Ch. Shamrock Acres Royal Oaks RFD
Ch. Shamrock Acres Britannia C.D., TD
Ch. Shamrock Acres Chantrelle, C.D.

Am./Can./Mex./World Ch. Franklin's Golden Mandigo C.D., WC

CH. LOCKERBIE BRIAN BORU, WC

(Ch. Lockerbie Kismet x Ch. Lockerbie Tackety Boots)

Whelped:	September 1, 1967
Breeder:	Helen Warwick
Owner:	Marjorie Brainard

The Sire of 61 AKC Champions:

Ch. Barnaby O'Brian C.D.
Ch. Rose's Monti
Ch. Tagalong's Camptorhynchus
Ch. Briary Bluebell
Ch. Wildwing's Mcduff
Ch. Jet's Tagalong Of Lockerbie
Ch. Winroc Janina, WC
Ch. Briary's Trace Of Brian
Ch. Roses Easter Star
Ch. Sierra Tagalong Buttercup
Ch. Brudstud's Brian's Brut
Ch. Brudstud's Barbaree
Ch. Brudstud's Bonnie Brae
Ch. Briary Brian's Song
Ch. Freeway Sweet Bippy C.D.X.
Ch. Briary Bonnie Briana
Ch. Briary's Glencoe MacBrian
Ch. Briary's Sure Shot Boru Too
Ch. Beckon Berry BB Of Willliston C.D.
Ch. Briary Bantry Bay
Ch. Briary Shillelagh
Ch. Sage Hill's Blarney Boru
Ch. Winroc's Move Over, WC
Ch. Aristes' Noche De Negro C.D.
Ch. Braemar Winter Rye
Ch. Aristes' Aurora Borealis C.D.
Ch. Briary Floradora
Ch. Brookland's Destiny C.D.
Ch. Vogue's Zechariah
Ch. Briarwood Tallulah
Ch. Jet's Liberty Belle

Ch. Briarwood's Fleetside Kye
Ch. Briary Blossom
Ch. HGLs Winsor Of Braemar
Ch. Briary Bracken
Ch. Braemar Thistle C.D.X.
Ch. Tagalong's Clickety Click
Ch. Tagalong's Nutmeg
Ch. Briary Brendan Of Rainell
Ch. Tagalong Ginger
Ch. Ravenwood Brigadier
Ch. Briary Barley
Ch. Elysium's Citizen Kane
Ch. Coal Creeks Briary Breakthru
Ch. Tagalong's Morning Glory
Ch. Elysium's Sailin Cat Ballou
Ch. Briary Bandolier
Ch. Borador's Bing Cherry
Ch. Balamar Briary Blithe
Ch. Briary Birch
Ch. Chucklebrook Black Irish
Ch. Braemar Lord Of Kuykendall
Ch. Elysium's Beau Geste
Ch. Chucklebrook Champagne Mist
Ch. Briary Andante
Am./Can. Ch. Campbellcroft's Angus C.D.
Ch. Sunnybrook Acres Rasta
Ch. Borador's Mr. Shook
Ch. Elysium's Bristol Cream
Ch. Briary Brenna Of Coal Creek
Ch. Lady Aberlyn Of Erinbrough

ENG. SH. CH./AM. CH. RECEIVER OF CRANSPIRE

(Dutch Ch. Cranspire Skytrain x Polly's Pride Of Genisval)

Whelped:	December 19, 1981
Breeders:	Miss Coddington & Mr. Shortland
Owners:	June Kagawa, Kendall Herr & Ken Hunter
	(now owned by Marc Gad in France)

The Sire of 60 AKC Champions:

Ch. Trentham Harvester Of Cranspire
Ch. Chafern Court Star Of Fabracken
Ch. Springfield's Mrs. Beeton
Ch. Boradors Ridgeway Resolution
Ch. Kresland's Almond At Lochiel
Ch. Cricklades Heather
Ch. Simmerdown's Montgomery

Ch. Old Union Reveille, JH
Ch. Putwyn True Britt
Ch. Jollymuff John Hardy
Ch. Jollymuff Omnie Wise
Ch. Donallys Adeline
Ch. Snowden Hill's Top Notc
Ch. Tweedcroft Rainbow Receiver

Ch. Snowden Hill's Blackmail
Ch. Dickendalls Ruffy, SH
Ch. Midnight's Morning Sunshine
Ch. Snowden Hill's Honey Bear
Ch. Graewalls Bette Davis
Ch. Snowden Hill's Right Stuff
Ch. Snowden Hill's Picadilly Lily
Ch. Sailin's Received Our Boo-Tee
Ch. Snowden Hill Duchess Of York
Ch. Blooming-Tails TGO
Ch. Cricklades True Believer
Ch. Lyndhurst Pampas
Ch. Springfield's Inselheim Tory
Ch. Breezy Wide Receiver
Ch. Donally's Chance Reception
Ch. Hawkett's Country Heir C.D.
Ch. Jagersbo Walking Stick
Ch. Sailin's Proud Dimension
Ch. Lannmarks Liberty Char-Don
Ch. Dickendall Moorwood Tiger
Ch. Boltwood Analore Crackle
Ch. Cinderhill Happy Talk
Ch. Fernwood Sug'rbaba Carlinton

Ch. Delight Creme De Menthe
Ch. Graemoor Bombay
Ch. Winalot's Doll
Ch. Wheatland Barnum Jul
Ch. Finchingfield Dust Devil
Ch. Misti-Dawn Analore Sojourn
Ch. Foxley Mallard O'Bollinbrook
Ch. Jollymuff Jack Of Diamonds
Ch. Finchingfield Excalibur
Ch. Scherwood's Novel Idea
Ch. Jagersbo Splash Down
Ch. Ebonylane's Rupert Of The Key
Ch. Broad Reach Message Received
Ch. Dickendall Davron Expose
Ch. Jollymuff Little Sadie
Ch. Ashlyn's Egan Of Linamia C.D.
Ch. Lakelets Brett Maverick
Ch. Inselheim Peria
Ch. Dickendall Davron Cee Dee
Ch. Dove Hills Shiloh
Ch. Hawkett's Impressive Mere C.D.
Ch. Dickendall Buckstone Apple, JH
Ch. Oaklea Bobby Dazzler

ENG./AM. CH. SANDYLAND'S MIDAS

(Eng. Ch. Reanacre Mallardhurn Thunder x Eng. Ch. Sandylands Truth)

Whelped: July 5, 1965
Breeder: Gwen Broadley
Owner: Mrs. Grace Lambert/Kenneth Golden

The Sire of 53 AKC Champions:

Ch. Genie Of Pine Cone
Ch. Baroke's All Hallow's Eve
Ch. Houyhnhnm's Miranda
Ch. Houyhnhnm's Marshall
Ch. Baroke's Noel Adam
Am./Can.Ch. Sebastian Of Anderscroft C.D.
Ch. Spenrock Sans Souci
Ch. Windfall Golden Lance
Ch. Anderscroft Roustabout
Ch. Jo-Dean's Dreamdust Daiquiri
Ch. Spenrock Phantomshire Amber
Ch. Gairloch's Lucifer C.D.
Ch. Silvershoe Tawny Sunbeam
Ch. Spenrock Spun Candy
Ch. Torquay's Scorpio
Am./Bda. Ch. Tawny Tim Of Mandalay
Ch. Wimberway's Odin
Ch. Holly Of Park Hill
Ch. Phantomshire's Widgeon
Ch. Shelbrook Nimrod
Ch. Abracadabra Xavier
Ch. Abracadabra Xabrina
Ch. Almar's Bobo Quivari
Ch. Pine Needles Golden Bear
Ch. Dickendall's Flip Flop C.D.X., WC
Ch. Malloch's Brick Of Gold
Ch. Almar's Chance

Ch. Ama's Houyhnhnm Gift Of Hope
Ch. Driftwood's Honeysuckle
Ch. Somersett Circe Minx C.D.X.
Ch. Pine Needles Paragon
Ch. Signal Hill Miss Priss
Ch. Shookstown Gimlet
Ch. Almar's Licorice
Ch. Jollymuff Honey Pot
Ch. Almar's Jezebel
Ch. Jollymuff Questionmark C.D.
Ch. Sandylands Viscum Honeysuckle
Ch. Yarrow's The Magus
Ch. Jen-Mic Lenard
Ch. Glebe House Phineas Fog
Ch. Ben Of Killingworth
Ch. Adidas Jeep
Ch. Baroke's Frolickin' Fantasy
Ch. Driftwood's Padstow
Ch. Glebe House Merrymaid
Ch. Yarrow's Dantine
Ch. Blackwatch Tapioca
Ch. Cedarhill Autumn Sunday
Ch. Jollymuff Bicentennial
Ch. Blackwatch Goldigger
Ch. Adidas Johnny Unitas C.D.
Ch. Spenrock's Hello Dolly

CH. JAYNCOURT AJOCO JUSTICE

(Eng. Ch. Ballyduff Marketeer x Am.,/Eng. Ch. Jayncourt Star Performer)

Whelped:	June 5, 1977
Breeders:	Mr. & Mrs. P. Palmer
Owners:	Anthony Heubel, Jr. & Janet Farmilette

The Sire of 38 AKC Champions:

Ch. Andercroft Mijans Bravo Jazz
Ch. Mijan's All That Jazz
Ch. Finchingfield Navigator
Ch. Mijan's Aint Misbehaving
Ch. Caballero Marangue
Ch. Valleywood's Kannonball Kate
Ch. Beechcrofts Dover
Ch. Rainell's Clancy Of Cork
Ch. Mijans Rocky Mountain High
Ch. Rainell's Little Miss Mornin
Ch. Beechcroft Gingess Khan,WC
Ch. Beechcrofts Skylark
Ch. Finchingfiled's Notorious
Ch. Larowe's Catch A Magic Moment
Ch. Larowe's Curtain Call
Ch. Mijans Golden Poppy
Ch. Finchingfield Chauncy Clarke
Ch. Larowe's Capella Of Janroy C.D.
Ch. Beechcrofts Meadowlark

Ch. Rainell's Dynasty
Ch. Finchingfield Celtic Caper, WC
Ch. Car-Nel's Shadrack Amazement
Ch. Carenna's Star Spencer
Ch. Shadowvale's Just So
Ch. Vision Skylark Of Braemar
Ch. Springfield's Black Rod
Am./Can. Ch.Briarcreek Erinbrough Jude
Am./Bda. Ch. Rainell's Sweet Emily
Ch. Carenna's Amos Starshine C.D.
Ch. Shadowvale's Jill At Ranbourne
Ch. Campbellcroft Sparke O'Delby C.D.
Ch. Hennings Mill Justus
Ch. Griffin's Special Friend
Ch. Sunnybrook Acres Lady Jane
Ch. Albelarm Florida Sun
Ch. Vision's Ky Trace Of Braemar
Ch. Kerrymark Kellygreen Cobb
Ch. Jaquins Cloud Croft

CH. ROYAL OAKS VIP O'SHAMROCK ACRES C.D., WC

(Ch. Shamrock Acres Light Brigade x Ch. Shamrock Acres Royal Oaks Wag C.D.)

Whelped:	April 2, 1969
Breeders:	Mr. & Mrs. Charles Allen
Owners:	Betsy N. Getz, Aymes Kennels

The Sire of 34 AKC Champions:

Ch. Aymes Devonshire Cream
Ch. Aymes Camenbert
Ch. Aymes Hollandaise
Ch. Aymes English Toffey
Ch. Aymes Bristol Cream
Ch. Shamrock Acres Cameo
Ch. Shamrock Acres Commander
Ch. Timbrland Golden Star
Ch. Bailiwick Copyright
Ch. Randolph's Golden Nugget
Ch. Aymes Alexander
Ch. Shamrock Acres Suncountry Sky
Ch. Shamrock Acres Rebel Rouser
Ch. Jake From Silver Oaks
Ch. Shamrock Acres Bonanza
Ch. Bucklamb Buster Of Starline C.D.
Ch. Lugar Macho Of Greenbriar

Ch. Birchdale Extra Light Son
Ch. Greenbriars Summer Dream
Ch. Shamrock Acres Vip Peso
Ch. Peachykeen's Dandy
Ch. Drumlin's Copper Penny
Ch. Lucar's Breckin Of Greenbriar
Ch. Peachykeen's Buttermilk Sky
Ch. Mt. Gilead's Peachykeen Bunker
Ch. Shamrock Acres Sonny Bear
Ch. Wyndoe's Hollidaze Snow Bird
Ch. Drumlin Alyster
Ch. Peachykeen Play Misty For Me
Ch. Alii O'koolau's Erin
Ch. Bailiwick Talent Show
Ch. Shamrock Acres Classified
Ch. Moonshadows Bread And Butter
Ch. Salute's Kissin' Cousin C.D.

CH. MARSHLAND BLITZ

(Ch. Allegheny's Eclipse x Ch. Marshland Paisley Broone)

Whelped:	January 16, 1984
Breeders:	Dennis Emken & Lorraine McKerracher
Owners:	Dennis & Pam Emken

The sire of 32 AKC Champions:

Ch. Sweetbriar MacLeod
Ch. Broad Reach Yardly

Ch. Welly-Bobs Black Tuxedo
Ch. Mandigos Bruiser Of Woodstok

Ch. Broad Reach Trace Of Grace	Ch. Snowden And Franklin's Ivy
Ch. Broad Reach Motie, JH	Ch. Valleywood Nighthawk
Ch. Broad Reach Dade's Final Fling	Ch. Franklin Hills Apple Strudel
Ch. Rocky Acres Bit Of Lace	Ch. Springharbor Silhouette
Ch. Avalon's Invincible	Ch. Snowden Hill's Miss Clairol
Ch. Belquest High Hopes	Ch. Broad Reach Blossom
Ch. Val-Lee's Hell-On-Wheels	Ch. Chelons Irish Mist
Ch. Accipiter Peggy Sue At Elk Run	Ch. Silkwoods Angelina's Dream
Ch. Kadenjas Black Onyx	Ch. Crossfield's Winnie
Ch. Paisley's Precious Hannah	Ch. Driftwood's Sergeant Pepper
Ch. Sandbar's Private Eye	Ch. Graemoor Tim
Ch. Avalon's Egyptian Queen	Ch. Marshland Glitz
Ch. Elk Run Aura Lee Of Greenglen	Ch. Devon's Rough Magic T.D., JH
Ch. Elk Run Epic In Black	Ch. Delight Heir Of Elendil

AM/.CAN. CH. SHAMROCK ACRES SONIC BOOM
(Ch. Whygin Gold Bullion x Ch. Whygin Gentle Julia Of Avec)

Whelped: July 29, 1962
Breeders: Mr. & Mrs. James McCarthy
Owners: Mrs. Sally B. McCarthy & James McCarthy

The Sire of 32 AKC Champions:

Ch. Siridan's Ochre Brigadier	Ch. Jenny's Little Molly Brown
Ch. Shamrock Acres Happy Holiday	Ch. Shamrock Acres Shadow Boxer
Ch. Shamrock Acres Black Button	Ch. Shamrock Acres Snuffy Smith
Ch. Sunburst Blackfoot Nell	Ch. Could Be's Black Pepper
Ch. Shamrock Acres Night Watch	Ch. Concho's Danny Boy
Ch. Shamrock Acres Dark Cloud	Ch. Could Be's Black Angus
Ch. Shamrock Acres High Gun	Ch. Concho's Cotton Candy C.D.
Ch. Shamrock Acres Kissin Cousin C.D.	Ch. Concho's Black Molasses
Ch. Shamrock Acres Kelly Black C.D.	Ch. Shamrock Acres Late Date
Ch. Shamrock Acres Royal Oaks Wag C.D.	Ch. Ecco-System's Patonia
Ch. Shamrock Acres Sandune	Ch. Harmony Lanes' Black Onyx
Ch. Ham's Queen Of Spades	Ch. Shamrock Acres Buttercup II
Ch. Shamrock Acres Nick O'Time	Ch. Summer Camp Bugalou
Ch. Shamrock Acres By Jiminy	Ch. Warbonnet's Sierra Tiger
Ch. Shamrock Acres Twiggy	Ch. Warbonnet Honeysuckle C.D.X.
Ch. Shamrock Acres Spring Tonic	Ch. Shamrock Acres Miss Non Stop

AM./MEX./CAN. CH. FRANKLIN'S GOLDEN MANDIGO C.D.
(Ch. Shamrock Acres Light Brigade x Ch. Franklin's Tally Of Burywood)

Whelped: July 16, 1972
Breeder: Mrs. B. W. Ziessow
Owners: John C. Jenny & Laurel E. Jenny

The Sire of 30 AKC Champions:

Ch. Sandbar Country Minny	Ch. Janrod's Little Miss Muffet
Ch. Sandbar's Chadwick	Ch. Mandigo's Rocky Mt Sunset C.D.
Ch. Boatswain's Dandy Lion	Ch. Mandigo's Lady Sunshine
Ch. Ramblin's Seven And Seven	Ch. Bench Mark Solar Energy C.D.
Ch. Mandigo's Annabel Lee	Ch. Benchmark Scremn' Yela Zonker
Ch. Mandigo's Heather Of Sunrise	Ch. Mandigo's Chelsea Morning
Ch. Mandigo's Simmerdown Destiny	Ch. Bench Mark's Arrogance C.D.
Ch. Tex's Tinn Lizzie	Ch. Janwood's Lady Perkins
Ch. Ramblin's Tequila N' Lemon	Ch. Charisma's Lone Star Rick
Ch. Sangin's Majestic Ruffian C.D.	Ch. Janwood's Tigger Tremayne
Ch. Barking Heights Buck O Sun	Ch. Araplan Mandigo's Manda
Ch. Mandigo's Nick-A-But	Ch. Benchmark's Cover Girl
Ch. Mandigo's Wind River Amber	Ch. Sunderbys Sir Winston Pooh
Ch. Mandigo's Golden Nugget	Ch. Trinity Valleys China Doll
Ch. Dulce Golden Rode Dust	Ch. Labradese Blue Boy V Ojibwa C.D.X.

Chapter 3

Top Producing Dams

The following lists include dams with 12 or more champions:

AM./CAN. CH. WHYGIN CAMPAIGN PROMISE
(Ch. Wildfield Micky Finn x Ch. Whygin The Bedford Brat)

Whelped: November 22, 1959
Breeder: Helen W. Ginnel
Owners: Mr. & Mrs. J. McCarthy

The Dam of 17 Champions:

Ch. Shamrock Acres Delta Waters
Ch. Shamrock Acres Good News
Ch. Shamrock Acres Shawn
Ch. Shamrock Acres Black Button
Ch. Shamrock Acres Hi Jinx Ii
Ch. Shamrock Acres Kelly Black
Ch. Shamrock Acres Nick O'time
Ch. Shamrock Acres Twiggy
Ch. Shamrock Acres Snuffy Smith

Ch. Ralston Of Shamrock Acres
Ch. Shamrock Acres Royal Oaks Wag C.D.
Ch. Shamrock Acres Glory Bee
Ch. Shamrock Acres Night Watch
Ch. Shamrock Acres Dark Cloud
Ch. Shamrock Acres Kissin Cousin
Ch. Shamrock Acres By Jiminy
Ch. Shamrock Acres One Way Ticket

CH. FRANKLIN'S TALLY OF BURYWOOD
(Ch. Franklin's Sun Star x Ch. Franklin's Spring Dawn)

Whelped: July 13, 1967
Breeder: Mrs. B. W. Ziessow
Owners: Mrs. B.W. Ziessow & Russell R. Kingsbury

The Dam of 16 AKC Champions:

Ch. Franklin's Corbi Of Limerick
Ch. Franklin's Whirlaway Of Barbella
Ch. Franklin's Top Of The Morning
Ch. Burywood Hurricane
Ch. Franklin's Hickory Grove
Ch. Franklin's Chance Play
Ch. Franklin's Winter Wheat
Ch. Roxanne Norton Of Burywood

Ch. Winacko's Abraham Of Burywood
Ch. Shamrock Norton Of Burywood
Ch. Franklin's Tell Tale Maggie
Ch. Franklin's Secretariat
Ch. Franklin's Bug-A-Boo
Ch. Franklin's Bailiwick Rally C.D.
Ch. Franklin's Ruffian
Am./Can. Ch. Franklin's Golden Mandigo C.D.

ENG./AM. CH. KENBARA JILL
(Halsinger Madford March x Sandylands Kaprice)

Whelped: January 15, 1965
Breeder: Mrs. B. M. Vipond
Owner: Mrs. R. W. Clark, Jr.

The Dam of 14 AKC Champions:

Ch. Springfield Faust
Ch. Springfield Musette
Ch. Springfield Tosca
Ch. Springfield Violetta
Ch. Springfield Beatrice
Ch. Springfield Cabaret
Ch. Springfield Cassandra

Ch. Springfield Peer Jill
Ch. Springfield Oliver
Ch. Kimvalley Kenbara Mr Softee
Ch. Springfield Dickens
Ch. Springfield Mimi
Ch. Springfield Salad Daze C.D.X.
Ch. Springfield Mister Roberts

AM./CAN./BDA. CH. SPENROCK BANNER
(Ch. Lockerbie Sandylands Tarquin x Ch. Sandylands Spungold)

Whelped:	June 30, 1964
Breeder:	Dorothy Francke
Owner:	Edwin A. Churchill, VMD

The Dam of 13 AKC Champions:

Ch. Spenrock Sans Souci
Ch. Spenrock Phantomshire Amber
Ch. Spenrock Spun Candy
Ch. Spenrock Bohemia Champagne
Ch. Spenrock Cajun
Ch. Spenrock's Topaz
Ch. Spenrock's Cognac

Ch. Spenrock's Cardigan Bay
Am./Can. Ch. Spenrock's Top Gallant
Ch. Spenrock's Hello Dolly
Ch. Spenrock Anthony Adverse
Ch. Spenrock Boomerang
Ch. Spenrock Ambassador

CH. WHYGIN GENTLE JULIA OF AVEC
(Ch. Whygin Gold Bullion x Ch. Whygin Black Gambit Of Avec)

Whelped:	June 27, 1959
Breeder:	Helen W. Ginnel
Owner:	Mrs. Sally McCarthy

The Dam of 13 AKC Champions:

Ch. Shamrock Acres Jim Dandy
Ch. Shamrock Acres Sugar
Ch. Shamrock Acres Sonic Boom
Ch. Shamrock Acres Casey Jones C.D.
Ch. Shamrock Acres Snow Of Whygin
Ch. Shamrock Acres Hurry Up
AFC/Ch. Shamrock Acres Simmer Down

Ch. Shamrock Acres Sparkle Plenty C.D.
Ch. Whygin Luck Of Shamrock Acres
Ch. Shamrock Acres Twenty Carats
Ch. Shamrock Acres Ebony Lancer
Ch. Shamrock Acres Sunny Side Up
Ch. Shamrock Acres Golden Rod

CH. SHAMROCK ACRES COTTON CANDY
(Ch. Shamrock Acres Light Brigade x Ch. Whygin Dawn Of Shamrock Acres)

Whelped:	February 1, 1966
Breeder:	Mr. & Mrs. James McCarthy
Owner:	Mrs. James R. Getz

The Dam of 12 AKC Champions:

Ch. Aymes Equal Times
Ch. Aymes First Fling
Ch. Aymes Prairie Gold
Ch. Aymes Shannon
Ch. Aymes Annie Of Broadfen
Ch. Aymes Triple Threat

Ch. Aymes Devonshire Cream
Ch. Aymes Michael Collier
Ch. Aymes Camenbert
Ch. Aymes Hollandais
Ch. Aymes English Toffee
Ch. Aymes Bristol Cream

Appendices

 Bibliography

 Index

Bibliography

Coode, Carole, **Labrador Retrievers Today**, New York: Maxwell MacMillan International, Howell Book House, 1993.

Dalgano, Mary, **Early History of the Labrador Dog**, O'Connor, ACT, Aust.: Self-published, 1987.

Hatton, Joseph and Rev. M. Harvy, **Newfoundland: Its History, Its Present Condition and Its Prospects in the Future**, Boston: Doyle and Whittle, 1883.

Herz, Henre, **Mes voyages en Amérique**, Paris: Achille Faure, 1866.

Howe, Lorna Countess, **The Popular Labrador Retriever**, 3rd Edition, London: Popular Dogs, 1961.

Howley, James P., **The Beothucks or Red Indians: The Aboriginal Inhabitants of Newfoundland** (1915), Toronto: Coles Publishing Co., 1974.

Jukes, J.B., **Excursions in and about Newfoundland During the years 1839 and 1840**, Vol. 2, 1942, Toronto: Canadian House, 1969.

Kennedy, Capt. W.R., **Sporting Notes in Newfoundland**, St. John's: J.C. Withers, 1881.

The Labrador Retriever Club , **The Labrador Retriever Club 1916-1991: A Celebration of 75 Years**, England: The Labrador Retriever Club, 1991

Little, C.C., **The Inheritance of Coat Color in Dogs**: New York, Howell Book House, Inc., 1973.

Martin, Nancy, **Legends In Labradors**, Pennsylvania: Self-Published, 1980.

Middleton, Sir John, **Letter to Sir Leonard Outerbridge**, 11 December 1983.

The Midland Counties Labrador Retriever Club, **Midland Counties Labrador Retriever Club Yearbook**, Midland Counties Labrador Retriever Club, 1990

Millais, J.G., **Newfoundland and Its Untrodden Ways**, London: Longmans, Green and Co., 1907.

New Zealand Kennel Gazette, "Movement in the Labrador," November 1986, pp. 89-93.

Pure-Bred Dogs, American Kennel Gazette, October 1993, pp. 175-176.

Pure-Bred Dogs, American Kennel Gazette, December 1993, pp. 124-127.

Pure-Bred Dogs, American Kennel Gazette, Events Calendar April 1994, p. 133.

Pure-Bred Dogs, American Kennel Gazette, June 1994, pp. 123-127.

Retriever International, "The Australian Field Trial," by Mr. Charles Ball, Fall 1984, vol. 23, pg. 8.

Retriever International, "Inheritance of Coat Color in the Labrador Retriever," by Joe W. Templeton and Andrew P. Stewart, Spring (1981), vol. 9, pp. 24-29, Summer (1981) vol 10, pp. 26-33.

Roslin-Williams, Mary, **The Dual-Purpose Labrador**, London: Pelham Books, 1969.

Schlintz, Irene C. Khatoonian, **The Top Producers 1965-1978, Labrador Retrievers**, California: H.I.S. Publications, 1978.

Scott, Lord George and Sir John Middleton, **The Labrador Dog Its Home and History**, London: H.F. & B. Witherby Ltd., 1936.

Scott, Lord George and Sir John Middleton, **Stud Book of the Duke of Buccleuch's Labrador Retrievers** (1931), London, Peregrin Books, 1990.

Tuck, James A., **Ancient People of Port au Choix, Newfoundland Social and Economic Studies No. 17**, St. John's Institute of Social and Economic Research, Memorial University, 1976.

Warwick, Helen, **The New Complete Labrador Retriever**, New York; Howell Book House, 1986.

Whitbourne, Richard, **A Discourse and Discovery of New-Found-Land** (1620), Amsterdam: Da Capo Press, 1971.

Wolters, Richard A., **The Labrador Retriever, The History . . . The People**, Los Angeles; Peterson Prints, 1981.

In appreciation . . .

How kind and generous everyone has been! If it were not for Mike Clarke, computer wizard and very helpful son of my friend, Joan Clarke (Trelawny), I'd still be puzzling over Word Perfect and DOS for Dummies. He surely saved me from computer chaos and guided me through the unfamiliar use of the equipment part of this endeavor. Many thanks, Mike!

Marianne Foote was another savior who spent untold hours and days in the editing process with me. I appreciate all she has done.

My thanks to Joan Read and Mary Swan who have been so generous with old photos, scrapbooks and memories. In England, Mrs. Jo Coulson, Secretary/Treasurer of The Labrador Retriever Club, and Mrs. Sue Hill, Secretary of the Midland Counties Labrador Retriever Club, both deserve a thank you for their advice and help.

In addition, I am most grateful to all the Labrador people in other countries who wrote articles for me about the breed in their homelands. I know it was a lot of work, but I am truly appreciative. Of course, I am indebted to my American friends for their write-ups as well.

To my friends, Chris Watt and Jim Schoenfeld, many thanks for your photographic help.

Over one thousand photographs and many kennel profiles were sent to me; unfortunately a book has only limited capacity, so many deletions had to be made. I thank everyone sincerely and wish I could have included more material.

—Nancy Martin

Index

314 ■ Appendices

Additional photos:
Chessa (yellow)
Labrador puppies in all three colors
Ch. Shadowvales Statesman C.D.X.,
    TDI (black)
Ch. Sandylands Marshal, JH
Am./Mex. Int. Ch. JanWood's Secret
    Agent (black)
Scrimshaw Placido Flamingo
    (yellow)
World Winner/Am. Ch. Misti-Dawn
    Analore Sojourn (yellow)
Ch. Chucklebrook Fannie Farmer
    (chocolate)
Ch. Chucklebrook Mouse Feathers
    (chocolate)
Swed./Am. Ch. Puhs Superman
    (chocolate)
Ch. Meadowrock's Fudge of Ayr, WC
    (chocolate)